Table of Contents

Introduction 13
Indian Instant Pot Breakfast Recipes 14
    Potato Masala 14
    Rave Upma 14
    Aloo Paratha 15
    Potato Poha 17
    Kanda Poha 17
    Methi Paratha 18
    Poori Masala 18
    Oats Upma 19
    Tomato Upma 19
    Semiya Upma 20
    Chura Matar 20
    Sweet Pongal 21
    Sweet Dalia 21
    Kadala Curry 22
    Paneer Butter Masala 22
    Oats Porridge 23
    Oats Khichdi 23
    Bhindi Masala 24
    Gajar Matar 24
    Aloo Capsicum 25
    Jeera Aloo 25
    Aloo Moongre Ki Sabzi 26
    Bharwa Karela 26
    Kurkuri Bhindi 27
    Banana Moong Dal 27
    Mango Moong Dal 28
    Sweet Potato Dhal 28
    Carrot Rasam and Moong Dal 29
    Tomato Rice 29
    Paneer Spread 30
    Green Dosa 30
    Veggie Masala 31
    Green Peas Masala Rice 31
    Spinach and Lentils Rice 32
    Broken Wheat Upma 32
    Millet Upma 33
    Sabudana Knichdi 33
    Bread Upma 34
    Indian Farro Masala 34
    Healthy Kheer 35

    Peach and Mango Lassi 35
    Aloo Egg Curry 36
    Quinoa Poha 36
    Mushrooms Korma 37
    Poha Bowls with Sprouts 37
    Ragi and Kale Idli 38
    Beans Masala 38
    Fruit Masala 39
    Banana Salad 39
    Rose Rice Bowls 39
    Rice Salad 40
    Apricot Rava Pudding 40
    Bell Pepper Omelet 41
    Masala Omelet 41
    Figs and Tomatoes Salad 42
    Millet Pongal 42
    Apple Ragi Halwa 43
    Ragi Malt Java 43
    Egg and Broccoli Bhurji 43
Indian Instant Pot Lunch Recipes 44
    Paneer Butter Masala 44
    Aloo Baingan Masala 44
    Palak Paneer 45
    Dum Aloo 45
    Veggie Khichdi 46
    Veggie Pulao 46
    Buttery Chicken 47
    Chicken Biryani 47
    Chicken Masala 48
    Goat Curry 48
    Lamb Rogan Josh 49
    Pork Vindaloo 49
    Shrimp Curry 50
    Chana Masala 50
    Keema Matar 51
    Toor Dal 51
    Rice with Lamb 52
    Potato and Pea Curry 52
    Shrimp Biryani 53
    Sookha Kana Chana 54
    Langar Dal 54
    Masala Pasta 55
    Kidney Beans Curry 55
    Chicken Masala 56

Avial 56
Chicken Soup 57
Cream of Broccoli 57
Mulligatawny Soup 58
Curry Cauliflower and Broccoli Soup 58
Palak Soup 59
Indian Fish Soup 59
Aloo Ki Kadhi 60
Beans and Rutabaga Soup 60
Tomato Soup 61
Spicy Cabbage Soup 61
Curry Turkey Soup 62
Turkey and Coriander Soup 62
Coconut Shrimp Stew 63
Beef Stew 63
Veggie Stew 64
Ghee Carrot Pudding 64
Chickpeas and Tomatoes Masala 65
Mutton Stew 65
Broccoli Junka 66
Zucchini Curry 66
Zucchini and Peas Curry 67
Squash and Lentils Stew 67
Turnips Soup 68
Balkan Bean Stew 68
Green Beans Curry 69
Indian Instant Pot Side Dish Recipes 70
   Mushroom Mix 70
   Okra Mix 70
   Turmeric Aloo 71
   Coconut Veggies 71
   Cumin Potatoes 72
   Cabbage Thoran 72
   Veggie Sabjee 73
   Aromatic Rice Mix 73
   Spicy Rice 74
   Spiced Quinoa 74
   Quinoa Curry 75
   Quinoa Pilaf 75
   Quinoa and Chickpeas Mix 76
   Beet Sabzi 76
   Beet Rice 77
   Beet Poriyal 77
   Beet Thoran 78

Beet and Carrot Poriyal	78
Green Peas Mix	79
Spiced Peas	79
Peas Pulao	80
Peas and Mushrooms	80
Gajar Matar	81
Hara Bhara Kabab	81
Matar Ka Nimona	82
Eggplant Bhurtha	82
Baingan Ka Bharta	83
Parsnips Mix	83
Cauliflower Mix	84
Spiced Gobi	84
Spicy Gobi Mix	85
Creamy Cauliflower Mix	85
Brussels Sprouts Subzi	86
Spiced Brussels Sprouts	86
Curried Brussels Sprouts	87
Kale Salad	87
Spiced Greens	88
Mango and Kale Mix	88
Turmeric Broccoli Mix	89
Citrus Cauliflower Mix	89
Orange Pulao	90
Narangi Pulao	90
Rice and Kale	91
Garlic Rice Mix	91
Asparagus Rice Mix	91
Spicy Eggplant Mix	92
Ginger Broccoli and Orange Mix	92
Saffron Red Cabbage	93
Cabbage Rice	93
Creamy Beans and Rice	94
Tomato Salad	94
Beets and Almonds	95
Spicy Artichokes and Rice	95
Spicy Tomatoes	96
Endives and Tomatoes Mix	96
Endives and Walnuts Mix	97
Endives with Orange Mix	97
Indian Cumin Asparagus	98
Turmeric Fennel and Rice	98
Peas and Fennel Mix	98
Indian Instant Pot Snack and Appetizer Recipes	99

Chili Paneer	99
Okra Bowls	99
Khara Biscuits	100
Pyaaz Chutney	100
Tomato Chutney	101
Garlic Dip	101
Minty Dip	101
Garam Masala Hummus	102
Avocado Raita	102
Tamarind Dip	103
Cashew Dip	103
Capsicum Masala	104
Peppers Dip	104
Marinated Shrimp Bowls	105
Spicy Shrimp Mix	105
Cumin Eggplant and Tomato Bowls	106
Hot Shrimp and Peppers Salad	106
Spinach and Avocado Dip	107
Spinach Spread	107
Beans Dip	108
White Beans Spread	108
Turmeric Shrimp Salad	109
Curd Chicken Salad	109
Chicken Chutney Salad	110
Mango Salad	110
Cucumber and Mango Salad	111
Turkey Bowls	111
Potato Dip	112
Cheese Dip	112
Endives Dip	113
Saffron Shrimp	113
Lentils Dip	114
Chickpea Dip	114
Turmeric Onion Dip	115
Zucchini Salad	115
Spiced Broccoli Spread	116
Hot Cauliflower Dip	116
Zucchini Dip	117
Corn and Leeks Bowls	117
Warm Cucumber Salad	118
Barley and Turmeric Salad	118
Barley and Olives Salad	119
Broccoli Bites	119
Quinoa, Almonds and Avocado Salad	120

Barley and Chickpea Bowls	120
Thyme Lentils and Tomatoes Bowls	121
Mushroom Dip	121
Mushroom and Broccoli Dip	122
Creamy Mushroom Spread	122
Shrimp and Green Beans Bowls	123
Indian Instant Pot Fish and Seafood Recipes	**124**
Fish Tikka	124
Fish Pulusu	124
Chili Fish Mix	125
Salmon Curry	125
Cod and Tomato Bowls	126
Cod Curry	126
Salmon and Broccoli	127
Charred Salmon	127
Lemon Cod and Rice	128
Shrimp and Lime Rice	128
Spiced Cod	129
Seafood Salad	129
Trout and Sauce	130
Cod and Cauliflower	130
Salmon and Chili Sauce	131
Indian Salmon and Asparagus	131
Cod and Butter Sauce	132
Turmeric Salmon and Lime Sauce	132
Indian Halibut	133
Simple Masala	133
Spicy Tuna	134
Turmeric Tuna	134
Ginger Trout and Tomatoes	135
Chives Tuna Curry	135
Salmon, Spinach and Coconut Mix	136
Tilapia, Tomatoes and Radish Saad	136
Sea Bass with Fennel	137
Shrimp and Radish Curry	137
Shrimp and Okra	138
Shrimp and Spiced Potatoes	138
Tuna and Avocado Mix	139
Tuna and Turmeric Green Beans Mix	139
Lemongrass Shrimp and Corn	140
Cardamom Shrimp and Zucchinis	140
Fenugreek Tuna and Mushroom Curry	141
Tilapia Masala	141
Spicy Tilapia	142

Tilapia Curry 142
Classic Indian Sea Bass Mix 143
Sea Bass and Lentils 143
Tandoori Sea Bass 144
Spiced Mussels 144
Curry Clams 145
Spicy Tamarind Clams 145
Crab Curry 146
Spicy Crab and Eggplant Mix 146
Mustard Seed Mahi Mahi 147
Mahi Mahi Tikka 147
Fish and Onions Paste 148
Cod and Cilantro Chutney 148
Coriander Cod Mix 149
Indian Instant Pot Poultry Recipes 150
Spiced Yogurt Turkey 150
Cilantro Turkey and Lemon Mix 150
Turkey Meatballs and Sauce 151
Citrus Turkey and Spiced Broccoli 151
Cinnamon Turkey and Cauliflower 152
Curry Chicken Thighs 152
Ginger Chicken Mix 153
Masala Chicken and Peppers 153
Cumin Chicken and Artichokes 154
Curry Chicken and Eggplants 154
Cardamom Turkey Mix 155
Cinnamon Chicken and Rice Mix 155
Ginger Chicken and Sweet Potatoes 156
Turkey with Spiced Potatoes 156
Coconut Chicken and Tomatoes 157
Sage Chicken and Mango 157
Curry Turkey, Asparagus and Tomatoes 158
Creamy Chicken Mix 158
Chicken, Avocado and Turmeric Rice 159
Cinnamon Turkey and Green Beans 159
Chicken and Masala Fennel 160
Turkey and Lime Sauce 160
Cumin Chicken with Tomato Chutney 161
Hot Chicken and Pineapple Mix 161
Chicken and Turmeric Zucchini Mix 162
Fenugreek Chicken Mix 162
Turkey, Cauliflower and Rice Mix 163
Cocoa Turkey and Beans 163
Chicken Meatballs Curry 164

Paprika Turkey Mix.. 164
Chicken and Lime Turmeric Carrots.. 165
Chicken and Zucchini Rice Mix... 165
Cheesy Turkey and Rice... 166
Chicken, Tomatoes and Mushrooms.. 166
Turkey and Masala Corn 167
Chicken and Chickpeas Mix 167
Turkey and Curried Lentils 168
Turkey, Chickpeas and Zucchinis 168
Chicken with Turmeric Cabbage... 169
Coriander Chicken Masala... 169
Chives Chicken and Broccoli 170
Chicken with Turmeric Beets and Broccoli.. 170
Chicken with Avocado and Cucumber Mix 171
Chicken with Cauliflower and Pomegranate Mix 171
Garlic Turkey, Tomatoes and Rice 172
Hot Cayenne Chicken Mix.. 172
Turkey with Turmeric Yogurt Mix.. 173
Turkey with Chili Black Beans... 173
Chicken Wings and Turmeric Sauce 174
Turkey and Chili Asparagus.. 174
Chicken with Coriander Broccoli Sauté 175
Chicken, Zucchini and Mushrooms Curry 175
Chicken and Endives Rice Mix.. 176
Lime Turmeric Chicken Wings.. 176
Turkey Bowls... 177
Turkey with Brussels Sprouts Rice... 177
Creamy Turkey and Peas Mix 178
Chicken with Chili Onions... 178
Masala Turkey with Nutmeg Potatoes... 179
Chicken, Rice and Mango Mix... 179
Coconut Turkey and Carrots Rice 180
Indian Instant Pot Meat Recipes 180
Beef Curry.. 180
Ribs Curry.. 181
Coconut Pork Mix.. 181
Madras Beef Mix.. 182
Ginger Beef Curry 182
Beef with Veggies Mix.. 183
Aromatic Beef 183
Lemony Beef Mix... 184
Beef and Lentils Curry 184
Pork with Red Lentils Mix 185
Kheema Masala.. 185

Beef and Peas	186
Coconut Beef and Cilantro Mix	186
Saag Gosht	187
Spicy Beef	187
Beef and Veggies Curry	188
Beef with Squash Curry	188
Indian Beef and Pumpkin Mix	189
Beef with Lemony Scallions	189
Cheesy Beef and Rice	190
Beef with Cinnamon Zucchini Mix	190
Cumin Beef	191
Beef and Beets Mix	191
Lamb Curry	192
Spiced Lamb Bowls	192
Creamy Lamb with Carrots Curry	193
Lamb with Coconut Green Beans	193
Spiced Lamb with Corn	194
Lamb with Spiced Sprouts	194
Beef with Chili Quinoa	195
Indian Lamb Chops	195
Minty Lamb Mix	196
Spiced Lamb and Cucumber	196
Turmeric Lamb with Beets	197
Indian Pork Chops	197
Pork Chops with Allspice Spinach	198
Pork and Tomato Chutney	198
Cocoa Pork Chops and Green Beans	199
Pork with Cinnamon Carrots Mix	199
Sweet Pork Chops	200
Pork with Broccoli	200
Pork Chops and Turmeric Cauliflower	201
Coriander Pork with Almonds	201
Mustard and Cumin Pork Chops	202
Paprika Pork with Nutmeg Potatoes	202
Pandi Masala	203
Pork Indaad	203
Hot Pork Mix	204
Orange Pork Mix	204
Ginger Pork Mix	205
Cocoa Pork and Tomatoes	205
Ema Datshi	206
Pork with Bamboo Mix	206
Kaleez Ankiti	207
Pork Chili Mix	207

Pork Meatballs Mix 208
Tamarind Pork... 208
Hot BBQ Ribs 209
Spicy Pork and Artichokes... 209
Beef and Creamy Turmeric Potatoes 210
Indian Instant Pot Vegetable Recipes 211
    Masala Artichokes 211
    Turmeric Artichokes... 211
    Creamy Artichokes and Coconut 212
    Spiced Asparagus... 212
    Cinnamon Artichokes and Rice 212
    Almond Asparagus Mix... 213
    Ginger Asparagus... 213
    Spiced Green Beans 214
    Green Beans and Orange Sauce 214
    Coconut Beets 215
    Hot Brussels Sprouts 215
    Walnuts Bell Peppers Mix 216
    Minty Peppers... 216
    Bell Peppers and Potatoes Mix 217
    Coriander Peppers Mix 217
    Beets with Yogurt 218
    Dill Potatoes.. 218
    Creamy Potatoes... 219
    Garlic Potato Masala 219
    Turmeric Zucchini 220
    Cayenne Zucchinis Mix... 220
    Potato and Zucchini Masala 221
    Spinach Mix 221
    Spiced Okra... 222
    Turmeric Broccoli and Onions... 222
    Nutmeg Cauliflower Mix.. 223
    Hot Spinach and Potato Mix 223
    Cinnamon Potato Mix 224
    Coconut Fennel Mix 224
    Masala Endives... 225
    Spinach and Okra Mix... 225
    Creamy Potato and Apples Mix 226
    Eggplant Masala 226
    Spiced Eggplant Mix 227
    Lime Zucchinis and Eggplant Mix 227
    Coconut Eggplants 228
    Coconut Tomatoes... 228
    Zucchini and Cauliflower Mix... 229

Turmeric Kale	229
Cocoa Zucchinis and Peppers	230
Orange Zucchinis	230
Tomatoes and Citrus Rice	231
Allspice Zucchini Mix	231
Spiced Zucchinis and Carrots	232
Cumin Potato and Carrots Mix	232
Cardamom Beets	233
Minty Tomatoes Mix	233
Spinach with Broccoli	234
Beets and Onions Mix	234
Basil Potato and Cream	235
Indian Instant Pot Dessert Recipes	**236**
Gajar Ka Halwa	236
Aam Shrikhand	236
Payasam	237
Pistachio Phirni	237
Indian Kulfi	237
Rice Kheer	238
Mixed Fruits	238
Gehun Ki Kheer	239
Ada Pradhaman	239
Pistachio Parfait	239
Saffron Zucchini Pudding	240
Turmeric Pear Bowls	240
Banana and Rice Pudding	240
Turmeric Apples	241
Grapes Rice	241
Cocoa Grapes Mix	241
Cranberries with Pistachios Cream	242
Carrots Pudding	242
Apples Quinoa Pudding	243
Almond Pudding	243
Coconut and Rice	243
Saffron Lime Cream	244
Raisins Pudding	244
Banana and Avocado Mix	244
Lemon Grapes and Bananas	245
Saffron Cauliflower Rice Pudding	245
Sweet Wheat Bowls	245
Sweet Potatoes Pudding	246
Lime Apples Bowls	246
Orange Cream	246
Raspberries and Rice	247

Turmeric Carrot Cream 247
Cardamom Pears Cream 247
Ginger Cauliflower Rice 248
Turmeric Blackberries Bowls 248
Apple Quinoa Mix 248
Avocado Cream 249
Apricots Rice 249
Zucchinis Rice 249
Dates Quinoa 250
Coconut Banana Mix 250
Walnuts Cream 250
Coconut Strawberry Mix 251
Pineapple Pudding 251
Coconut Parfait 251
Cardamom Pudding 252
Saffron Chocolate Cream 252
Rhubarb Quinoa 252
Mango and Banana Mix 253
Nutmeg Pumpkin Mix 253
Conclusion 254

Introduction

Cooking in an instant pot is such a fun activity. You get to make all your favorite meals with minimum effort and time consumption. The instant pot is truly the future in the kitchen. It's such an innovative and original kitchen appliances used by millions of people all over the world. The meals you get to prepare using the instant pot taste so delicious and they are all so rich and flavored.

So, get your own instant pot today and cook some of the best meals ever.
If you need some meal ideas, then this recipes collection is what you really need.
We bring to you the best instant pot recipes: Indian ones! It will be the best culinary trip you'll ever take.

India is all about cultures, occupations, soils, religions, flavors and textures. Indian cuisine is a diverse and such an exotic one. It's such an amazing cuisine, full of intense tastes and colors. The ingredients you get to use in Indian cuisine combine perfectly, and the dishes are all spiced and flavored.
If you choose to cook Indian meals, you'll get to play with so many interesting and exotic ingredients and you'll discover different and new tastes.

All in all, the Indian cuisine is exceptional and you should take your time and discover its amazing dishes. We can assure you that the Indian meals you'll make in the instant pot will taste so good.

So, get your hands on a copy of this great Indian instant pot recipes collection and create magical culinary feasts in the comfort of your own kitchen.
Discover India today and make healthy and rich meals using the instant pot.
Enjoy cooking and have fun in the kitchen!

Indian Instant Pot Breakfast Recipes

Potato Masala

Preparation time: *10 minutes* | ***Cooking time:*** *20 minutes* | ***Servings:*** *4*

Ingredients:

- 4 gold potatoes, peeled and cubed
- ½ teaspoon mustard seeds
- 1 tablespoon chana dal, soaked in ¼ cup hot water for 30 minutes and drained
- 2 big yellow onions, chopped,
- 1 teaspoon ginger, grated
- 10 curry leaves
- 2 green chilies, chopped
- A pinch of asafetida powder
- ¼ teaspoon turmeric powder
- ½ cup water
- 4 tablespoons coriander, chopped
- Salt and black pepper to the taste

Directions:

Set the Instant pot on Sauté mode, add the mustard seeds and brown them for 2 minutes. Add the potatoes, onions, ginger and the other ingredients, toss, put the lid on and cook on High for 18 minutes. Release the pressure naturally for 10 minutes, divide the masala into bowls and serve.

Nutrition: calories 100, fat 0.6, fiber 4.7, carbs 22.3, protein 2.8

Rave Upma

Preparation time: *10 minutes* | ***Cooking time:*** *15 minutes* | ***Servings:*** *3*

Ingredients:

- 1 cup fine rava(cream of wheat)
- 1 green chili, chopped
- 1 yellow onion, chopped
- 1 teaspoon chana dal
- 1 teaspoon urad dal
- 2 and ½ cups water
- 1 teaspoon ginger, grated
- ½ teaspoon cumin seeds
- 1 teaspoon mustard seeds
- 10 curry leaves
- 12 cashews, chopped
- 2 tablespoons coriander
- 2 teaspoon sugar
- 2 tablespoons ghee, melted
- Salt and black pepper to the taste

Directions:

Set the Instant pot on Sauté mode, add the rava, and heat up for 2 minutes. Add the ghee and whisk well. Add the chana dal and urad dal, stir and cook for 2 minutes. Add the cumin, mustard seeds, cashews and curry leaves, stir and cook for 2 minutes more. Add the chili and the remaining ingredients, toss, put the lid on and cook on High for 9 minutes. Release the pressure naturally for 10 minutes, divide the mix between plates and serve.

Nutrition: calories 200, fat 12, fiber 2.6, carbs 20.8, protein 3.6

Aloo Paratha

Preparation time: 40 minutes | Cooking time: 30 minutes | Servings: 9

Ingredients:
For the stuffing:
- 4 potatoes, peeled and cubed
- ½ cup water
- 2 green chilies, chopped
- ½ teaspoon Punjabi garam masala
- ½ teaspoon red chili powder
- 1 teaspoon dry mango powder
- 2 teaspoons coriander, chopped
- Salt and black pepper to the taste
- 2 tablespoons ghee, melted
- Cooking spray

For the paratha dough:
- 2 cups whole wheat flour
- A pinch of salt
- 2 teaspoons vegetable oil
- Water as required
- Yogurt for serving

Directions:
Set the instant pot on Sauté mode, add 2 tablespoons ghee, heat it up, add the chilies, garam masala and chili powder and sauté for 2 minutes. Add the potatoes and the other ingredients for the stuffing except the cooking spray, stir, put the lid on and cook on High for 15 minutes. Release the pressure naturally for 10 minutes, cool the mix down and mash it a bit with a potato masher. In a bowl, combine the flour with the vegetable oil and the other ingredients for the dough, stir, knead well and leave aside for 30 minutes. Shape 2 balls out of this dough, flatten them well on a working surface in round shapes. Add the potato mix in the center of one circle, put the other one on top, press well and seal the edges. Heat up a pan with cooking spray over medium high heat, add the paratha, cook for 6 minutes on each side, transfer to a platter and serve with yogurt on top.

Nutrition: calories 203, fat 4.4, fiber 3.3, carbs 36.6, protein 4.6

Onion Rava Dosa

Preparation time: *20 minutes* | ***Cooking time:*** *20 minutes* | ***Servings:*** *6*

Ingredients:

- ½ cup semolina
- ½ cup rice flour
- 2 tablespoons whole wheat flour
- 1 green chili, minced
- 1 yellow onions, chopped
- 6 curry leaves, chopped
- 1 teaspoon ginger, grated
- 2 cups buttermilk
- 10 black peppercorns, crushed
- 1 tablespoon coriander, chopped
- Salt to the taste

For tempering the dosa:

- 1 teaspoon cumin seeds, ground
- ½ teaspoons mustard seeds
- 1 teaspoon vegetable oil
- 2 tablespoons ghee, melted

Directions:

Heat up a pan with 1 teaspoon oil over medium-high heat, add cumin and mustard seeds and toast for 3 minutes. In a bowl, combine the seeds mix with the semolina, rice flour and the other ingredients except the melted ghee, stir well, cover the bowl and leave aside for 20 minutes. Set the instant pot on Sauté mode, add the ghee and heat it up. Pour the dosa batter, spread into the pot, put the lid on and cook on High for 15 minutes. Release the pressure naturally for 10 minutes, divide the dosa between plates and serve for breakfast.

Nutrition: calories 200, fat 6.4, fiber 1.7, carbs 29.6, protein 6

Potato Poha

Preparation time: 10 minutes | Cooking time: 20 minutes | Servings: 6

Ingredients:
- 1 and ½ cups parched rice
- 2 green chilies, chopped
- ½ teaspoon turmeric powder
- 2 tablespoons peanuts, chopped
- 1 yellow onion, chopped
- 1 potato, peeled and cubed
- 1 teaspoon mustard seeds
- 1 teaspoon cumin seeds
- 8 curry leaves, chopped
- 2 tablespoons coconut, grated
- 1 tablespoons coriander, chopped
- 2 tablespoons vegetable oil
- 1 teaspoon sugar
- Salt to the taste

Directions:
Set the Instant pot on Sauté mode, add the oil, heat it up, add the mustard, cumin seeds and curry leaves, stir and toast for 3 minutes. Add the rice, turmeric and peanuts, toss and brown for 3 minutes more. Add the chilies and the other ingredients, put the lid on and cook on High for 14 minutes. Release the pressure naturally for 10 minutes, divide everything between plates and serve.

Nutrition: calories 327, fat 7.4, fiber 2.7, carbs 58.4, protein 6.3

Kanda Poha

Preparation time: 10 minutes | Cooking time: 10 minutes | Servings: 2

Ingredients:
- 1 and ½ cups red beaten rice
- 1 yellow onion, chopped
- ½ teaspoon turmeric powder
- 1 teaspoon mustard seeds
- 2 and ½ tablespoons peanuts, chopped
- 12 curry leaves, chopped
- 1 green chili, chopped
- 1 teaspoon sugar
- 2 tablespoons vegetable oil
- Salt to the taste

Directions:
Set the Instant pot on Sauté mode, add the oil, heat it up, add the mustard seeds and the rice and brown for 3 minutes. Add the turmeric and the onion and brown for 2 minutes more. Add the rest of the ingredients, put the lid on and cook on Low for 5 minutes. Release the pressure naturally for 10 minutes, divide the mix between plates and serve for breakfast.

Nutrition: calories 899, fat 20.5, fiber 6.1, carbs 56.7, protein 17.1

Methi Paratha

Preparation time: 10 minutes | Cooking time: 10 minutes | Servings: 8

Ingredients:
- 2 cups whole wheat flour
- 1 cup fenugreek leaves, chopped
- 2 green chilies, chopped
- 8 garlic cloves, minced
- 1 cup water
- 2 teaspoons vegetable oil
- 2 tablespoons ghee, melted

Directions:
In a bowl, combine the flour with the fenugreek and the other ingredients except the ghee, and knead a smooth dough. Shape medium balls out of this mix and flatten them on a working surface. Set the Instant pot on Sauté mode, add the ghee, heat it up, add the parathas, cook for 4 minutes on each side, divide between plates and serve for breakfast.

Nutrition: calories 228, fat 6.1, fiber 6.4, carbs 37.9, protein 8.6

Poori Masala

Preparation time: 10 minutes | Cooking time: 23 minutes | Servings: 4

Ingredients:
- 2 big gold potatoes, peeled and cubed
- 1 yellow onion, chopped
- 2 tomatoes, chopped
- 2 teaspoons ginger, grated
- 2 green chilies, chopped
- 10 curry leaves, chopped
- 1 teaspoon cumin seeds
- 1 teaspoon mustard seeds
- 2 teaspoons chana dal
- 1 teaspoon urad dal
- ½ teaspoon turmeric powder
- 10 cashews, chopped
- 2 teaspoons gram flour
- 1 and ½ cusp water
- 2 tablespoons coriander, chopped
- 2 tablespoons vegetable oil
- Salt to the taste

Directions:
Set the Instant pot on Sauté mode, add the oil, heat it up, add the chilies, curr leaves, cumin, mustard seeds, chana dal, urad dal and turmeric and cook for 5 minutes. Add the cashews and brown them for 3 minutes more. Add the potatoes and the other ingredients, put the lid on and cook on High for 15 minutes. Release the pressure naturally for 10 minutes, divide everything between plates and serve.

Nutrition: calories 167, fat 10.7, fiber 3.9, carbs 16.6, protein 3.4

Oats Upma

Preparation time: 10 minutes | Cooking time: 20 minutes | Servings: 4

Ingredients:

- 1 cup quick oats
- ¼ cup onions, chopped
- ¼ cup French beans, chopped
- ¼ cup carrots, chopped
- ¼ cup green peas
- 8 curry leaves, chopped
- 1 teaspoon cumin seeds
- 1 teaspoon mustard seeds
- 1 teaspoon chana dal
- 10 peanuts, chopped
- ½ teaspoon ginger, grated
- 2 tablespoons coriander, chopped
- 2 green chilies, chopped
- 1 and ½ cups water
- Salt to the taste
- 1 and ½ tablespoons ghee, melted

Directions:

Set the instant pot on Sauté mode, add the ghee, heat it up, add the oats, curry leaves, cumin seeds, mustard seeds, chana dal and peanuts and cook for 5 minutes. Add the other ingredients, put the lid on and cook on High for 15 minutes. Release the pressure naturally for 10 minutes, divide everything between plates and serve.

Nutrition: calories 247, fat 12.4, fiber 8, carbs 28.2, protein 8.2

Tomato Upma

Preparation time: 10 minutes | Cooking time: 20 minutes | Servings: 2

Ingredients:

- 1 cup cream of wheat
- 2 tablespoons ghee, melted
- 1 teaspoon cumin seeds
- 1 teaspoon urad dal
- 1 teaspoon mustard seeds
- 1 teaspoon chana dal
- 2 red chilies, minced
- 1 yellow onion, chopped
- A pinch of asafetida powder
- 2 large tomatoes, roughly chopped
- 1 teaspoon ginger, grated
- 6 curry leaves, chopped
- ½ teaspoon red chili powder
- ¼ teaspoon turmeric powder
- 2 and ½ cups water
- Salt to the taste

Directions:

Set the instant pot on Sauté mode, add the ghee, heat it up, add the cream of wheat, cumin, urad dal, mustard seed, chana dal and chilies, stir and cook for 5 minutes. Add the onion and the other ingredients, put the lid on and cook o High for 15 minutes. Release the pressure naturally for 10 minutes, divide the mix between plates and serve.

Nutrition: calories 269, fat 14.8, fiber 6.5, carbs 31.7, protein 5.9

Semiya Upma

***Preparation time:** 10 minutes | **Cooking time:** 15 minutes | **Servings:** 3*

Ingredients:
- 1 cup whole wheat vermicelli
- 2 tablespoons vegetable oil
- ½ teaspoon mustard seeds
- ½ teaspoon cumin seeds
- 1 yellow onion, chopped
- ½ teaspoon ginger, grated
- 1 green chili, chopped
- 1 red chili, chopped
- 8 curry leaves, chopped
- 2 cups water
- ½ teaspoon sugar
- 2 tablespoons coriander, chopped
- Salt to the taste

Directions:
Set the instant pot on Sauté mode, add the oil, heat it up, add the mustard and cumin seeds and brown for 2 minutes. Add the onion, ginger and the chilies, stir and sauté for 2 minutes more. Add the vermicelli and the other ingredients, put the lid on and cook on High for 11 minutes. Release the pressure naturally for 10 minutes, divide everything between plates and serve for breakfast.

Nutrition: calories 136, fat 10, fiber 2.3, carbs 10.5, protein 2.1

Chura Matar

***Preparation time:** 10 minutes | **Cooking time:** 15 minutes | **Servings:** 2*

Ingredients:
- 1 and ½ cups flattened rice
- ½ cup green peas
- 1 teaspoon cumin seeds
- 1 tablespoon vegetable oil
- 2 green chilies, chopped
- 1 teaspoon ginger, grated
- 1 cup water
- ½ teaspoon black pepper
- ½ teaspoon garam masala
- ½ cup coriander, chopped
- 1 teaspoon lemon juice
- 12 cashews, chopped

Directions:
Set the instant pot on Sauté mode, add the oil, heat it up, add the cumin, chilies and ginger and cook for 2 minutes Add the rice and cook for 2 minutes more. Add the rest of the ingredients, put the lid on and cook on High for 11 minutes more. Release the pressure naturally for 10 minutes, divide everything between plates and serve for breakfast.

Nutrition: calories 285, fat 16, fiber 4, carbs 30.4, protein 7.1

Sweet Pongal

Preparation time: 5 minutes | Cooking time: 15 minutes | Servings: 4

Ingredients:
- ½ cup white rice
- ½ cup split mung lentils
- 3 cups water
- ½ cup jaggery, grated mixed with ½ cup water
- 12 cashews, chopped
- 5 tablespoons ghee, melted
- ½ teaspoon cardamom powder

Directions:
In your Instant pot, combine the rice with the lentils and the other ingredients, toss, put the lid on and cook on High for 15 minutes. Release the pressure fast for 5 minutes, divide everything into bowls and serve for breakfast.

Nutrition: calories 293, fat 19.2, fiber 2.5, carbs 26.1, protein 4.9

Sweet Dalia

Preparation time: 15 minutes | Cooking time: 20 minutes | Servings: 4

Ingredients:
- 1 tablespoon ghee, melted
- ½ cup dalia
- 2 cups water
- 1 and ½ cups milk
- 1/3 cup sugar
- ½ teaspoon cardamom
- 1 tablespoon almonds, chopped
- 1 tablespoon cashews

Directions:
Set the instant pot on Sauté mode, add the ghee, heat it up, add the dalia and roast for 4 minutes. Add the water, put the lid on and cook on High for 6 minutes. Release the pressure naturally for 10 minutes, add the rest of the ingredients, put the lid back on and cook on High for 10 minutes more. Release the pressure fast for 5 minutes, divide the mix between plates and serve.

Nutrition: calories 364, fat 12.3, fiber 3.4, carbs 7, protein 3.4

Kadala Curry

Preparation time: 10 minutes | Cooking time: 25 minutes | Servings: 4

Ingredients:

- 1 cup black chickpeas, soaked in water overnight and drained
- 2 cups water
- ½ teaspoon fennel seeds
- 1-inch cinnamon, crushed
- 4 cloves, crushed
- 1 teaspoon nutmeg, ground
- ½ cup coconut, grated mixed with ½ cup water
- 1/3 cup shallots, chopped
- 1 teaspoon ginger, grated
- 2 green chilies, chopped
- 12 curry leaves, chopped
- ½ teaspoon mustard seeds
- 1 teaspoon red chili powder
- ¼ teaspoon turmeric powder
- 1 teaspoon coriander powder
- 2 tablespoons coconut oil
- Salt to the taste

Directions:

Set the instant pot on Sauté mode, add the oil, heat it up, add the fennel cinnamon, cloves and nutmeg, stir and cook for 2 minutes. Add the coconut, shallots, ginger, chilies and the curry leaves, stir and cook for 2 minutes more. Add the chickpeas and the other ingredients, toss, put the lid on and cook on High for 20 minutes. Release the pressure naturally for 10 minutes, divide everything into bowls and serve.

Nutrition: calories 342, fat 11.4 fiber 3.4, carbs 15.5, protein 6.6

Paneer Butter Masala

Preparation time: 10 minutes | Cooking time: 30 minutes | Servings: 4

Ingredients:

- 20 cashews, chopped
- 4 tomatoes, chopped
- 2 tablespoons butter
- 4 garlic cloves, mined
- 1-inch ginger, grated
- 1 Indian bay leaf
- 1 teaspoon red chili powder
- 1 and ½ cups water
- 2 green chilies, chopped
- 1 teaspoon garam masala
- 1 cup cottage cheese, diced
- 2 tablespoons whipping cream
- 1 teaspoon sugar
- Salt to the taste
- 2 tablespoons coriander, chopped

Directions:

Set the instant pot on sauté mode, add the butter, heat it up, add the garlic, ginger, bay leaf, garam masala and the chili powder, stir and cook for 5 minutes. Add the cashews and the other ingredients, toss, put the lid on and cook on High for 25 minutes. Release the pressure naturally for 10 minutes, divide everything into bowls and serve for breakfast.

Nutrition: calories 208, fat 13.6, fiber 2.2, carbs 12.8, protein 10.8

Oats Porridge

Preparation time: 5 minutes | Cooking time: 20 minutes | Servings: 4

Ingredients:
- 1 cup rolled oats
- 2 cups water
- 1 cup milk
- 2 tablespoons sugar

Directions:
In your instant pot, combine the water with the oats and the other ingredients, put the lid on and cook on High for 20 minutes. Release the pressure fast for 5 minutes, stir the mix, divide it into bowls and serve.

Nutrition: calories 131, fat 2.6, fiber 2.1, carbs 22.8, protein 4.7

Oats Khichdi

Preparation time: 10 minutes | Cooking time: 15 minutes | Servings: 2

Ingredients:
- 2 tablespoons ghee, melted
- 1 yellow onion, chopped
- 1 teaspoon cumin seeds
- ½ teaspoon ginger, grated
- 1/3 cup tomatoes, chopped
- 1 green chili, chopped
- 1/3 cup potatoes, peeled and chopped
- 1/3 cup carrots, chopped
- ¼ cup green peas
- 1/3 cup rolled oats
- 1/3 cup moong lentils
- ¼ teaspoon red chili powder
- ¼ teaspoon turmeric powder
- 2 and ½ cups water
- Salt to the taste

Directions:
Set the instant pot on Sauté mode, add the ghee, heat it up, add the cumin, ginger, chili, chili powder and turmeric, stir and cook for 5 minutes. Add the onion and the other ingredients, toss, put the lid on and cook on High for 10 minutes. Release the pressure naturally for 10 minutes, divide everything into bowls and serve.

Nutrition: calories 253, fat 6.7, fiber 3.5, carbs 22.4, protein 6.7

Bhindi Masala

***Preparation time:** 10 minutes | **Cooking time:** 20 minutes | **Servings:** 2*

Ingredients:
- 2 tablespoons vegetable oil
- 10 ounces bhindi (okra)
- 1 yellow onion, chopped
- 1 teaspoon ginger and garlic paste
- 2 tomatoes, chopped
- 1 teaspoon coriander powder
- ½ teaspoon red chili powder
- ½ teaspoon fennel powder
- ½ teaspoon turmeric powder
- ½ teaspoon garam masala
- ½ teaspoon dry mango powder
- Salt to the taste
- 2 tablespoons coriander, chopped

Directions:
Set the instant pot on Sauté mode, add the oil, heat it up, add the ginger and garlic paste, coriander powder, chili powder, fennel, turmeric, mango powder and garam masala, toss and cook for 5 minutes. Add the rest of the ingredients, put the lid on and cook on High for 15 minutes. Release the pressure naturally for 10 minutes, divide everything into bowls and serve for breakfast.

Nutrition: calories 245, fat 7.8, fiber 2.4, carbs 22.5, protein 2.5

Gajar Matar

***Preparation time:** 5 minutes | **Cooking time:** 25 minutes | **Servings:** 4*

Ingredients:
- 4 carrots, sliced
- 1 cup green peas
- 1 teaspoon cumin, ground
- 1-inch ginger, grated
- 2 chili peppers, chopped
- ¼ teaspoon garam masala
- ½ teaspoon red chili powder
- 2 tablespoons vegetable oil
- ½ cup water
- 1 tablespoon coriander, chopped
- Salt to the taste

Directions:
Set the Instant pot on Sauté mode, add the cumin, ginger, chilies, garam masala and chili powder, stir and cook for 5 minutes. Add the carrots and the other ingredients, toss, put the lid on and cook on High for 20 minutes. Release the pressure fast for 5 minutes, divide the mix into bowls and serve for breakfast.

Nutrition: calories 300, fat 7.7, fiber 3.4, carbs 15.6, protein 5.7

Aloo Capsicum

Preparation time: 10 minutes | Cooking time: 20 minutes | Servings: 3

Ingredients:
- 4 capsicums, chopped
- 3 potatoes, peeled and cubed
- ½ teaspoon turmeric powder
- ½ teaspoon red chili powder
- 1 teaspoon mango powder
- 1 teaspoon garam masala
- 2 tablespoons vegetable oil
- Salt to the taste

Directions:
Set the instant pot on Sauté mode, add the oil, heat it up, add the turmeric, chili powder, mango powder and garam masala, toss and cook for 5 minutes. Add the rest of the ingredients, put the lid on and cook on High for 15 minutes. Release the pressure naturally for 10 minutes, divide the mix between plates and serve.

Nutrition: calories 254, fat 9.7, fiber 6.2, carbs 39.2, protein 4.8

Jeera Aloo

Preparation time: 10 minutes | Cooking time: 12 minutes | Servings: 5

Ingredients:
- 6 potatoes, peeled and cubed
- Salt to the taste
- 3 tablespoons vegetable oil
- 2 teaspoons cumin seeds
- 3 green chilies, chopped
- ½ teaspoon turmeric powder
- ½ teaspoon red chili powder
- ¼ cup coriander, chopped
- 4 teaspoons lemon juice

Directions:
Set the Instant pot on Sauté mode, add the oil, heat it up, add the cumin, chilies, turmeric and chili powder, stir and cook for 2 minutes. Add the rest of the ingredients, put the lid on and cook on High for 10 minutes. Release the pressure naturally for 10 minutes, divide everything between plates and serve.

Nutrition: calories 245, fat 11.4, fiber 3.5, carbs 15.5, protein 3.6

Aloo Moongre Ki Sabzi

Preparation time: 10 minutes | Cooking time: 20 minutes | Servings: 4

Ingredients:
- ¼ pound radish pods
- 2 potatoes, peeled and cubed
- ½ teaspoon chili powder
- 1 teaspoon turmeric powder
- ¼ teaspoon garam masala powder
- 3 tablespoons mustard oil
- Salt to the taste
- 1 teaspoon mango powder

Directions:
Set the Instant pot on Sauté mode, add the oil, heat it up, add the chili powder, turmeric, and garam masala, stir and cook for 5 minutes. Add the potatoes and the other ingredients, put the lid on and cook on High for 15 minutes. Release the pressure naturally for 10 minutes, divide everything into bowls and serve.

Nutrition: calories 245, fat 11.3, fiber 5.4, carbs 13.2, protein 3.4

Bharwa Karela

Preparation time: 10 minutes | Cooking time: 20 minutes | Servings: 4

Ingredients:
- 1 teaspoon turmeric powder
- 1 teaspoon red chili powder
- ¼ teaspoon punjam garam masala
- 1 teaspoon mango powder
- 1 teaspoon fennel powder
- 2 yellow onions, chopped
- 3 tablespoons vegetable oil
- 1 tablespoon coriander, chopped
- Salt to the taste
- 12 small karela

Directions:
Set the instant pot on Sauté mode, add the oil, heat it up, add the turmeric, chili powder, garam masala, mango powder and fennel powder, stir and cook for 5 minutes. Add the rest of the ingredients, put the lid on and cook on High for 15 minutes. Release the pressure naturally for 10 minutes, divide everything into bowls and serve for breakfast.

Nutrition: calories 300, fat 14.6, fiber 3.5, carbs 12.5, protein 4.6

Kurkuri Bhindi

Preparation time: 10 minutes | Cooking time: 20 minutes | Servings: 4

Ingredients:
- 1 pound okra (bhindi), sliced
- 1 teaspoon coriander powder
- ½ teaspoon turmeric powder
- 1 teaspoon cumin powder
- 1 teaspoon chili powder
- 1 teaspoon mango powder
- 1 teaspoon garam masala powder
- 1 teaspoon chaat masala
- 2 tablespoons vegetable oil
- ½ cup water
- Salt to the taste

Directions:
In your instant pot, combine the okra with the coriander, turmeric and the other ingredients, put the lid on and cook on High for 20 minutes. Release the pressure naturally for 10 minutes, divide everything into bowls and serve for breakfast.

Nutrition: calories 245, fat 9.8, fiber 3.4, carbs 15.6, protein 7.6

Banana Moong Dal

Preparation time: 10 minutes | Cooking time: 10 minutes | Servings: 4

Ingredients:
- 8 bananas, peeled and sliced
- ½ cup yellow moong dal
- 1 yellow onion, chopped
- 5 garlic cloves, minced
- ½ teaspoon ginger, grated
- 2 green chilies, chopped
- ¼ tablespoon turmeric powder
- 1 tablespoon cumin seeds
- 1 tablespoon coconut spice powder
- ½ tablespoon coriander, chopped
- ½ tablespoon red chili powder
- 1 tablespoon curry powder
- 3 tablespoons vegetable oil
- Juice of 1 lime
- ¼ cup water

Directions:
Set the instant pot on Sauté mode, add the moong dal, ginger, chilies, turmeric, cumin, coconut powder, coriander, chili and curry powder, stir and cook for 5 minutes. Add the bananas and the other ingredients, put the lid on and cook on High for 5 minutes. Release the pressure naturally for 10 minutes, divide the mix into bowls and serve for breakfast.

Nutrition: calories 470, fat 20.8, fiber 7.9, carbs 72.2, protein 6

Mango Moong Dal

Preparation time: 5 minutes | **Cooking time:** 20 minutes | **Servings:** 4

Ingredients:
- ¼ cup mung dal
- 1 teaspoon chili powder
- 1 teaspoon turmeric powder
- 1 green mango, peeled and cubed
- Salt to the taste
- 1 teaspoon nigella seeds
- 2 tablespoons ghee, melted
- 1 teaspoon mustard seeds
- 2 red chilies, minced
- 1 shallot, chopped

Directions:
Set the Instant pot on Sauté mode, add the mung dal, chili and turmeric powder and cook for 2 minutes. Add the mango and the other ingredients, put the lid on and cook on High for 18 minutes. Release the pressure fast for 5 minutes, divide the dal into bowls and serve for breakfast.

Nutrition: calories 300, fat 15.4, fiber 3.4, carbs 17.6, protein 11.2

Sweet Potato Dhal

Preparation time: 10 minutes | *Cooking time:* 17 minutes | *Servings:* 4

Ingredients:
- 2 garlic cloves, minced
- 1 red onion, chopped
- 1 tablespoon sesame oil
- 1 teaspoon ginger, grated
- 1 red chili, chopped
- 2 teaspoons turmeric powder
- 1 teaspoon cumin, ground
- 2 sweet potatoes, peeled and cut into chunks
- 1 cup red lentils
- 2 cups veggie stock
- ½ tablespoon basil, chopped

Directions:
Set the instant pot on Sauté mode, add the oil, heat it up, add the garlic, onion, ginger, chili, turmeric and the cumin and sauté for 2 minutes. Add the sweet potatoes and the other ingredients, put the lid on and cook on High for 15 minutes. Release the pressure naturally for 10 minutes, divide everything into bowls and serve for breakfast.

Nutrition: calories 314, fat 12.5, fiber 5.4, carbs 22, protein 1.9

Carrot Rasam and Moong Dal

Preparation time: 10 minutes | Cooking time: 10 minutes | Servings: 4

Ingredients:
- 14 baby carrots, peeled and sliced
- 2 tomatoes, chopped
- 2 tablespoons yellow moong dal
- 1 tablespoon ghee, melted
- ¼ tablespoon turmeric powder
- Salt to the taste
- Juice of ½ lime
- 2 cups water
- 4 garlic cloves, mined
- 1-inch ginger, grated

Directions:
Set the instant pot on sauté mode, add the ghee, heat it up, add the moong dal, turmeric, garlic and ginger and sauté for 2 minutes. Add the carrots and the other ingredients, put the lid on and cook on High for 8 minutes. Release the pressure naturally for 10 minutes, divide the mix into bowls and serve for breakfast.

Nutrition: calories 344, fat 15.5, fiber 3.5, carbs 23.4, protein 5.67

Tomato Rice

Preparation time: 10 minutes | Cooking time: 20 minutes | Servings: 4

Ingredients:
- 1 cup basmati rice, soaked in 1 and ½ cups water
- ½ cup yellow moong dal, soaked for 30 minutes and drained
- 2 tomatoes, chopped
- 1 potato, peeled and cubed
- 2 green chilies, chopped
- 1 tablespoon garlic and ginger paste
- 1 shallot, chopped
- 4 cloves, ground
- 3 cardamom, crushed
- 2 bay leaves
- ½ tablespoon cumin seeds
- 3 tablespoons vegetable oil
- ½ tablespoon sambar powder
- Salt to the taste

Directions:
Set the instant pot on Sauté mode, add the oil, heat it up, add the chilies, garlic paste, shallot, cloves, cardamom, bay leaves and cumin seeds, stir and sauté for 5 minutes. Add the rice and the other ingredients, put the lid on and cook on High for 15 minutes. Release the pressure naturally for 10 minutes, divide the mix into bowls and serve for breakfast.

Nutrition: calories 244, fat 11.7, fiber 4.5, carbs 18.9, protein 3.4

Paneer Spread

Preparation time: 10 minutes | Cooking time: 15 minutes | Servings: 4

Ingredients:
- 1 cup grated paneer
- 1 cup milk
- ½ cup jaggery
- ¼ tablespoon pistachios, chopped
- 3 tablespoons semolina
- 1 tablespoon ghee, melted
- 4 cardamom, ground
- 2 cups water

Directions:
Grease a steel bowl with the ghee, add all the ingredients except the water inside and whisk well. Put the water in the instant pot, add the trivet inside, add the bowls, put the lid on and cook on High for 15 minutes. Release the pressure naturally for 10 minutes, whisk the mix, cool down and serve as a breakfast spread.

Nutrition: calories 300, fat 14.5, fiber 4.5, carbs 17.4, protein 4.9

Green Dosa

Preparation time: 10 minutes | Cooking time: 12 minutes | Servings: 6

Ingredients:
- 3 cups cauliflower florets
- 2 potatoes, peeled and cubed
- ½ cup green peas
- 1 carrot, chopped
- 1 yellow onion, chopped
- 1 tablespoon green chili paste
- 4 garlic cloves, minced
- 1 tablespoon ginger, grated
- 1 tablespoon red chili powder
- 1 tablespoon coriander, chopped
- 1 tablespoon cumin powder
- 1 tablespoon dry mango powder
- 2 tablespoons vegetable oil
- ¼ tablespoon turmeric powder
- Salt to the taste
- ½ tablespoons mustard seeds
- 1 tablespoon cumin, ground

Directions:
Set the instant pot on Sauté mode, add the oil, heat it up, add the chili paste, garlic, ginger, chili powder, coriander, cumin, mango and turmeric powder, mustard seeds and cumin and sauté for 3 minutes. Add the rest of the ingredients, put the lid on and cook on High for 9 minutes. Release the pressure naturally for 10 minutes, divide everything into bowls and serve for breakfast.

Nutrition: calories 355, fat 16.5, fiber 3.5, carbs 18.2, protein 3.4

Veggie Masala

Preparation time: 10 minutes | Cooking time: 20 minutes | Servings: 4

Ingredients:
- 1 cup basmati rice
- 2 tablespoons masala paste
- 1 and ½ cups water
- Salt to the taste
- 2 tablespoons ghee, melted
- 1 yellow onion, chopped
- 1 cup cauliflower florets
- 1 cup green beans, trimmed and halved
- 2 carrots, sliced
- 1 red bell pepper, chopped
- 2 potatoes, peeled and cubed
- 2 tomatoes, chopped
- 1 tablespoon mint, chopped
- 24 soya granules, toasted

Directions:
Set the instant pot on Sauté mode, add the ghee, heat it up, add the masala paste, onion, cauliflower and the other ingredients except the rice and water, stir and sauté for 4 minutes. Add the remaining ingredients, put the lid on and cook on High for 16 minutes. Release the pressure naturally for 10 minutes, divide everything between plates and serve.

Nutrition: calories 288, fat 11.2, fiber 4.65, carbs 12.4, protein 5.4

Green Peas Masala Rice

Preparation time: 10 minutes | Cooking time: 20 minutes | Servings: 4

Ingredients:
- 1 and ¼ cups basmati rice, soaked for 30 minutes and drained
- 2 and ½ cups water
- ½ cup green peas
- 2 green chilies, chopped
- ½ cup yellow onion, chopped
- ½ cup tomatoes, chopped
- 4 garlic cloves, minced
- 2 teaspoons coriander seeds
- 3 cloves, crushed
- 1-inch cinnamon stick
- ½ teaspoon fennel seeds, ground
- ¼ teaspoon turmeric powder
- 1 teaspoon cumin seeds
- 2 tablespoons vegetable oil
- Salt to the taste

Directions:
Set the instant pot on Sauté mode, add the oil, heat it up, add the garlic, coriander, cloves, cinnamon , fennel, turmeric and cumin seeds, stir and cook for 4 minutes. Add the rest of the ingredients, put the lid on and cook on High for 16 minutes. Release the pressure naturally for 10 minutes, divide the mix between plates and serve.

Nutrition: calories 436, fat 8.1, fiber 3.6, carbs 81.4, protein 8.4

Spinach and Lentils Rice
Preparation time: *10 minutes* | ***Cooking time:*** *20 minutes* | ***Servings:*** *4*

Ingredients:
- 1 cup basmati rice
- 1 and ½ cups water
- ½ cup chana dal
- 4 handfuls spinach, chopped
- 1 tablespoon coriander, chopped
- 1 tablespoon mint, chopped
- 2 tomatoes, cubed
- 1 yellow onion, sliced
- 1 potato, peeled and cubed
- ½ tablespoon ginger, grated
- 1 tablespoon biryani masala
- Salt to the taste
- 1 tablespoon garam masala
- 2 tablespoons vegetable oil

Directions:
Set the instant pot on Sauté mode, add the oil, heat it up, add the ginger, onion, biryani masala, salt and garam masala, stir and cook for 4 minutes. Add the rice and the other ingredients, put the lid on and cook on High for 16 minutes. Release the pressure naturally for 10 minutes, divide everything into bowls and serve for breakfast.

Nutrition: calories 355, fat 11.4, fiber 3.5, carbs 25.4, protein 4.6

Broken Wheat Upma
Preparation time: *10 minutes* | ***Cooking time:*** *20 minutes* | ***Servings:*** *4*

Ingredients:
- 1 cup broken wheat rava
- ¼ cup water
- ¼ cup yellow onion, chopped
- ¼ cup carrot, chopped
- ¼ cup green beans, trimmed and chopped
- ¼ cup cauliflower florets
- ½ teaspoon mustard seeds
- ½ teaspoon cumin seeds
- 6 curry leaves, chopped
- 1 teaspoon ginger, grated
- 2 teaspoons green chilies, minced
- ¼ teaspoon turmeric powder
- 1 teaspoon vegetable oil
- 1 teaspoon ghee, melted
- 2 tablespoons coriander, chopped
- Salt to the taste

Directions:
Set the instant pot on Sauté mode, add the oil and the ghee, heat them up, add the mustard seeds, cumin seeds, curry leaves, ginger, chilies, and the turmeric, stir and sauté for 5 minutes. Ad the wheat rava and the other ingredients, put the lid on and cook on High for 15 minutes. Release the pressure naturally for 10 minutes, divide the mix into bowls and serve for breakfast.

Nutrition: calories 400, fat 13.54, fiber 4.5, carbs 22.4, protein 4.9

Millet Upma

Preparation time: 10 minutes | Cooking time: 20 minutes | Servings: 4

Ingredients:

- 1 cup mixed millet
- ¼ cup carrot, chopped
- 1 yellow onion, chopped
- ¼ cup water
- ¼ cup French beans, chopped
- ¼ cup cauliflower florets
- ½ teaspoon mustard seeds
- 5 curry leaves, chopped
- ½ teaspoon cumin seeds
- 2 green chilies, chopped
- 1 teaspoon ginger, grated
- ¼ teaspoon turmeric powder
- 1 tablespoon ghee, melted
- 2 tablespoon coriander, chopped
- Salt to the taste

Directions:

Set the instant pot on Sauté mode, add the ghee, heat it up, add mustard seeds, curry leaves, cumin, chilies, ginger, and turmeric, stir and cook for 5 minutes Add the millet and the remaining ingredients, put the lid on and cook on High for 15 minutes. Release the pressure naturally for 10 minutes, divide the mix into bowls and serve for breakfast.

Nutrition: calories 299, fat 11.2, fiber 4.5, carbs 16.7, protein 5.6

Sabudana Knichdi

Preparation time: 10 minutes | Cooking time: 25 minutes | Servings: 4

Ingredients:

- 1 cup water
- 1 cup sabudana (tapioca pearls)
- 1 potato, peeled and cubed
- ½ teaspoons mustard seeds
- ½ teaspoon cumin seeds
- 1 yellow onion, chopped
- 2 green chilies, chopped
- 1 teaspoon ginger, grated
- ¼ teaspoon turmeric powder
- Juice of 1 lemon
- ¼ cup peanuts, roasted and chopped
- 2 tablespoons vegetable oil
- 2 tablespoons coriander, chopped
- Salt to the taste

Directions:

Set the instant pot on Sauté mode, add the oil, heat it up, add the mustard seeds, cumin seeds, chilies, ginger, turmeric and the peanuts and cook for 5 minutes. Add the rest of the ingredients, put the lid on and cook on High for 20 minutes. Release the pressure naturally for 10 minutes, divide the mix into bowls and serve for breakfast.

Nutrition: calories 388, fat 11.9, fiber 3.5, carbs 22, protein 6.7

Bread Upma

Preparation time: 5 minutes | Cooking time: 20 minutes | Servings: 4

Ingredients:
- 10 bread slices, toasted and cubed
- ¼ cup vegetable stock
- 2 yellow onions, chopped
- 3 tomatoes, chopped
- 1 teaspoon sambar powder
- 2 green chilies, chopped
- 1 teaspoon turmeric powder
- 4 curry springs, chopped
- 1 teaspoon mustard seeds
- Salt to the taste
- 2 tablespoons butter
- 1 tablespoon coriander, chopped

Directions:
Set the instant pot on Sauté mode, add the butter, heat it up, add the sambar powder, turmeric, curry springs, mustard seeds and salt, stir and cook for 5 minutes. Add the bread and the other ingredients, put the lid on and cook on High for 15 minutes. Release the pressure fast for 5 minutes, divide everything into bowls and serve.

Nutrition: calories 399, fat 11, fiber 6.7, carbs 15.6, protein 5.6

Indian Farro Masala

Preparation time: 10 minutes | Cooking time: 25 minutes | Servings: 4

Ingredients:
- 2 cups water
- 2 cups farro
- 1 cup corn
- 1 cup cauliflower florets
- 1 tablespoon vegetable oil
- 2 tablespoons chaat masala
- 2 yellow onions, chopped
- 6 garlic cloves, minced
- 1 tablespoon cumin, ground
- 2 tablespoons coriander, ground
- ½ tablespoon turmeric powder
- Juice of ½ lemon
- 1 tablespoon sugar
- 1 tablespoon cilantro, chopped
- 1 tablespoon chili powder

Directions:
Set the instant pot on Sauté mode, add the oil, heat it up, add the onions, garlic, masala, cumin, coriander, turmeric, and chili powder, stir and cook for 5 minutes. Add the farro and the other ingredients, toss, put the lid on and cook on High for 20 minutes. Release the pressure naturally for 10 minutes, divide the mix into bowls and serve for breakfast.

Nutrition: calories 165, fat 5, fiber 5, carbs 7, protein 10

Healthy Kheer

Preparation time: 10 minutes | Cooking time: 15 minutes | Servings: 4

Ingredients:

- ½ cup rolled oats
- 1 and ½ cups water
- 3 tablespoons almonds, chopped
- A pinch of cardamom, ground
- 3 teaspoons flax seed, ground
- A pinch of nutmeg, ground
- 1 teaspoon sugar
- 2/3 cup milk

Directions:

In your instant pot, combine the oats with the water and the other ingredients, put the lid on and cook on High for 15 minutes. Release the pressure naturally for 10 minutes, divide into bowls and serve for breakfast.

Nutrition: calories 188, fat 6, fiber 4, carbs 6, protein 9

Peach and Mango Lassi

Preparation time: 5 minutes | Cooking time: 5 minutes | Servings: 4

Ingredients:

- 2 mangoes, peeled, seeded and cubed
- 2 peaches, stones removed and cubed
- 1 cup yogurt
- ½ cup skim milk
- 1 teaspoon ginger, grated
- 4 mint leaves, chopped
- ½ cup water

Directions:

In your instant pot, combine the mangoes with the peaches and the other ingredients, put the lid on and cook on High for 5 minutes Release the pressure fast for 5 minutes, blend the mix using an immersion blender, divide into bowls and serve for breakfast.

Nutrition: calories 171, fat 8, fiber 4, carbs 6, protein 5

Aloo Egg Curry

***Preparation time:** 10 minutes | **Cooking time:** 25 minutes | **Servings:** 4*

Ingredients:
- 4 eggs
- 1 and ½ tablespoons ghee, melted
- 3 green cardamoms
- ½ teaspoon cumin, ground
- 2 cups yellow onions, chopped
- 1 tomato cubed
- 2 teaspoons ginger garlic paste
- A pinch of turmeric powder
- Salt to the taste
- 1 teaspoon garam masala
- 1 teaspoon red chili powder
- 4 potatoes, peeled and cubed
- 2 tablespoons coriander, chopped

Directions:

Set the instant pot on Sauté mode, add the ghee, heat it up, add the cardamom, cumin, onion, ginger paste, turmeric, salt, garam masala, and chili powder and cook for 5 minutes. Add the rest of the ingredients, toss, put the lid on and cook on High for 20 minutes. Release the pressure naturally for 10 minutes, divide into bowls and serve for breakfast.

Nutrition: calories 200, fat 8, fiber 4, carbs 6, protein 8

Quinoa Poha

***Preparation time:** 10 minutes | **Cooking time:** 15 minute | **Servings:** 3*

Ingredients:
- ½ cup quinoa, rinsed
- 1 teaspoon mustard seeds
- 1 tablespoon vegetable oil
- 2 teaspoons ginger, grated
- 1 potato, peeled and cubed
- 1 yellow onion, chopped
- 2 green chilies, chopped
- 6 curry leaves, chopped
- Salt to the taste
- ½ cup water
- ½ cup peas
- 1 teaspoon coriander powder
- ½ teaspoon chili powder
- 1 teaspoon turmeric powder
- 2 tablespoons cilantro, chopped
- 1 teaspoon lime juice

Directions:

Set the instant pot on Sauté mode, add the oil, heat it up, add the mustard seeds, ginger, chilies, curry leaves, salt, coriander, chili powder and turmeric powder, stir and cook for 3 minutes. Add the quinoa and the other ingredients, toss, put the lid on and cook on High for 12 minute. Release the pressure naturally for 10 minutes, stir the quinoa mix, divide into bowls, and serve.

Nutrition: calories 250, fat 4.8, fiber 4.5, carbs 11.6, protein 10

Mushrooms Korma

Preparation time: 10 minutes | *Cooking time:* 20 minutes | *Servings:* 3

Ingredients:

- ½ cup yellow onions, chopped
- 1 potato, peeled and cubed
- 1 cup mushrooms, sliced
- 1 tablespoon mint, chopped
- 1 green chili, chopped
- 1 teaspoon ginger garlic paste
- 1 teaspoon garam masala
- 1 teaspoon turmeric powder
- ½ teaspoon red chili powder
- ¼ cup yogurt
- 1 tablespoon coriander, chopped
- 2 tablespoons vegetable oil

Directions:

Set the instant pot on Sauté mode, add the oil, heat it up, add the mushrooms, chili, ginger paste, garam masala, turmeric and red chili powder, stir and cook for 3 minutes. Add rest of the ingredients, put the lid on and cook on High for 17 minutes. Release the pressure naturally for 10 minutes, divide the mix between plates and serve for breakfast.

Nutrition: calories 200, fat 12, fiber 6, carbs 7.7, protein 9

Poha Bowls with Sprouts

Preparation time: 10 minutes | *Cooking time:* 20 minutes | *Servings:* 2

Ingredients:

- 1 cup flattened rice
- Salt to the taste
- 1 teaspoon sugar
- 1 teaspoon lemon juice
- 1 tablespoon ghee, melted
- ½ teaspoon mustard seeds
- 4 curry leaves, chopped
- 2 green chilies, minced
- ½ cup potato, peeled and cubed
- ¼ cup veggie stock
- 1 teaspoon turmeric powder
- ½ cup yellow onion, chopped
- 1 tablespoon coriander, chopped
- ½ cup peanuts, chopped
- ½ teaspoon chaat masala
- A pinch of black pepper
- ¼ cup cumin powder
- 1 cup green moong sprouts
- ¼ cup tomato, cubed

Directions:

Set the instant pot on Sauté mode, add the ghee, heat it up, add mustard seeds, curry leaves, chili, turmeric, coriander, peanuts, chaat masala, black pepper and cumin powder, stir and cook for 5 minutes. Add the rest of the ingredients, toss, put the lid on and cook on High for 15 minutes. Release the pressure naturally for 10 minutes, divide the mix into bowls and serve.

Nutrition: calories 263, fat 11.8, fiber 5.5, carbs 9.7, protein 1.1

Ragi and Kale Idli

Preparation time: 30 minutes | Cooking time: 12 minutes | Servings: 3

Ingredients:
- 1 cup urad dal, soaked in ½ cup water for 30 minutes
- ¼ cup poha
- 2 cups ragi flour
- 4 methi seeds
- 8 kale leaves, chopped
- Salt to the taste
- Cooking spray

Directions:
In a bowl, combine the urad dal with the poha and the other ingredients except the cooking spray, stir well and shape medium cakes out of this mix. Grease the instant pot with the cooking spray, add the cakes inside, put the lid on and cook on High for 12 minutes. Release the pressure naturally for 10 minutes, divide the cakes between plates and serve for breakfast.

Nutrition: calories 260, fat 12, fiber 5, carbs 6.6, protein 8.3

Beans Masala

Preparation time: 10 minutes | Cooking time: 20 minutes | Servings: 4

Ingredients:
- 1 teaspoon mustard seeds
- 2 teaspoons urad dal
- 1 curry leaf, chopped
- 2 cups French beans, trimmed
- ½ cup yellow onion, chopped
- ½ teaspoon turmeric powder
- 1 tablespoon vegetable oil
- Salt to the taste
- 4 shallots, chopped
- 3 garlic cloves, minced
- 3 tablespoons coconut, shredded
- 1 tablespoon coriander seeds
- 1 teaspoon jeera
- 2 red chilies, chopped
- 2 tablespoons coriander, chopped

Directions:
In your instant pot, combine the mustard seeds with the oil, curry leaf and the other ingredients, toss, put the lid on and cook on High for 20 minutes. Release the pressure naturally for 10 minutes, stir the mix, divide it into bowls and serve.

Nutrition: calories 480, fat 9.8, fiber 3.5, carbs 16.8, protein 6

Fruit Masala

Preparation time: 5 minutes | Cooking time: 10 minutes | Servings: 4

Ingredients:
- 1 teaspoon black peppercorns
- 2 teaspoons coriander seeds
- 1 teaspoon pomegranate seeds, dried
- ½ teaspoon ajowan seeds
- ¼ teaspoon chili powder
- 1 papaya, peeled and cubed
- Juice for 2 limes
- 1 pineapple, peeled and cubed
- 4 bananas, peeled and cubed
- A handful mint, chopped

Directions:
In your instant pot, combine the peppercorns with the coriander and the other ingredients, put the lid on and cook on High for 10 minutes. Release the pressure fast for 5 minutes, divide everything into bowls and serve for breakfast.

Nutrition: calories 173, fat 4.3, fiber 2, carbs 7.5, protein 5

Banana Salad

Preparation time: 5 minutes | Cooking time: 6 minutes | Servings: 2

Ingredients:
- 2 green chilies, chopped
- 2 bananas, peeled and sliced
- 2 cups curd
- ¼ teaspoon red chili powder
- ½ tablespoon sugar
- 1 tablespoon coriander

Directions:
In your instant pot, combine the bananas with the chilies and the other ingredients, put the lid on and cook on High for 6 minutes. Release the pressure fast for 5 minutes, divide into bowls and serve for breakfast.

Nutrition: calories 257, fat 4,8, fiber 4, carbs 11.6, protein 8.10

Rose Rice Bowls

Preparation time: 10 minutes | Cooking time: 20 minutes | Servings: 4

Ingredients:
- 1 and ½ cups basmati rice
- 1 teaspoon cardamom, ground
- 3 cups milk
- 1 teaspoon rosewater
- 2 tablespoons sugar
- 3 tablespoons pistachios

Directions:
In your instant pot, combine the rice with the cardamom and the other ingredients, toss, put the lid on and cook on High for 20 minutes. Release the pressure naturally for 10 minutes, divide the mix into bowls and serve for breakfast.

Nutrition: calories 180, fat 11, fiber 5.4, carbs 8.4, protein 7

Rice Salad

Preparation time: 10 minutes | Cooking time: 30 minutes | Servings: 6

Ingredients:
- 2 cups basmati rice
- 4 cups water
- Salt to the taste
- ½ cup vegetable oil
- 1/3 cup rice vinegar
- 1 tablespoon sesame oil
- 2 tablespoons ginger, grated
- 1 and ¼ cups mango, peeled and cubed
- 1 cup cucumber, cubed
- ½ cup scallions, chopped
- ¼ cup cilantro, chopped

Directions:
Set your instant pot on Sauté mode, add the oil, heat it up, add the scallions and sauté for 5 minutes. Add the rice, water and the other ingredients, toss, put the lid on and cook on High for 25 minutes. Release the pressure naturally for 10 minutes, divide the mix into bowls and serve for breakfast.

Nutrition: calories 320, fat 14, fiber 1, carbs 45, protein 4

Apricot Rava Pudding

Preparation time: 10 minutes | Cooking time: 20 minutes | Servings: 3

Ingredients:
- 1 and ½ cups milk
- ½ cup sugar
- 4 tablespoons semolina (rava)
- ½ cup strawberries, chopped
- 4 apricot, stones removed and cubed
- 2 tablespoons pecans, chopped

Directions:
In your instant pot, combine the sugar with the milk and the other ingredients, toss, put the lid on and coo on High for 20 minutes. Release the pressure naturally for 10 minutes, divide the mix into bowls and serve for breakfast.

Nutrition: calories 190, fat 5.4, fiber 4.2, carbs 8.6, protein 1

Bell Pepper Omelet

Preparation time: 10 minutes | Cooking time: 10 minutes | Servings: 2

Ingredients:
- 2 eggs, whisked
- 1 tomato, cubed
- 1 yellow onion , chopped
- 1 green bell pepper, chopped
- Salt and the black pepper to the taste
- 1 cup water
- Cooking spray

Directions:
In a bowl, mix the eggs with the other ingredients except the cooking spray and the water and whisk well Grease a pan that fits your instant pot with cooking spray and pour the omelet mix inside. Add the water to your instant pot, add the trivet inside, add the pan with the omelet mix, put the lid on and cook on High for 10 minutes. Release the pressure naturally for 10 minutes, divide the omelet between plates and serve.

Nutrition: calories 271, fat 12, fiber 5, carbs 5.6, protein 7.8

Masala Omelet

Preparation time: 10 minutes | Cooking time: 12 minutes | Servings: 4

Ingredients:
- 4 eggs, whisked
- 2 tablespoons milk
- A pinch of turmeric powder
- 2 tablespoons butter, melted
- 1 green bell pepper, chopped
- 1 tomato, cubed
- 1 potato, boiled, peeled and cubed
- 12 coriander stems, chopped
- 1 green chili pepper, chopped
- Salt and black pepper to the taste

Directions:
Set the instant pot on Sauté mode, add the butter, melt it, add the bell pepper, tomato, potato, coriander and chili pepper, stir and sauté for 2 minutes. Add the rest of the ingredients, toss, spread, put the lid on and cook on High for 10 minutes. Release the pressure naturally for 10 minutes, divide the omelet between plates and serve for breakfast.

Nutrition: calories 342, fat 6.4, fiber 5.3, carbs 9.6, protein 9

Figs and Tomatoes Salad

Preparation time: 5 minutes | Cooking time: 8 minutes | Servings: 4

Ingredients:
- 1 cup spinach, torn
- 5 figs, cut into quarters
- 10 cherry tomatoes, halved
- 1 cucumber, sliced
- ¼ cup red wine vinegar
- 1 teaspoon mustard
- ¼ cup vegetable oil
- Salt and black pepper to the taste

Directions:
In your instant pot, combine the spinach with the figs and the other ingredients, toss, put the lid on and cook on Low for 8 minutes. Release the pressure fast for 5 minutes, divide into bowls and serve for breakfast.

Nutrition: calories 161, fat 7, fiber 3.3, carbs 6.5, protein 5

Millet Pongal

Preparation time: 10 minutes | Cooking time: 20 minutes | Servings: 2

Ingredients:
- ¼ cup moong dal, soaked for 2 hours and drained
- ¼ cup millet, soaked for 2 hours and drained
- 1 and ½ cups water
- 2 tablespoons brown rice
- 4 peppercorns
- 4 cashews, chopped
- ¼ teaspoon cumin, ground
- 1 green chili, chopped
- Salt to the taste
- 1 teaspoon ginger, grated
- 1 teaspoon turmeric powder
- 2 teaspoons ghee, melted

Directions:
In your instant pot, combine the moong dal with the millet and the other ingredients, toss, put the lid on and cook on High for 20 minutes. Release the pressure naturally for 10 minutes, stir the mix, divide it into bowls and serve for breakfast.

Nutrition: calories 370, fat 11.6, fiber 4, carbs 9.8, protein 6.5

Apple Ragi Halwa

Preparation time: 10 minutes | Cooking time: 10 minutes | Servings: 2

Ingredients:

- 4 tablespoons ragi flour
- 1 cup water
- 1 big apple, cored and cubed
- 1 teaspoon ghee, melted
- 2 teaspoons jaggery

Directions:

In your instant pot, combine the apple with the ghee and the other ingredients, toss, put the lid on and cook on High for 10 minutes. Release the pressure naturally for 10 minutes, blend the mix using an immersion blender, divide into bowls and serve for breakfast.

Nutrition: calories 128, fat 2.4, fiber 9.1, carbs 33.6, protein 1.1

Ragi Malt Java

Preparation time: 10 minutes | Cooking time: 10 minutes | Servings: 2

Ingredients:

- ¼ cup ragi flour (millet flour)
- 1 and ½ cups water
- 1 and ½ tablespoons sugar
- 1 and ½ cups milk
- 2 teaspoons ghee, melted
- A pinch of cardamom powder
- 1 tablespoon almonds, chopped

Directions:

In your instant pot, mix the ragi flour with the water and the other ingredients, put the lid on and cook on High for 10 minutes. Release the pressure naturally for 10 minutes, stir the mix, divide it into bowls and serve.

Nutrition: calories 272, fat 8.5, fiber 4, carbs 11.7, protein 6

Egg and Broccoli Bhurji

Preparation time: 10 minutes | Cooking time: 20 minutes | Servings: 4

Ingredients:

- 3 eggs, whisked
- 1 cup broccoli florets, chopped
- Salt to the taste
- 2 yellow onions, chopped
- 2 tomatoes, cubed
- 1 teaspoon turmeric powder
- 5 garlic cloves, minced
- 2 teaspoons red chili powder
- 2 tablespoons coriander, chopped
- 2 tablespoons vegetable oil

Directions:

Set the instant pot on Sauté mode, add the oil, heat it up, add the onions, garlic, chili powder and turmeric, stir and cook for 5 minutes. Add the whisked eggs and the other ingredients, toss, put the lid on and cook on High for 15 minutes. Release the pressure naturally for 10 minutes, divide the mix between plates and serve for breakfast.

Nutrition: calories 290, fat 7.2, fiber 2, carbs 5.8, protein 7

Indian Instant Pot Lunch Recipes

Paneer Butter Masala

Preparation time: 10 minutes | *Cooking time:* 20 minutes | *Servings:* 4

Ingredients:
- 1 pound paneer, cut into chunks
- 1 teaspoon cumin seeds
- 2 tablespoons butter
- 1 yellow onions, chopped
- 1 tablespoon ginger, grated
- 1 tablespoon garlic, minced
- 4 tomatoes, cubed
- ¼ cup cashews, chopped
- 2 tablespoons fenugreek leaves, chopped
- ¼ cup water
- ¼ cup coconut cream
- 1 tablespoon honey
- Salt to the taste
- 1 teaspoon red chili powder
- ½ teaspoon turmeric powder

Directions:
In your instant pot, combine the butter with the cumin and all the other ingredients except the paneer, cream and honey, toss, put the lid on and cook on High for 15 minutes. Release the pressure naturally for 10 minutes, add the paneer, cream and honey, toss, set the machine on Sauté mode again, cook for 5 minutes more, divide into bowls and serve for lunch.

Nutrition: calories 387, fat 22.7, fiber 5.9, carbs 38.5

Aloo Baingan Masala

Preparation time: 10 minutes | *Cooking time:* 20 minutes | *Servings:* 6

Ingredients:
- 2 and ½ tablespoons mustard oil
- 1 cup red bell peppers, chopped
- 1 cup yellow onion, chopped
- 1 cup green chilies, chopped
- 1-inch ginger, grated
- 5 garlic cloves, minced
- 4 tomatoes, cubed
- 10 cashews, chopped
- 8 baby eggplants, halved
- 3 potatoes, peeled and cubed
- ½ cup veggie stock
- 1 teaspoon cumin seeds
- 1 teaspoon coriander powder
- 1 teaspoon turmeric powder
- 2 teaspoons cayenne pepper
- 1 teaspoon garam masala
- Salt to the taste
- 1 tablespoons mint, chopped

Directions:
Set the instant pot on Sauté mode, add the oil, heat it up, add the onion, chilies, ginger, garlic, cumin, coriander, turmeric, cayenne and garam masala, toss and cook for 5 minutes. Add the remaining ingredients, put the lid on and cook on High for 15 minutes. Release the pressure naturally for 10 minutes, divide the mix into bowls and serve for lunch.

Nutrition: calories 392, fat 9.8, fiber 32.5, carbs 74.8, protein 12.1

Palak Paneer

Preparation time: 10 minutes | Cooking time: 15 minutes | Servings: 4

Ingredients:
- 1 pound spinach, torn
- 1 teaspoon cumin seeds
- 1 tablespoon ghee, melted
- 2 cups paneer, cubed
- 1 yellow onion, chopped
- 1 green chili pepper, minced
- 1-inch ginger, grated
- 5 garlic cloves, minced
- 1 tomato, cubed
- ¼ cup water
- 1 teaspoon garam masala
- ½ teaspoon turmeric powder
- 1 teaspoon coriander powder
- Salt to the taste

Directions:
Set the instant pot on Sauté mode, add the ghee, heat it up, add the onion, chili pepper, ginger, garlic, garam masala, turmeric, coriander and cumin seeds, stir and cook for 4 minutes. Add the rest of the ingredients, put the lid on and cook on High for 11 minutes. Release the pressure naturally for 10 minutes, divide the mix into bowls and serve.

Nutrition: calories 337, fat 16.4, fiber 5.7, carbs 36, protein 14.2

Dum Aloo

Preparation time: 10 minute | Cooking time: 20 minutes | Servings: 4

Ingredients:
- 10 baby potatoes, peeled and halved
- 1 yellow onion, chopped
- 2 tablespoons ghee, melted
- 2 teaspoons ginger, grated
- 2 teaspoons garlic, minced
- 2 tomatoes, crushed
- 1 teaspoon garam masala
- 1 tablespoon red chili powder
- ½ teaspoon turmeric powder
- 10 cashews, chopped
- ¼ cup milk
- Salt to the taste
- 1 tablespoon cilantro, chopped

Directions:
In a blender, combine the cashews with the milk, pulse well and transfer to a bowl. Set the instant pot on Sauté mode, add the ghee, heat it up, add the onion, garlic, ginger, garam masala, chili powder, turmeric powder and cashew paste, stir and cook for 5 minutes. Add the remaining ingredients, put the lid on and cook on High for 15 minutes. Release the pressure naturally for 10 minutes, divide into bowls and serve.

Nutrition: calories 202, fat 11.3, fiber 4.8, carbs 52, protein 5.7

Veggie Khichdi

Preparation time: 10 minutes | Cooking time: 20 minutes | Servings: 4

Ingredients:
- ½ cup moong lentils
- ½ cup white rice
- 3 cups water
- 1 tablespoon ghee, melted
- ½ teaspoon cumin seeds
- ½ tablespoon ginger, grated
- 1 yellow onion, chopped
- 1 tomato cubed
- 1 tablespoon cilantro, chopped
- 1 potato, peeled and cubed
- ½ cup carrot, chopped
- ½ cup green peas
- ¼ teaspoon turmeric powder
- ½ teaspoon cayenne pepper

Directions:
Set the instant pot on Sauté mode, add the ghee, heat it up, add the cumin, ginger, turmeric and cayenne, stir and cook for 3 minutes. Add the lentils and the other ingredients, toss, put the lid on and cook on High for 17 minutes more. Release the pressure naturally for 10 minutes, divide everything between plates and serve for lunch.

Nutrition: calories 208, fat 5.2, fiber 7.6, carbs 12, protein 8.2

Veggie Pulao

Preparation time: 10 minutes | Cooking time: 20 minutes | Servings: 4

Ingredients:
- 1 cup basmati rice
- 1 green chili pepper, chopped
- 1 tablespoon ghee, melted
- ½ tablespoon ginger, grated
- ½ cup yellow onion, chopped
- ½ tablespoon garlic, minced
- Salt to the taste
- ½ cup tomato, cubed
- 1 potato, peeled and cubed
- 2 cups mixed carrots and green beans, roughly chopped
- 1 and ½ cups water
- ½ teaspoon turmeric powder
- ½ teaspoon garam masala
- 1 bay leaf
- 1 teaspoon cumin seeds

Directions:
Set the instant pot on Sauté mode, add the ghee, heat it up, add the ginger, chili pepper, garlic, turmeric, garam masala, bay leaf and cumin seeds, stir and cook for 5 minutes. Add the rice and the other ingredients, stir, put the lid on and cook on High for 15 minutes. Release the pressure naturally fro 10 minutes, divide the mix into bowls and serve.

Nutrition: calories 344, fat 12.5, fiber 4.5, carbs 16.5, protein 3.5

Buttery Chicken

Preparation time: 10 minutes | Cooking time: 20 minutes | Servings: 4

Ingredients:
- 14 ounces canned tomatoes, cubed
- 5 garlic cloves, minced
- 2 teaspoons ginger, grated
- ½ teaspoon cayenne pepper
- 1 teaspoon turmeric powder
- 1 teaspoon smoked paprika
- Salt to the taste
- 1 teaspoon cumin, ground
- 1 teaspoon garam masala
- 1 pound chicken thighs, boneless, skinless
- 4 ounces butter, soft
- 4 ounces coconut cream
- ½ cup cilantro, chopped

Directions:
Set the instant pot on Sauté mode, add the butter, melt it, add the garlic, ginger, cayenne, turmeric, paprika, cumin and garam masala, stir and cook for 3 minutes. Add the chicken and the rest of the ingredients, put the lid on and cook on High for 17 minutes. Release the pressure naturally for 10 minutes, divide everything between plates and serve.

Nutrition: calories 340, fat 20, fiber 1, carbs 16.3, protein 25

Chicken Biryani

Preparation time: 30 minutes | Cooking time: 30 minutes | Servings: 4

Ingredients:
For the marinade:
- 2 teaspoons garam masala
- 1 tablespoon ginger, grated
- 1 tablespoon garlic, grated
- 1 tablespoon red chili powder
- ½ teaspoon turmeric powder
- ¼ cup cilantro, chopped
- ¼ cup mint, chopped
- 2 tablespoons lemon juice
- 1 cup yogurt
- Salt to the taste
- 2 pounds chicken thighs, skinless and boneless

For the remaining ingredients:
- 3 cups basmati rice
- 3 tablespoons ghee, melted
- 2 yellow onions, chopped
- 2 bay leaves
- 1 teaspoon saffron powder

Directions:
In a bowl, combine the ingredients for the marinade with the chicken, toss and keep in the fridge for 30 minutes. Set the instant pot on Sauté mode, add the ghee, heat it up, add the chicken mix, rice, bay leaves, onions and the saffron, put the lid on and cook on High for 30 minutes. Release the pressure naturally for 10 minutes, divide the mix into bowls and serve.

Nutrition: calories 383, fat 16.7, fiber 4.5, carbs 66, protein 7.5

Chicken Masala

***Preparation time:** 10 minutes | **Cooking time:** 20 minutes | **Servings:** 4*

Ingredients:

- 1 pound chicken breast, skinless, boneless and halved
- ¼ cup yogurt
- 2 teaspoons red chili powder
- 1 tablespoon lime juice
- 1 tablespoon garlic, minced
- 1 tablespoon ginger, grated
- ½ teaspoon turmeric powder
- 1 teaspoon garam masala
- 2 tablespoons ghee, melted
- 1 cup yellow onion, chopped
- 1 cup tomato puree
- ½ cup water
- ½ cup heavy cream
- 1 tablespoon fenugreek leaves, dried
- 1 tablespoon cilantro, chopped

Directions:

In a bowl, mix the chicken with the yogurt, chili powder, lime juice, garlic, ginger, turmeric and garam masala, toss and keep in the fridge for 10 minutes. Set the instant pot on Sauté mode, add the ghee, heat it up, add the chicken breasts and the onion and cook for 5 minutes. Add the rest of the ingredients, put the lid on and cook on High for 15 minutes. Release the pressure naturally for 10 minutes, divide the mix into bowls and serve.

Nutrition: calories 305, fat 15.6 fiber 3.2, carbs 14, protein 27.7

Goat Curry

***Preparation time:** 10 minutes | **Cooking time:** 30 minutes | **Servings:** 4*

Ingredients:

- 1 pound goat meat, bone-in
- ½ tablespoon garlic, minced
- ½ tablespoon ginger, grated
- 1 green chili pepper, chopped
- 3 tablespoons ghee, melted
- 1 tomato, cubed
- 1 tablespoon lemon juice
- ½ teaspoon cumin seeds
- 6 cloves
- 6 black peppercorns
- 1 bay leaf
- 1 black peppercorns
- ¼ teaspoon turmeric powder
- 1 teaspoon cayenne pepper
- ¼ cup water

Directions:

Set the instant pot on Sauté mode, add the ghee, heat it up, add the garlic, ginger, chili pepper, cumin, peppercorns, cloves, bay leaf, turmeric and cayenne, toss and cook for 5 minutes. Add the meat and brown it for 5 minutes more. Add the rest of the ingredients, put the lid on and cook on High for 20 minutes. Release the pressure naturally for 10 minutes, divide the curry into bowls and serve for lunch.

Nutrition: calories 253, fat 13.5, fiber 2, carbs 8.34, protein 24.65

Lamb Rogan Josh

Preparation time: 30 minutes | *Cooking time:* 20 minutes | *Servings:* 4

Ingredients:
- 1 pound leg of lamb, cubed
- 1 red onion, chopped
- 4 garlic cloves, minced
- 2 teaspoons ginger, grated
- ¼ cup yogurt
- 1 tablespoon tomato paste
- 2 teaspoons garam masala
- ¼ cup cilantro, chopped
- Salt to the taste
- ½ teaspoon cinnamon powder
- 1 teaspoon turmeric powder
- ¼ cup water

Directions:
In a bowl, combine the lamb meat with the onion and the other ingredients, toss and keep in the fridge for 30 minutes. Transfer the whole mix to your instant pot, put the lid on and cook on High for 20 minutes. Release the pressure naturally for 10 minutes, divide everything into bowls and serve for lunch.

Nutrition: calories 327, fat 12.4, fiber 2.3, carbs 15.6, protein 17

Pork Vindaloo

Preparation time: 10 minutes | *Cooking time:* 35 minutes | *Servings:* 6

Ingredients:
- 5 red chilies, chopped
- 1 teaspoon turmeric powder
- 2 teaspoons cumin seeds
- 1 teaspoon black pepper
- 6 cardamom pods
- 8 cloves
- ½ teaspoon mustard seeds
- 1 tablespoon ginger, grated
- 1 tablespoon garlic, minced
- 2 teaspoons tamarind paste
- 1 teaspoon brown sugar
- ¼ cup apple cider vinegar
- 1 and ½ pounds pork ribs, cut into medium pieces
- 1 cup water
- 2 cups yellow onion, chopped
- 3 tablespoons vegetable oil

Directions:
Set the instant pot on Sauté mode, add the oil, heat it up, add the onion, chilies, turmeric, cumin, black pepper, cardamom, cloves, mustard seeds and tamarind paste, stir and cook for 5 minutes. Add the meat and brown it for 5 minutes more. Add the rest of the ingredients, put the lid on and cook on High for 25 minutes. Release the pressure naturally for 10 minutes, divide everything into bowls and serve.

Nutrition: calories 374, fat 22.2, fiber 3, carbs 18.3, protein 26

Shrimp Curry

Preparation time: 5 minutes | Cooking time: 15 minutes | Servings: 4

Ingredients:
- 1 pound shrimp, peeled and deveined
- 1 green chili pepper, chopped
- 1 teaspoon mustard seeds
- 1 tablespoon vegetable oil
- 1 cup yellow onion, chopped
- ½ tablespoon ginger, grated
- ½ tablespoon garlic, minced
- 1 cup tomato, chopped
- 4 ounces coconut milk
- 1 tablespoon lime juice
- ½ teaspoon turmeric powder
- ½ teaspoon garam masala
- ½ teaspoon red chili powder
- ¼ cup cilantro, chopped

Directions:
Set the instant pot on Sauté mode, add the oil, heat it up, add the onion, ginger, garlic, turmeric, garam masala, and chili powder, stir and cook for 3 minutes. Add the shrimp and the rest of the ingredients, put the lid on and cook on High for 12 minutes. Release the pressure fast for 5 minutes, divide the mix into bowls and serve for lunch.

Nutrition: calories 226, fat 10, fiber 5.4, carbs 8.5, protein 12.4

Chana Masala

Preparation time: 10 minutes | Cooking time: 40 minutes | Servings: 4

Ingredients:
- 2 cups chickpeas
- 2 tablespoons vegetable oil
- 1 bay leaf
- 1 yellow onion, chopped
- 2 teaspoons garlic, minced
- 2 teaspoons ginger, grated
- 2 tomatoes, chopped
- 2 teaspoons coriander powder
- 2 teaspoons dried mango powder
- 2 teaspoons cumin powder
- Salt to the taste
- 1 teaspoon garam masala
- 1 teaspoon turmeric powder
- 2 cups water

Directions:
Set the instant pot on Sauté mode, add the oil, heat it up, add the onion, garlic and ginger and sauté for 5 minutes. Add the coriander, mango powder, cumin, garam masala and turmeric and cook for 5 minutes more. Add the rest of the ingredients, put the lid on and cook on High for 30 minutes. Release the pressure naturally for 10 minutes, divide the mix into bowls and serve.

Nutrition: calories 300, fat 13.45, fiber 4.5, carbs 16.5, protein 3.6

Keema Matar

Preparation time: 10 minutes | *Cooking time:* 20 minutes | *Servings:* 4

Ingredients:
- 2 tablespoons ghee, melted
- 1 yellow onion, chopped
- 4 teaspoons garlic, minced
- 1 green chili, minced
- 1 teaspoon ginger, grated
- 1 tablespoon coriander powder
- 1 teaspoon sweet paprika
- ½ teaspoon cumin, ground
- ½ teaspoon garam masala
- ½ teaspoon turmeric powder
- ¼ teaspoon cardamom, ground
- 1 pound beef meat, ground
- 14 ounces canned tomatoes, chopped
- 2 cup peas
- 1 tablespoon cilantro, chopped

Directions:
Set the instant pot on Sauté mode, add the ghee, heat it up, add the garlic, chili and ginger, stir and cook for 5 minutes. Add the coriander, cumin, garam masala, turmeric and cardamom, stir and cook for 5 minutes more. Add the rest of the ingredients, put the lid on and cook on High for 10 minutes. Release the pressure naturally for 10 minutes, divide the mix into bowls and serve.

Nutrition: calories 320, fat 13.5, fiber 4.6, carbs 16.5, protein 3.5

Toor Dal

Preparation time: 10 minutes | *Cooking time:* 15 minutes | *Servings:* 4

Ingredients:
- 1 cup split peas, soaked in water for 20 minutes and drained
- 1 tablespoon vegetable oil
- 1 teaspoon cumin seeds
- 1 Serrano pepper, chopped
- Salt to the taste
- ½ cup onion masala
- ½ teaspoon garam masala
- 1 tablespoon cilantro, chopped
- 3 cups water

Directions:
Set the instant pot on Sauté mode, add the oil, heat it up, add the cumin, Serrano pepper, onion masala and garam masala, stir and cook for 3 minutes. Add the rest of the ingredients, put the lid on and cook on High for 12 minutes. Release the pressure naturally for 10 minutes, divide the mix into bowls and serve for lunch.

Nutrition: calories 320, fat 11.3, fiber 4.6, carbs 18.4, protein 4.5

Rice with Lamb

Preparation time: 10 minutes | Cooking time: 30 minutes | Servings: 4

Ingredients:
- 1 cup brown rice, soaked in water for 10 minutes and drained
- 2 tablespoons vegetable oil
- 5 cardamom pods
- 4 cloves
- ½ teaspoon cinnamon powder
- 2 bay leaves
- ½ teaspoon fennel seeds
- ½ teaspoon cumin seeds
- 1 pound lamb stew meat, cubed
- 4 teaspoons garlic, minced
- 1 yellow onion, chopped
- 2 teaspoons ginger, grated
- 2 teaspoons coriander powder
- Salt to the taste
- 1 teaspoon garam masala
- 2 teaspoons sweet paprika
- ¼ teaspoon turmeric powder
- 1 cup water
- 1 tablespoon mint, chopped

Directions:
Set the instant pot on Sauté mode, add the oil, heat it up, add the cardamom, cloves, cinnamon, bay leaves, fennel and cumin, stir and cook for 2 minutes. Add the garlic, onion, ginger, coriander, garam masala, paprika and turmeric and sauté for 3 minutes more. Add the meat and brown it for 5 minutes more. Add the rest of the ingredients, put the lid on and cook on High for 20 minutes more. Release the pressure naturally for 10 minutes, divide the mix into bowls and serve.

Nutrition: calories 338, fat 16.7, fiber 3.5, carbs 20.4, protein 14.3

Potato and Pea Curry

Preparation time: 10 minutes | Cooking time: 15 minutes | Servings: 4

Ingredients:
- 1 teaspoon cumin seeds
- 2 tablespoons vegetable oil
- ½ cup onion masala
- 1 Serrano pepper, minced
- Salt to the taste
- 1 pound potatoes, peeled and cubed
- ½ teaspoon garam masala
- 2 cups peas
- 1 and ½ cups water

Directions:
Set the instant pot on Sauté mode, add the oil, heat it up, add the onion masala, Serrano pepper and garam masala, stir and cook for 2 minutes. Add the potatoes and the other ingredients, toss, put the lid on and cook on High for 13 minutes. Release the pressure naturally for 10 minutes, divide the mix into bowls and serve.

Nutrition: calories 300, fat 11.2, fiber 4.5, carbs 18.4, protein 6.6

Shrimp Biryani

Preparation time: 10 minutes | *Cooking time:* 26 minutes | *Servings:* 4

Ingredients:

- 1 cup basmati rice, soaked in water and drained
- 2 tablespoons ghee, melted
- 1 tablespoon cashews, chopped
- 1 tablespoon raisins
- 2 red onions, chopped
- 3 cloves
- 4 cardamom pods
- ½ teaspoon cumin seeds
- 2 teaspoons ginger, grated
- 2 teaspoons garlic, minced
- 1 green chili, chopped
- 20 curry leaves
- 1 tomato, chopped
- 1 teaspoon garam masala
- 1 teaspoon sweet paprika
- Salt to the taste
- ½ teaspoon turmeric powder
- 1 cup water
- 1 pound shrimp, peeled and deveined
- 1 tablespoon cilantro, chopped
- 1 tablespoon mint, chopped

Directions:

Set the instant pot on Sauté mode, add the ghee, heat it up, add the cloves, cardamom, cumin, ginger, garlic, chili, curry leaves, garam masala, paprika and turmeric, stir and cook for 6 minutes. Add the onion, stir and cook for 10 minutes more. Add the rest of the ingredients, except the cilantro and the mint, put the lid on and cook on High for 10 minutes. Release the pressure naturally for 10 minutes, add the cilantro and the mint, stir, divide into bowls and serve for lunch.

Nutrition: calories 311, fat 11.3, fiber 5.6, carbs 16.4, protein 13.4

Sookha Kana Chana

Preparation time: 10 minutes | *Cooking time:* 35 minutes | *Servings:* 4

Ingredients:

- 2 cups brown chickpeas, soaked overnight and drained
- ½ teaspoon cumin seeds
- 2 tablespoons ghee, melted
- ½ teaspoon black mustard seeds
- 1 black cardamom
- ½ teaspoon coriander powder
- Salt to the taste
- ½ teaspoon dried mango powder
- ½ teaspoon turmeric powder
- ½ teaspoon garam masala
- 1/3 teaspoon sweet paprika
- ¼ teaspoon black salt
- 1 cup water
- 1 tablespoon cilantro, chopped

Directions:

Set the instant pot on Sauté mode, add the ghee, heat it up, add the cumin, mustard seeds, cardamom, coriander, mango powder, turmeric, garam masala, paprika and black salt, stir and cook for 5 minutes. Add the rest of the ingredients, put the lid on and cook on High for 30 minutes. Release the pressure naturally for 10 minutes, divide the mix into bowls and serve for lunch.

Nutrition: calories 300, fat 12.4, fiber 4.5, carbs 15.5, protein 5.6

Langar Dal

Preparation time: 10 minutes | *Cooking time:* 30 minutes | *Servings:* 4

Ingredients:

- 2 tablespoons ghee, melted
- 1 cup urad dal, soaked overnight in cold water and drained
- 1 teaspoon cumin seeds
- ¼ cup chana dal, rinsed
- 1 cup onion masala
- 3 cups water
- Salt to the taste
- A pinch of cayenne pepper
- 1 and ½ teaspoon garam masala
- 1 tablespoon cilantro

Directions:

Set the instant pot on Sauté mode, add the ghee, heat it up, add the urad dal, cumin and chana dal, stir and cook for 2 minutes. Add the rest of the ingredients, put the lid on and cook on High for 28 minutes. Release the pressure naturally for 10 minutes, divide into bowls and serve.

Nutrition: calories 300, fat 11.2, fiber 3.4, carbs 14.5, protein 4.5

Masala Pasta

Preparation time: 10 minutes | Cooking time: 10 minutes | Servings: 3

Ingredients:
- 2 cups elbow macaroni
- ½ cup bell pepper, chopped
- ½ cup carrots, chopped
- ½ cup red onion, chopped
- 1 and ¾ cups water
- 1 cup onion, masala
- ½ teaspoon garam masala
- 2 tablespoons ghee, melted
- Salt to the taste
- 1 tablespoon cilantro, chopped

Directions:
In your instant pot, mix the macaroni with the bell pepper and the other ingredients except the cilantro, put the lid on and cook on High for 10 minutes. Release the pressure naturally for 10 minutes, divide the mix between plates, sprinkle the cilantro on top and serve for lunch.

Nutrition: calories 355, fat 15.4, fiber 4.5, carbs 17.4, protein 3.5

Kidney Beans Curry

Preparation time: 10 minutes | Cooking time: 45 minutes | Servings: 4

Ingredients:
- 2 cups red kidney beans, soaked overnight and drained
- 1 Serrano pepper, chopped
- 1 yellow onion, chopped
- 3 tablespoons ghee, melted
- 2 teaspoons garlic, minced
- 1 bay leaf
- 2 teaspoons ginger, grated
- 1 teaspoon garam masala
- 1 teaspoon coriander powder
- Salt to the taste
- ½ teaspoon turmeric powder
- 1 teaspoon sweet paprika
- A pinch of cayenne pepper
- 2 cup tomato puree
- 2 cups water
- 1 tablespoon cilantro, chopped

Directions:
Set the instant pot on Sauté mode, add the ghee, heat it up, add the pepper, onion, garlic, bay leaf, ginger, garam masala, coriander, turmeric, paprika and cayenne, stir and cook for 10 minutes. Add the rest of the ingredients, put the lid on and cook on High for 35 minutes. Release the pressure naturally for 10 minutes, divide the mix into bowls and serve for lunch.

Nutrition: calories 400, fat 13.4, fiber 4.5, carbs 22.3, protein 4.5

Chicken Masala

Preparation time: 10 minutes | Cooking time: 20 minutes | Servings: 4

Ingredients:
- ¼ cup vegetable oil
- 4 cloves
- 3 green cardamom
- 1 black cardamom
- ½ star anise
- ½ teaspoon cumin seeds
- 2 pounds chicken thighs, skinless, boneless and cut into quarters
- 1 teaspoon coriander powder
- Salt to the taste
- 1 and ¼ cup onion masala
- 1 yellow onion, chopped
- 1 teaspoon garam masala
- 1 tablespoon cilantro, chopped

Directions:
Set the instant pot on Sauté mode, add the oil, heat it up, add the cloves, cardamom, star anise, cumin seeds, coriander and the chicken, stir and cook for 5 minutes. Add the rest of the ingredients, put the lid on and cook on High for 15 minutes. Release the pressure naturally for 10 minutes, divide the mix into bowls and serve.

Nutrition: calories 563, fat 30.5, fiber 0.6, carbs 2.7, protein 66

Avial

Preparation time: 10 minutes | Cooking time: 10 minutes | Servings: 4

Ingredients:
- ½ teaspoon black mustard seeds
- 1 tablespoon coconut oil, melted
- 30 curry leaves
- ½ cup carrots, sliced
- ½ cup peas
- ½ cup corn
- ½ cup okra, trimmed and halved
- ½ cup coconut, grated
- 2/3 cup water
- 1 green chili pepper, chopped
- Salt to the taste
- ½ teaspoon cumin, ground
- ¼ teaspoon turmeric powder
- ½ cup yogurt

Directions:
Set the instant pot on Sauté mode, add the oil, heat it up, add the mustard seeds and curry leaves, stir and cook for 2 minutes. Add the rest of the ingredients, put the lid on and cook on High for 8 minutes. Release the pressure naturally for 10 minutes, divide the mix between plates and serve for lunch.

Nutrition: calories 322, fat 12.3, fiber 4.5, carbs 19.8, protein 5.6

Chicken Soup

Preparation time: 10 minutes | Cooking time: 30 minutes | Servings: 4

Ingredients:

- 1 pound chicken breast, skinless, boneless and cubed
- 1 cup mixed carrots, peas and potatoes, peeled and cubed
- 1 tablespoon ginger, grated
- ½ cup corn
- 2 tablespoons lemon juice
- 1 teaspoon ghee, melted
- 4 peppercorns
- 1 bay leaf
- 4 cloves

Directions:

Set your instant pot on sauté mode, add the ghee, heat it up, add the peppercorns, bay leaf, ginger and cloves, stir and cook for 5 minutes. Add the meat, stir and brown for 5 minutes more. Add the other ingredients, toss, put the lid on and cook on High for 20 minutes. Release the pressure naturally for 10 minutes, divide into bowls and serve.

Nutrition: calories 373, fat 14, fiber 4, carbs 13.4, protein 18

Cream of Broccoli

Preparation time: 10 minutes | Cooking time: 15 minutes | Servings: 4

Ingredients:

- 2 cups broccoli florets
- 1 potato, peeled and cubed
- 1 yellow onion, chopped
- 4 garlic cloves, minced
- ½ cup milk
- Salt to the taste
- 1 tablespoon cream
- 1 tablespoon ghee, melted
- ¼ teaspoon oregano, dried
- 1 teaspoon turmeric powder
- ½ teaspoon garam masala

Directions:

Set your instant pot on sauté mode, add the ghee, heat it up, add the onion, garlic, oregano, turmeric and garam masala, stir and cook for 2 minutes. Add the rest of the ingredients, put the lid on and cook on High for 13 minutes. Release the pressure naturally for 10 minutes, blend the soup using an immersion blender, divide into bowls and serve.

Nutrition: calories 311, fat 12, fiber 4.5, carbs 11.7, protein 9

Mulligatawny Soup

Preparation time: 10 minutes | *Cooking time:* 35 minutes | *Servings:* 6

Ingredients:
- 1 yellow onion, chopped
- ¼ cup ghee, melted
- 1 red chili pepper, minced
- 1 carrot, peeled and cubed
- 2 teaspoons ginger, grated
- 3 garlic cloves, minced
- 2 apples, peeled, cored and cubed
- 1 tablespoon curry powder
- 14 ounces canned tomatoes, chopped
- Salt to the taste
- 1 teaspoon cumin, ground
- ½ teaspoon cinnamon powder
- ½ teaspoon sweet paprika
- ¼ teaspoon cardamom, ground
- ½ teaspoon turmeric powder
- ½ teaspoon thyme, dried
- ½ cup red lentils, soaked overnight and drained
- 4 cups chicken stock
- 1 cup coconut milk
- 1 tablespoon cilantro, chopped

Directions:

Set your instant pot on sauté mode, add the ghee, heat it up, add the onion, chili pepper, ginger and garlic, stir and sauté for 5 minutes. Add the curry powder, cumin, cinnamon, paprika, cardamom, turmeric, thyme and salt, stir and cook for 5 minutes more. Add the rest of the ingredients, put the lid on and cook on High for 25 minutes. Release the pressure naturally for 10 minutes, divide the soup into bowls, and serve.

Nutrition: calories 383, fat 12, fiber 5.4, carbs 11.7, protein 10

Curry Cauliflower and Broccoli Soup

Preparation time: 10 minutes | *Cooking time:* 25 minutes | *Servings:* 4

Ingredients:
- 1 pound cauliflower florets
- 2 cups broccoli florets
- 3 garlic cloves, minced
- 1 yellow onion, chopped
- 14 ounces coconut cream
- 2 cups chicken stock
- 1 tablespoon red curry paste
- 2 tablespoons chives, chopped

Directions:

In your instant pot, combine the cauliflower with the broccoli and all the other ingredients, toss, put the lid on and cook on High for 25 minutes. Release the pressure naturally for 10 minutes, blend using an immersion blender, ladle into bowls and serve.

Nutrition: calories 291, fat 4.6, fiber 4, carbs 9.7, protein 6.7

Palak Soup

Preparation time: 10 minutes | Cooking time: 20 minutes | Servings: 2

Ingredients:

- 2 cups spinach, chopped
- 3 garlic cloves, minced
- 1 tablespoon gram flour
- ¼ cup yellow onion, chopped
- ¼ teaspoon cumin powder
- 1 bay leaf
- 2 cups water
- 1 tablespoon olive oil
- Salt to the taste
- A pinch of black pepper

Directions:

Set your instant pot on sauté mode, add the oil, heat it up, add the onion, garlic, cumin and bay leaf, stir and cook for 5 minutes. Add the rest of the ingredients, put the lid on and cook on High or 15 minutes. Release the pressure naturally for 10 minutes, blend the soup with an immersion blender, ladle into bowls and serve.

Nutrition: calories 199, fat 4.5, fiber 4, carbs 9.6, protein 11

Indian Fish Soup

Preparation time: 10 minutes | Cooking time: 25 minutes | Servings: 4

Ingredients:

- 1 tablespoon sunflower oil
- 2 teaspoons black mustard seeds
- 1 tablespoon curry powder
- 10 curry leaves, chopped
- 1 teaspoon turmeric powder
- 2 red chilies, chopped
- 1-inch ginger, grated
- 2 garlic cloves, minced
- 1 yellow onion, chopped
- ½ cup basmati rice
- 1 tablespoon mango chutney
- 3 cups chicken stock
- 1 pound white fish fillets, boneless, skinless and cubed
- 15 ounces coconut milk
- Salt and black pepper to the taste
- Juice of 2 limes
- 1 teaspoon garam masala
- 1 tablespoon coriander, chopped

Directions:

Set your instant pot on sauté mode, add oil, heat it up, add the mustard seeds, curry powder, curry leaves, turmeric, chilies, ginger, garlic and onion, stir and sauté for 10 minutes. Add the fish and the rest of the ingredients except the coriander, put the lid on and cook on High for 15 minutes. Release the pressure naturally for 10 minutes, ladle into bowls and serve with the coriander sprinkled on top.

Nutrition: calories 291, fat 8.3, fiber 2, carbs 8.5, protein 9

Aloo Ki Kadhi

Preparation time: 10 minutes | Cooking time: 20 minutes | Servings: 4

Ingredients:
- 6 cups gold potatoes, peeled and cubed
- 2 tablespoons ghee, melted
- ½ cup yogurt
- 1 teaspoon cumin seeds
- ¼ teaspoon fenugreek seeds
- Salt and black pepper to the taste
- 1 bay leaf
- 2 teaspoons ginger paste
- 1 red chili, chopped
- 2 tablespoons cilantro, chopped
- ¼ teaspoon garam masala

Directions:
Set your instant pot on Sauté mode, add the oil, heat it up, add the cumin seeds, fenugreek seeds, bay leaf, ginger paste, chili and garam masala, stir and cook for 5 minutes. Add the potatoes and the rest of the ingredients, put the lid on and cook on High for 15 minutes. Release the pressure naturally for 10 minutes, blend the soup using an immersion blender, divide into bowls and serve.

Nutrition: calories 310, fat 7.4, fiber 4, carbs 11.6, protein 11

Beans and Rutabaga Soup

Preparation time: 10 minutes | Cooking time: 20 minutes | Servings: 4

Ingredients:
- 1 tablespoon ghee, melted
- 2 cups carrots, peeled and cubed
- 2 cups celery, chopped
- 30 ounces hominy, drained
- 6 cups water
- 15 ounces kidney beans, rinsed and drained
- 4 cups rutabaga, cubed
- Salt to the taste

Directions:
Set your instant pot on Sauté mode, add the ghee, heat it up, add the carrots and the celery, stir and sauté for 2 minutes. Add the rest of the ingredients, stir, put the lid on and cook on High for 18 minutes. Release the pressure naturally for 10 minutes, divide the soup into bowls and serve.

Nutrition: calories 385, fat 9.6, fiber 4, carbs 14.8, protein 10

Tomato Soup

Preparation time: 10 minutes | Cooking time: 20 minutes | Servings: 2

Ingredients:

- 4 tomatoes, peeled and chopped
- 3 garlic cloves, minced
- 1 Indian bay leaf
- 1 yellow onion, chopped
- 1 tablespoon butter
- 1 cup water
- 1 tablespoon cream
- ½ tablespoon sugar
- Salt and black pepper to the taste

Directions:

Set the instant pot on Sauté mode, add the butter, heat it up, add the garlic and the onion, stir and sauté for 5 minutes. Add the tomatoes and the other ingredients, put the lid on and cook on High for 15 minutes. Release the pressure naturally for 10 minutes, blend everything using an immersion blender, divide the soup into bowls and serve.

Nutrition: calories 280, fat 5.7, fiber 3, carbs 11.6, protein 7.4

Spicy Cabbage Soup

Preparation time: 10 minutes | Cooking time: 25 minutes | Servings: 6

Ingredients:

- 2 pounds green cabbage, shredded
- Salt and black pepper to the taste
- 1 cup tomatoes, chopped
- 1 yellow onion, chopped
- 4 garlic cloves, minced
- 2 tablespoons parsley, chopped
- 1 quart water
- 4 tablespoons lemon juice
- 1 teaspoon turmeric powder
- 1 tablespoon coriander powder

Directions:

In your instant pot, combine the cabbage with the tomatoes and all the other ingredients, put the lid on and cook on High for 25 minutes. Release the pressure naturally for 10 minutes, ladle the soup into bowls and serve.

Nutrition: calories 272, fat 6.4, fiber 4, carbs 11.7, protein 9

Curry Turkey Soup

Preparation time: 10 minutes | Cooking time: 25 minutes | Servings: 4

Ingredients:
- 2 tablespoons butter
- 1 cup celery, chopped
- 1 cup carrot, chopped
- 2 cups yellow onion, chopped
- 4 teaspoons yellow curry powder
- 4 cups chicken stock
- ¼ cup white rice
- 2 green apples, cored, peeled and cubed
- 2 bay leaves
- Salt to the taste
- 2 cups turkey meat, cooked, skinless, boneless and shredded
- ¼ cup heavy cream

Directions:

Set your instant pot on Sauté mode, add the butter, heat it up, add the onion, curry powder and bay leaves, stir and cook for 5 minutes. Add the rest of the ingredients, put the lid on and cook on High for 20 minutes. Release the pressure naturally for 10 minutes, divide the soup into bowls and serve.

Nutrition: calories 320, fat 15.4, fiber 4, carbs 16.7, protein 12.2

Turkey and Coriander Soup

Preparation time: 10 minutes | Cooking time: 25 minutes | Servings: 6

Ingredients:
- 3 cups turkey meat, cooked, skinless, boneless and shredded
- 1 quart water
- 2 garlic cloves, minced
- 1-inch ginger, grated
- 2 tablespoons curry powder
- 2 tablespoons vegetable oil
- 1 teaspoon cumin, ground
- 2 potatoes, peeled and cubed
- 3 carrots, sliced
- 1 cup coconut milk
- ¼ cup lime juice
- 1 tablespoon coriander, chopped

Directions:

Set your instant pot on Sauté mode, add the oil, heat it up, add the garlic, ginger, cumin, and curry powder, stir and sauté for 5 minutes. Add the rest of the ingredients except the coriander, put the lid on and cook on High for 20 minutes. Release the pressure naturally for 10 minutes, ladle the soup into bowls, sprinkle the coriander on top and serve.

Nutrition: calories 290, fat 7.5, fiber 4, carbs 11.8, protein 11

Coconut Shrimp Stew

Preparation time: 5 minutes | Cooking time: 15 minutes | Servings: 4

Ingredients:

- 1 pound shrimp, peeled and deveined
- 1 tablespoon vegetable oil
- 1 yellow onion, chopped
- 1 teaspoon ginger, grated
- 2 teaspoons turmeric powder
- 1 teaspoon coriander, ground
- 1 teaspoon cumin, ground
- 1 teaspoon sweet paprika
- 1 teaspoon curry powder
- ½ teaspoon chili powder
- 2 garlic cloves, mined
- 15 ounces coconut milk
- Salt to the taste
- 14 ounces tomato sauce

Directions:

Set the instant pot on Sauté mode, add the oil, heat it up, add the onion, ginger, turmeric, coriander, cumin, paprika, curry powder, chili powder and garlic, stir and sauté for 5-6 minutes. Add the rest of the ingredients, put the lid on and cook on High for 10 minutes. Release the pressure fast for 5 minutes, divide the stew into bowls and serve.

Nutrition: calories 376, fat 8.3, fiber 3, carbs 8, protein 11.3

Beef Stew

Preparation time: 10 minutes | Cooking time: 35 minutes | Servings: 4

Ingredients:

- 1 teaspoon mustard seeds
- 1 cup tomatoes, chopped
- 2 green chilies, minced
- 1 cup red onions, chopped
- 1 tablespoon chili powder
- 1 teaspoon fenugreek seeds
- 1 tablespoon garam masala
- 1 tablespoon coriander powder
- 2 teaspoons fennel powder
- 2 teaspoons cumin powder
- 1 teaspoon turmeric powder
- 1 tablespoon ginger garlic paste
- Salt to the taste
- 2 tablespoon s coconut oil
- 2 pounds beef stew meat, cubed
- 1 carrot, sliced
- 1 plantain, peeled and cubed
- 8 curry leaves
- 1 and ½ cups water

Directions:

Set your instant pot on Sauté mode, add the oil, heat it up, add the meat, onion, chilies and curry leaves, stir and brown for 5 minutes. Add the tomatoes, chili powder, fenugreek seeds and the rest of the ingredients, put the lid on and cook on High for 30 minutes. Release the pressure naturally for 10 minutes, divide the stew into bowls and serve.

Nutrition: calories 371, fat 13, fiber 4, carbs 22.8, protein 14

Veggie Stew

Preparation time: 10 minutes | Cooking time: 25 minutes | Servings: 4

Ingredients:
- 1 potato, peeled and cubed
- 1 carrot, peeled and cubed
- 1 yellow onion, chopped
- 1-inch ginger, grated
- 2 garlic cloves, minced
- 2 green chilies, chopped
- 2 curry leaves
- 2 tablespoons coconut oil
- Salt and black pepper to the taste
- ½ teaspoon erachii masala
- 1 cup water
- 1 cup milk

Directions:
Set your instant pot on Sauté mode, add the oil, heat it up, add the onion, garlic, ginger and the curry leaves, stir and cook for 5 minutes. Add the rest of the ingredients, put the lid on and cook on High for 20 minutes. Release the pressure naturally for 10 minutes, divide the stew into bowls and serve.

Nutrition: calories 264, fat 12, fiber 4, carbs 9, protein 18

Ghee Carrot Pudding

Preparation time: 10 minutes | Cooking time: 20 minutes | Servings: 4

Ingredients:
- 5 carrots, peeled and roughly grated
- 1 and ½ cups almond milk
- 1 cup coconut milk
- 1 tablespoon ghee, melted
- 2 tablespoons honey
- ½ teaspoon cardamom, ground
- ½ teaspoon ginger, grated
- ½ teaspoon cinnamon powder
- ½ teaspoon cloves, ground
- A pinch of salt
- 1 star anise
- ¼ cup cashews, chopped
- ¼ cup raisins

Directions:
Set your instant pot on Sauté mode, add the ghee, heat it up, add the carrots and ginger and sauté for 5 minutes. Add the rest of the ingredients, put the lid on and cook on High for 15 minutes. Release the pressure naturally for 10 minutes, divide the mix into bowls and serve.

Nutrition: calories 280, fat 12, fiber 5.5, carbs 9, protein 5.6

Chickpeas and Tomatoes Masala

Preparation time: 10 minutes | Cooking time: 25 minutes | Servings: 4

Ingredients:

- 1 yellow onion, chopped
- 1 pound chickpeas, rinsed and drained
- 20 ounces canned tomatoes, chopped
- 1 teaspoon oregano, dried
- ½ teaspoon turmeric powder
- ½ teaspoon garam masala
- ½ teaspoon coriander, ground
- 2 tablespoons ghee, melted
- A pinch of salt and black pepper
- ½ teaspoon red pepper flakes

Directions:

Set the instant pot on Sauté mode, add the ghee, heat it up, add the onion, oregano, turmeric garam masala and the coriander, stir and sauté for 5 minutes. Add all the other ingredients, put the lid on and cook on High for 20 minutes. Release the pressure naturally for 10 minutes, divide the mix into bowls and serve.

Nutrition: calories 280, fat 12, fiber 4.5, carbs 14.5, protein 7.8

Mutton Stew

Preparation time: 10 minutes | Cooking time: 30 minutes | Servings: 4

Ingredients:

- 1 pound mutton, cubed
- 4 cups water
- 1 tablespoon butter, melted
- 1 and ½ cups yellow onion, chopped
- 1 carrots, chopped
- ¼ cup potato, cubed
- 1 teaspoon nutmeg, ground
- 2 teaspoons turmeric powder
- ½ teaspoon chili powder

Directions:

Set your instant pot on Sauté mode, add the oil, heat it up, add onion, the meat, nutmeg, turmeric and chili powder, stir and cook for 5 minutes. Add the rest of the ingredients, put the lid on and cook on High for 25 minutes. Release the pressure naturally for 10 minutes, divide the mix into bowls and serve.

Nutrition: calories 382, fat 8.5, fiber 3, carbs 23.0, protein 15.4

Broccoli Junka

***Preparation time:** 5 minutes | **Cooking time:** 15 minutes | **Servings:** 4*

Ingredients:
- 1 yellow onion, chopped
- 2 tablespoons vegetable oil
- ½ teaspoon mustard seeds
- 1 tablespoon garlic-ginger paste
- ½ teaspoon cumin seeds
- 1 teaspoon turmeric powder
- 1 teaspoon chili powder
- 1 pound broccoli florets
- 2 teaspoons water
- Salt to the taste
- 3 tablespoons gram flour

Directions:
Set your instant pot on Sauté mode, add the oil, heat it up, add the onion, garlic paste, mustard and cumin seeds, stir and cook for 5 minutes. Add the broccoli and the rest of the ingredients, put the lid on and cook on High for 10 minutes. Release the pressure fast for 5 minutes, divide the stew into bowls and serve.

Nutrition: calories 272, fat 5.4, fiber 4, carbs 11.7, protein 8

Zucchini Curry

***Preparation time:** 10 minutes | **Cooking time:** 20 minutes | **Servings:** 2*

Ingredients:
- 2 zucchinis, cubed
- 1 tablespoon coconut oil
- ½ teaspoon mustard seeds
- ¼ teaspoon asafetida powder
- 2 garlic cloves, minced
- ½ teaspoon turmeric powder
- 1 teaspoon red chili powder
- 1 teaspoon cumin powder
- ½ teaspoon garam masala
- Salt to the taste
- ½ cup veggie stock

Directions:
Set your instant pot on Sauté mode, add the oil, heat it up, the mustard seeds and the garlic, stir and cook for 3 minutes. Add the zucchinis and the rest of the ingredients, put the lid on and cook on High for 17 minutes. Release the pressure naturally for 10 minutes, divide the stew into bowls and serve.

Nutrition: calories 265, fat 5.67, fiber 3, carbs 9, protein 5.1

Zucchini and Peas Curry

Preparation time: 10 minutes | *Cooking time:* 20 minutes | *Servings:* 4

Ingredients:

- 1 tablespoon coconut oil
- 1 yellow onion, chopped
- 2 garlic cloves, minced
- 1 teaspoon ginger, grated
- 2 zucchinis, cubed
- ½ teaspoon sweet paprika
- 2 tablespoons curry powder
- ½ teaspoon cumin, ground
- ½ teaspoon thyme, dried
- 1 cup green peas
- 14 ounces coconut milk
- ½ cup vegetable stock
- Salt to the taste
- ¼ cup cilantro, chopped

Directions:

Set your instant pot on Sauté mode, add the oil, heat it up, add the garlic, onion and the ginger, stir and sauté for 5 minutes. Add the zucchinis and the rest of the ingredients, put the lid on and cook on High for 15 minutes.. Release the pressure naturally for 10 minutes, divide the stew into bowls and serve.

Nutrition: calories 280, fat 12, fiber 4, carbs 11.8, protein 12

Squash and Lentils Stew

Preparation time: 10 minutes | *Cooking time:* 25 minutes | *Servings:* 8

Ingredients:

- 1 cup split pigeon peas
- 1 pound butternut squash, peeled and cubed
- 1 tomato, cubed
- 1 cup coconut, shredded
- ½ teaspoon turmeric powder
- ½ teaspoon cumin, ground
- 2 cups veggie stock
- 2 tablespoons vegetable oil
- 1 teaspoon mustard seeds
- ½ teaspoon red pepper flakes
- 1 garlic clove, minced
- Juice of 1 lime
- 1 tablespoon honey
- 1 tablespoon coriander, chopped

Directions:

Set your instant pot on Sauté mode, add the oil, heat it up, add the coconut, turmeric, cumin, mustard sees, pepper flakes and garlic, stir and cook for 5 minutes. Add the peas, squash and the remaining ingredients, put the lid on and cook on High for 20 minutes. Release the pressure naturally for 10 minutes, divide the stew into bowls and serve.

Nutrition: calories 282, fat 11.4, fiber 5.4, carbs 8, protein 12

Turnips Soup

Preparation time: 10 minutes | Cooking time: 20 minutes | Servings: 4

Ingredients:
- 2 cups zucchinis, cubed
- 2 cups turnips, cubed
- ½ cup water
- 1 tablespoon coconut oil
- ½ cup yellow onion, chopped
- 5 cups veggie stock
- 2 handfuls spinach, chopped
- 1 teaspoon lemon juice
- 1 tablespoon ginger, grated
- 2 tablespoons garlic, minced
- Salt to the taste

Directions:
Set the instant pot on Sauté mode, add the oil, heat it up, add the onion, ginger and the garlic, stir and sauté for 5 minutes. Add the turnips and the rest of the ingredients except the parsley, put the lid on and cook on High for 15 minutes. Release the pressure naturally for 10 minutes, divide the soup into bowls and serve.

Nutrition: calories 231, fat 13, fiber 3, carbs 8, protein 11.1

Balkan Bean Stew

Preparation time: 10 minutes | Cooking time: 30 minutes | Servings: 4

Ingredients:
- 2 tablespoons vegetable oil
- 2 garlic cloves, minced
- 1 yellow onion, chopped
- 2 teaspoons sweet paprika
- 2 bay leaves
- Salt and black pepper to the taste
- 1 cup mushrooms, sliced
- 7 ounces seitan, chopped
- 2 cups canned beans, drained
- 1 cup water
- 1 tablespoon parsley, chopped

Directions:
Set the pot on Sauté mode, add the oil, heat it up, add the onion, garlic, paprika and bay leaves, stir and sauté for 5 minutes. Add the beans and the rest of the ingredients except the parsley, put the lid on and cook on High for 25 minutes. Release the pressure naturally for 10 minutes, add the parsley, divide the stew into bowls and serve.

Nutrition: calories 272, fat 12, fiber 4, carbs 9, protein 11.3

Green Beans Curry

Preparation time: 10 minutes | Cooking time: 20 minutes | Servings: 4

Ingredients:

- 4 cups green beans, trimmed and halved
- 2 teaspoons vegetable oil
- 2 potatoes, cubed
- 3 garlic cloves, mined
- ½ teaspoon turmeric powder
- ¼ teaspoon asafetida powder
- Salt to the taste
- ½ teaspoon cumin, ground
- ¼ cup water
- 1 tablespoon lemon juice
- 1 tablespoon cilantro, chopped

Directions:

In your instant pot, combine the green beans with the oil and the all the other ingredients except the cilantro, put the lid on and cook on High for 20 minutes. Release the pressure naturally for 10 minutes, divide the stew into bowls and serve with the cilantro sprinkled on top.

Nutrition: calories 251, fat 13, fiber 5, carbs 9.8, protein 7.6

Indian Instant Pot Side Dish Recipes

Mushroom Mix

Preparation time: 5 minutes | *Cooking time:* 20 minutes | *Servings:* 4

Ingredients:
- 1 pound button mushrooms, halved
- 1 tablespoon ginger, grated
- 2 tablespoons vegetable oil
- 3 garlic cloves, minced
- 1 green chili, chopped
- 3 tablespoons yogurt
- 2 teaspoons coriander seeds
- 1 teaspoon tomato puree
- ½ teaspoon turmeric powder
- ½ teaspoon chili powder
- Salt to the taste

Directions:
Set the instant pot on Sauté mode, add the oil, heat it up, add the garlic, ginger and the chili, stir and sauté for 5 minutes. Add the rest of the ingredients, put the lid on and cook on High for 15 minutes more. Release the pressure fast for 5 minutes, divide the mix between plates and serve.

Nutrition: calories 103, fat 7.4, fiber 1.5, carbs 6.7, protein 4.6

Okra Mix

Preparation time: 5 minutes | *Cooking time:* 20 minutes | *Servings:* 4

Ingredients:
- 1 pound okra, trimmed and halved
- 1 teaspoon chili flakes
- 1 yellow onion, chopped
- 2 teaspoons coriander seeds
- 3 tablespoons mustard oil
- 1 teaspoon turmeric powder
- 1 teaspoon garam masala
- Salt to the taste
- 2 teaspoons dried mango powder

Directions:
Set the instant pot on Sauté mode, add the oil, heat it up, add the onion and sauté for 5 minutes. Add the okra and the other ingredients, put the lid on and cook on High for 15 minutes. Release the pressure fast for 5 minutes, divide the mix between plates and serve.

Nutrition: calories 151, fat 10.8, fiber 4.4, carbs 11.4, protein 2.6

Turmeric Aloo

Preparation time: 10 minutes | Cooking time: 20 minutes | Servings: 4

Ingredients:

- 1 teaspoon mustard seeds
- 1 tablespoon vegetable oil
- 1 yellow onion, chopped
- 5 curry leaves
- 1 teaspoon cumin seeds
- 2 green chilies, chopped
- ½ teaspoon red chili powder
- 1 teaspoon coriander seeds
- ½ teaspoon turmeric powder
- 2 potatoes, peeled and cut into chunks
- 1 teaspoon garam masala
- 1 tablespoon coriander, chopped

Directions:

Set the instant pot on Sauté mode, add the oil, heat it up, add the mustard seeds and the onion and sauté for 5 minutes. Add the curry leaves, cumin and the other ingredients, toss, put the lid on and cook on High for 15 minutes. Release the pressure naturally for 10 minutes, divide the mix between plates and serve.

Nutrition: calories 123, fat 4, fiber 3.5, carbs 20.2, protein 2.5

Coconut Veggies

Preparation time: 10 minutes | Cooking time: 20 minutes | Servings: 4

Ingredients:

- 1 red bell pepper, cut into chunks
- 1 green bell pepper, cut into chunks
- 1 tablespoon vegetable oil
- 10 mushrooms, halved
- 1 cup green beans, trimmed and halved
- 1 tablespoon cumin seeds
- 2 yellow onions, chopped
- 2 cups tomatoes, chopped
- Salt to the taste
- 1 teaspoon turmeric powder
- ½ tablespoon chili powder
- 2 green chilies, chopped
- 1 cup coconut cream
- 1 tablespoon garam masala

Directions:

Set the instant pot on Sauté mode, add the oil, heat it up, add the onions, cumin, turmeric, chili powder and green chilies, stir and cook for 5 minutes. Add the rest of the ingredients, put the lid on and cook on High for 15 minutes. Release the pressure naturally for 10 minutes, divide the mix between plates and serve.

Nutrition: calories 254, fat 18.8, fiber 6.4, carbs 21.4, protein 5.7

Cumin Potatoes

Preparation time: 10 minutes | Cooking time: 20 minutes | Servings: 4

Ingredients:
- 4 potatoes, peeled and roughly cubed
- 1 tablespoon coriander seeds
- 2 tablespoons vegetable oil
- 2 teaspoons cumin seeds
- 2 green chilies, chopped
- 1 teaspoon red chili powder
- 1 tablespoon ginger, grated
- ½ teaspoon turmeric powder
- Salt to the taste
- 2 teaspoons mango powder
- ¼ cup veggie stock

Directions:
In your instant pot, combine the potatoes with the oil and the other ingredients, put the lid on and cook on High for 20 minutes. Release the pressure naturally for 10 minutes, divide everything between plates and serve.

Nutrition: calories 300, fat 6.23, fiber 3.4, carbs 11.5, protein 5.5

Cabbage Thoran

Preparation time: 10 minutes | Cooking time: 15 minutes | Servings: 4

Ingredients:
- 2 red chilies, chopped
- 1 teaspoon cumin seeds
- 3 tablespoons coconut oil
- 2 tablespoons curry leaves, chopped
- 2 teaspoons black mustard seeds
- 1 tablespoon ginger, grated
- 1 pound green cabbage, shredded
- Salt to the taste
- ½ cup coconut, grated

Directions:
Set the instant pot on Sauté mode, add the oil, heat it up, add the chilies, cumin, curry leaves and mustard seeds, toss and cook for 2 minutes. Add the cabbage and the other ingredients, put the lid on and cook on High for 13 minutes. Release the pressure naturally for 10 minutes, divide everything between plates and serve.

Nutrition: calories 166, fat 14.3, fiber 4.1, carbs 9.9, protein 2.4

Veggie Sabjee

Preparation time: 10 minutes | Cooking time: 15 minutes | Servings: 4

Ingredients:
- 1 yellow bell pepper, roughly cubed
- 1 potato, peeled and roughly cubed
- 1 carrot, sliced
- ½ cup peas
- 2 tablespoons mustard oil
- 1 teaspoon cumin seeds
- 1 teaspoon mustard seeds
- 1 yellow onion, chopped
- 6 ounces canned tomatoes, chopped
- 2 garlic cloves, minced
- 1 tablespoon ginger, grated
- 1 teaspoon fenugreek leaves, dried
- 1 teaspoon turmeric powder
- Salt to the taste
- 1 teaspoon garam masala
- 1 tablespoon coriander, chopped

Directions:
Set the instant pot on Sauté mode, add the oil, heat it up, add cumin seeds, mustard seeds, onion, garlic, ginger, turmeric and garam masala, stir and cook for 3 minutes. Add the rest of the ingredients, put the lid on and cook on High for 12 minutes. Release the pressure naturally for 10 minutes, divide everything between plats and serve.

Nutrition: calories 200, fat 3.4, fiber 3.45, carbs 6.7, protein 3.4

Aromatic Rice Mix

Preparation time: 10 minutes | Cooking time: 30 minutes | Servings: 4

Ingredients:
- 2 cups basmati rice
- 6 cups water
- Salt to the taste
- 2 cardamom pods
- 2 cloves
- 3 tablespoons vegetable oil
- ½ teaspoon black mustard seeds
- ¼ teaspoon chili flakes
- ½ teaspoon cumin seeds
- 1 yellow onion, chopped
- 4 garlic cloves, minced
- ¼ teaspoon turmeric powder

Directions:
Set your instant pot on Sauté mode, add the oil, heat it up, add the onion and garlic, stir and sauté for 3 minutes Add the cardamom, cloves, mustard seeds, chili flakes and turmeric, stir and cook for 2 minutes more Add the rest of the ingredients, put the lid on and cook on High for 25 minutes Release the pressure naturally for 10 minutes, divide the mix between plates and serve as a side dish.

Nutrition: calories 351, fat 7, fiber 6, carbs 9.2, protein 6

Spicy Rice

Preparation time: 10 minutes | Cooking time: 25 minutes | Servings: 4

Ingredients:
- 1 and ½ cups basmati rice
- 2 tablespoons vegetable oil
- 1 tablespoon cumin seeds
- Salt to the taste
- 2 and ½ cups water
- 2 green cardamom pods
- 1 yellow onion, chopped
- 2 cloves
- 1 tablespoon chili powder
- 1 teaspoon turmeric powder

Directions:
Set your instant pot on Sauté mode, add oil, heat it up, add the onion, cloves, cardamom, chili powder and the turmeric, stir and cook for 5 minutes. Add the rest of the ingredients, toss, put the lid on and cook on High for 20 minutes. Release the pressure naturally for 10 minutes, divide the mix between plates and serve as a side dish.

Nutrition: calories 271, fat 4.5, fiber 5, carbs 11..6, protein 6

Spiced Quinoa

Preparation time: 5 minutes | Cooking time: 20 minutes | Servings: 4

Ingredients:
- 1 cup red quinoa
- 2 tablespoons vegetable oil
- 1 yellow onion, chopped
- 2 cups cauliflower florets
- 2 tablespoons chili peppers, chopped
- Salt to the taste
- ½ teaspoon turmeric powder
- ½ teaspoon red chili powder
- 1 and ½ teaspoon cumin, ground
- ½ cup peas
- 2 tablespoons lemon juice
- ½ cup cilantro, chopped
- 1 tablespoon cashews, chopped

Directions:
Set your instant pot on Sauté mode, add the oil, heat it up, add the onion, chili peppers, turmeric, chili powder, cumin and salt, stir and cook for 5 minutes. Add the quinoa and the rest of the ingredients, put the lid on and cook on High for 15 minutes. Release the pressure fast for 5 minutes, divide the mix between plates and serve as a side dish.

Nutrition: calories 182, fat 6, fiber 3, carbs 5.6, protein 4.5

Quinoa Curry

Preparation time: 5 minutes | Cooking time: 20 minutes | Servings: 4

Ingredients:
- 1 cup white quinoa
- 2 teaspoons tamari sauce
- 2 cups coconut milk
- 1 tablespoon curry powder
- 1 teaspoon cumin, ground

Directions:
In your instant pot, combine the quinoa with the tamari sauce and the other ingredients, put the lid on and cook on High for 20 minutes. Release the pressure fast for 5 minutes, stir the mix, divide it between plates and serve as a side dish.

Nutrition: calories 262, fat 6, fiber 4, carbs 6, protein 3.5

Quinoa Pilaf

Preparation time: 5 minutes | Cooking time: 20 minutes | Servings: 4

Ingredients:
- 1 cup quinoa
- 1 and ½ cups water
- 1 tablespoon vegetable oil
- ½ teaspoon turmeric powder
- ½ cup corn
- ½ cup carrot, sliced
- 1 green chili, chopped
- ½ teaspoon cumin seeds
- 1 bay leaf
- ¼ teaspoon black mustard seeds
- 1 tablespoon lime juice
- 1 cup tomato, chopped

Directions:
Set your instant pot on Sauté mode, add the oil, heat it up, add the corn, carrot, chili, cumin and black mustard seeds, stir and cook for 5 minutes. Add rest of the ingredients, put the lid on and cook on High for 15 minutes. Release the pressure fast for 5 minutes, divide between plates and serve.

Nutrition: calories 200, fat 8, fiber 4, carbs 6, protein 7

Quinoa and Chickpeas Mix

Preparation time: 5 minutes | Cooking time: 20 minutes | Servings: 6

Ingredients:

- 2 tablespoons ghee, melted
- 1 teaspoon smoked paprika
- 2 teaspoons chili powder
- 2 teaspoons cumin, ground
- 2 teaspoons garam masala
- ¼ teaspoon red pepper flakes
- 2 teaspoons curry powder
- 1 yellow onion, chopped
- 1 red bell pepper, chopped
- 1 tablespoon ginger, grated
- 3 garlic cloves, minced
- 1 cup quinoa
- 1 and ½ cups water
- 1 green chili, chopped
- 28 ounces canned chickpeas, drained and rinsed
- 14 ounces canned tomatoes, chopped
- 4 cups spinach leaves, chopped
- Salt to the taste

Directions:

Set your instant pot on Sauté mode, add the ghee, heat it up, add the onion, garlic, ginger, paprika, chili powder, cumin, garam masala, curry powder and pepper flakes, stir and cook for 5 minutes. Add the quinoa and the rest of the ingredients, toss, put the lid on and cook on High for 15 minutes. Release the pressure fast for 5 minutes, divide the mix between plates and serve as a side dish.

Nutrition: calories 280, fat 7, fiber 4.4, carbs 11.7, protein 6

Beet Sabzi

Preparation time: 10 minutes | Cooking time: 25 minutes | Servings: 4

Ingredients:

- 2 cups beets, peeled and cubed
- 2 tablespoons vegetable oil
- ¼ cup chicken stock
- ¼ teaspoon mustard seeds
- ½ teaspoon cumin seeds
- 2 red chilies, chopped
- 2 green chilies, chopped
- 10 curry leaves
- ¼ teaspoon turmeric powder
- 1 yellow onion, chopped
- ¼ cup coconut, grated
- Salt to the taste

Directions:

Set the instant pot on sauté mode, add the oil, heat it up, add the cumin, mustard, red and green chilies, curry leaves, onion and turmeric, stir and cook for 5 minutes. Add the remaining ingredients, put the lid on and cook on High for 20 minutes. Release the pressure naturally for 10 minutes, stir the mix, divide between plates and serve as a side dish.

Nutrition: calories 220, fat 8, fiber 4, carbs 6.6, protein 8

Beet Rice

Preparation time: 10 minutes | Cooking time: 25 minutes | Servings: 4

Ingredients:
- 1 cup basmati rice
- 2 cups water
- 2 tablespoons vegetable oil
- 3 green cardamom
- 1-inch cinnamon, crushed
- 3 cloves
- ½ teaspoon mustard seeds
- ½ teaspoon cumin seeds
- 1 yellow onion, chopped
- 8 curry leaves
- 2 beets, peeled and chopped
- 1 teaspoon ginger-garlic paste
- ¼ cup coriander, chopped
- 1 green chili, chopped
- ¼ teaspoon turmeric powder
- ¼ teaspoon red chili powder
- ½ teaspoon coriander powder
- Salt to the taste

Directions:
Set the instant pot on Sauté mode, add the oil, heat it up, add the cardamom, cinnamon, cloves, mustard seeds, cumin, onion, curry, and green chili, stir and cook for 5 minutes. Add the rest of the ingredients, toss, put the pressure lid on and cook on High for 20 minutes. Release the pressure naturally for 10 minutes, divide the mix between plates and serve as a side dish.

Nutrition: calories 281, fat 11.7, fiber 3, carbs 8.6, protein 4.7

Beet Poriyal

Preparation time: 10 minutes | Cooking time: 20 minutes | Servings: 2

Ingredients:
- 2 tablespoons coconut oil
- 2 cups beets, peeled and grated
- 1 green chili, chopped
- 10 curry leaves, chopped
- 1 teaspoon black mustard seeds
- 1 teaspoon urad dal
- 1 teaspoon asafetida
- ½ cup water
- 4 tablespoons coconut, grated
- Salt to the taste

Directions:
Set your instant pot on Sauté mode, add the oil, heat it up, add the chili, curry leaves, mustard seeds and asafetida, stir and cook for 5 minutes. Add the beets and the rest of the ingredients, stir, put the lid on and cook on High for 15 minutes. Release the pressure naturally for 10 minutes, divide between plates and serve as a side dish.

Nutrition: calories 184, fat 6, fiber 3, carbs 6, protein 6

Beet Thoran

***Preparation time:** 10 minutes | **Cooking time:** 20 minutes | **Servings:** 4*

Ingredients:
- 3 beets, peeled and grated
- ¼ cup chicken stock
- 1 teaspoon mustard seeds
- ½ cup coconut, grated
- ½ teaspoon cumin seeds
- 4 shallots, chopped
- 10 curry leaves, chopped
- 2 red chilies, chopped
- 1 green chili, chopped
- 1 teaspoon ginger, grated
- 1 teaspoon turmeric powder
- 1 teaspoon red chili powder
- 2 tablespoons coconut oil
- 1 teaspoon coriander powder
- Salt to the taste

Directions:
In your instant pot, combine beets with the mustard seeds, coconut, cumin and the other ingredients, toss, put the lid on and cook on High for 20 minutes. Release the pressure naturally for 10 minutes, divide between plates and serve as a side dish.

Nutrition: calories 200, fat 8, fiber 3, carbs 7, protein 8

Beet and Carrot Poriyal

***Preparation time:** 10 minutes | **Cooking time:** 20 minutes | **Servings:** 4*

Ingredients:
- 2 beets, peeled and cubed
- 1 green chili, minced
- 2 carrots, sliced
- 1 teaspoon mustard
- 1 teaspoon urad dal
- 10 curry leaves, chopped
- 1 teaspoon turmeric powder
- 1 tablespoon coconut oil
- 4 tablespoons coconut, grated
- Salt to the taste
- ¼ cup chicken stock

Directions:
Set your instant pot on sauté mode, add the oil, heat it up, add the chilies, mustard, urad dal, curry, and turmeric, stir and sauté for 5 minutes. Add the beets and the rest of the ingredients except the spinach, put the lid on and cook on High for 15 minutes. Release the pressure naturally for 10 minutes, divide the mix between plates and serve as a side dish.

Nutrition: calories 200, fat 5.7, fiber 5.4, carbs 6.7, protein 5

Green Peas Mix

Preparation time: 10 minutes | Cooking time: 25 minutes | Servings: 4

Ingredients:
- 1 cup peas
- 1 teaspoon ginger, grated
- 2 tablespoons curd
- 2 tablespoon milk powder
- ½ teaspoon turmeric powder
- 1 teaspoon red chili powder
- 1 teaspoon coriander powder
- 1 teaspoon cumin powder
- ½ teaspoon garam masala
- ½ teaspoon fenugreek leaves, dried
- 1 cup water
- Salt to the taste
- 4 tablespoons ghee, melted

Directions:
Set your instant pot on Sauté mode, add the ghee, heat up, add the ginger, turmeric, chili powder, coriander, cumin, garam masala and fenugreek leaves, stir and cook for 5 minutes. Add the rest of the ingredients, toss, put the lid on and cook on High for 20 minutes. Release the pressure naturally for 10 minutes, divide the mix between plates and serve as a side dish.

Nutrition: calories 185, fat 6, fiber 4, carbs 6, protein 5.8

Spiced Peas

Preparation time: 10 minutes | Cooking time: 25 minutes | Servings: 4

Ingredients:
- 1 cup paneer, cubed
- 1 cup peas
- 1 and ½ cups water
- ¼ teaspoon turmeric powder
- ½ teaspoon cumin seeds
- Salt to the taste
- ½ teaspoon red chili powder
- ½ teaspoon garam masala
- 1 tablespoon cream
- ½ teaspoon sugar
- 2 tablespoons ghee, melted
- Salt to the taste

Directions:
Set your instant pot on Sauté mode, add the ghee, heat it up, add the cumin, turmeric, chili powder, garam masala, sugar and the salt, stir and cook for 5 minutes. Add the rest of the ingredients, put the lid on and cook on High for 20 minutes. Release the pressure naturally for 10 minutes, divide between plates and serve as side dish.

Nutrition: calories 200, fat 7, fiber 2.3, carbs 5, protein 6

Peas Pulao

***Preparation time:** 10 minutes | **Cooking time:** 20 minutes | **Servings:** 4*

Ingredients:
- 1 cup basmati rice
- 1 cup peas
- ½ cup onion, chopped
- 3 tablespoons ghee, melted
- 2 cups water
- Salt to the taste
- 1 teaspoon cumin seeds
- 1 black cardamom
- 2 green cardamom
- 3 cloves
- 1 bay leaf

Directions:
Set the instant pot on Sauté mode, add the ghee, heat it up, add the onion and sauté for 5 minutes Add the peas and the rest of the ingredients, put the lid on and cook on High for 15 minutes Release the pressure naturally for 10 minutes, divide between plates and serve as a side dish.

Nutrition: calories 226, fat 5.4, fiber 5, carbs 8, protein 5

Peas and Mushrooms

***Preparation time:** 10 minutes | **Cooking time:** 20 minutes | **Servings:** 4*

Ingredients:
- ½ pound white mushrooms
- 1 cup peas
- 3 tomatoes, cubed
- 1 yellow onion, chopped
- 1 green chili, chopped
- ½ teaspoon chili powder
- ½ teaspoon turmeric powder
- ½ teaspoon garam masala
- 1 teaspoon coriander powder
- 1 teaspoon ginger-garlic paste
- 2 cups water
- Salt to the taste
- 2 tablespoons vegetable oil

Directions:
Set the instant pot on Sauté mode, add the oil, heat it up, add the onion and the chili, stir and sauté for 5 minutes. Add the rest of the ingredients, toss, put the lid on and cook on High for 15 minutes. Release the pressure naturally for 10 minutes, divide the mix between plates and serve as a side dish.

Nutrition: calories 175, fat 4, fiber 2, carbs 6, protein 8

Gajar Matar

Preparation time: 10 minutes | Cooking time: 20 minutes | Servings: 4

Ingredients:

- 4 carrots, sliced
- 1 cup green peas
- 1 teaspoon cumin seeds
- 1-inch ginger, grated
- 2 green chilies, chopped
- ½ teaspoon red chili powder
- ¼ teaspoon garam masala
- 2 tablespoons vegetable oil
- ½ cup water
- 1 tablespoon coriander, chopped
- Salt to the taste

Directions:

Set the instant pot on Sauté mode, add the oil, heat it up, add the cumin, ginger, chilies, chili powder and garam masala, stir and cook for 5 minutes. Add the rest of the ingredients, toss, put the lid on and cook on High for 15 minutes. Release the pressure naturally for 10 minutes, divide the mix between plates and serve as a side dish.

Nutrition: calories 200, fat 5.5, fiber 3.3, carbs 6, protein 7

Hara Bhara Kabab

Preparation time: 10 minutes | Cooking time: 20 minutes | Servings: 4

Ingredients:

- 2 cups spinach, torn
- 1 cup water
- 2 potatoes, peeled and cubed
- ½ cup green peas
- 4 tablespoons gram flour
- 1 green chili, chopped
- 1 teaspoon ginger, grated
- 1 teaspoon chaat masala
- 1 teaspoon dry mango powder
- 8 cashews, chopped
- Salt to the taste
- 2 tablespoons coconut oil

Directions:

Set the pot on sauté mode, add the oil, heat it up, add the flour, chili, ginger, chaat masala, mango powder and salt, whisk well and cook for 3 minutes. Add the rest of the ingredients, toss, put the lid on and cook on High for 17 minutes. Release the pressure naturally for 10 minutes, divide the mix between plates and serve as a side dish.

Nutrition: calories 262, fat 8.6, fiber 2, carbs 7.6, protein 4

Matar Ka Nimona

Preparation time: 10 minutes | Cooking time: 20 minutes | Servings: 4

Ingredients:
- 1 yellow onion, chopped
- 1 teaspoon garlic, minced
- ½ teaspoon ginger, grated
- 2 green chilies, chopped
- 1 cup peas
- 2 tablespoons mustard oil
- 1 yellow potato, cubed
- 1 bay leaf
- 3 cloves
- ½ teaspoon cumin seeds
- 1 tomato, cubed
- ½ teaspoon turmeric powder
- ½ teaspoon red chili powder
- ½ teaspoon coriander powder
- 2 tablespoons coriander, chopped
- 1 cup water
- ½ teaspoon garam masala

Directions:
Set your instant pot on Sauté mode, add the oil, heat it up, add the onion, garlic, ginger and the chilies and sauté for 5 minutes. Add the rest of the ingredients except the coriander, put the lid on and cook on High for 15 minutes. Release the pressure naturally for 10 minutes, divide the mix between plates and serve as a side dish with the coriander sprinkled on top.

Nutrition: calories 252, fat 6.4, fiber 2.5, carbs 6, protein 4.8

Eggplant Bhurtha

Preparation time: 10 minutes | Cooking time: 20 minutes | Servings: 4

Ingredients:
- 2 eggplants, roughly cubed
- ½ teaspoon turmeric powder
- ½ teaspoon cumin, ground
- 2 tablespoons vegetable oil
- ½ teaspoon cumin seeds
- 1 yellow onion, chopped
- ½ teaspoon coriander, ground
- 1 tomato, cubed
- 1 teaspoon ginger, grated
- ½ cup veggie stock

Directions:
In your instant pot, combine the eggplant with the oil, turmeric and the other ingredients, put the lid on and cook on High for 20 minutes. Release the pressure naturally for 10 minutes, divide the mix between plates and serve.

Nutrition: calories 200, fat 11.8, fiber 4, carbs 7, protein 5.6

Baingan Ka Bharta

Preparation time: 10 minutes | Cooking time: 20 minutes | Servings: 4

Ingredients:

- 2 eggplants, roughly cubed
- 1 yellow onion, chopped
- 2 tablespoons ghee, melted
- 1 teaspoon cumin seeds
- 1 teaspoon ginger, grated
- 5 garlic cloves, minced
- 1 chili pepper, chopped
- 2 teaspoons coriander powder
- ½ teaspoon garam masala
- ½ teaspoon turmeric powder
- ½ teaspoon sweet paprika
- 4 tomatoes, cubed
- 1 tablespoon cilantro, chopped

Directions:

Set your instant pot on Sauté mode, add the ghee, heat it up, add the cumin, ginger, garlic, chili pepper, coriander and garam masala, stir and cook for 5 minutes. Add the rest of the ingredients, put the lid on and cook on High for 15 minutes. Release the pressure naturally for 10 minutes, divide the mix between plates and serve as a side dish.

Nutrition: calories 162, fat 4, fiber 4, carbs 6.9, protein 5.7

Parsnips Mix

Preparation time: 10 minutes | Cooking time: 20 minutes | Servings: 4

Ingredients:

- 1 pound parsnips, peeled and cut into sticks
- ½ cup chicken stock
- Salt to the taste
- 2 tablespoons coconut oil
- 3 carrots, peeled and cut into sticks
- ½ teaspoon garam masala

Directions:

In your instant pot, combine the parsnips with the carrots and the other ingredients, put the lid on and cook on High for 20 minutes. Release the pressure naturally for 10 minutes, divide the mix between plates and serve as a side dish.

Nutrition: calories 142, fat 2, fiber 4, carbs 9, protein 4

Cauliflower Mix

Preparation time: 10 minutes | Cooking time: 15 minutes | Servings: 4

Ingredients:
- 1 pound cauliflower florets
- 1 teaspoon cumin seeds
- ½ teaspoon mustard seeds
- 1 teaspoon garam masala
- 1 teaspoon sage, dried
- Salt and black pepper to the taste
- 1 tablespoon coriander, chopped
- ¼ cup coconut cream

Directions:
In your instant pot, mix the cauliflower with the cumin, mustard seeds and the other ingredients, toss, put the lid on and cook on High for 15 minutes. Release the pressure naturally for 10 minutes, divide the mix between plates and serve as a side dish.

Nutrition: calories 242, fat 4, fiber 3, carbs 6, protein 4.5

Spiced Gobi

Preparation time: 5 minute | Cooking time: 20 minutes | Servings: 4

Ingredients:
- 1 pound cauliflower florets
- 3 tablespoons ghee, melted
- 1 yellow onion, chopped
- 4 garlic cloves, minced
- 3 tablespoons curd
- ½ teaspoon red chili powder
- ¼ teaspoon turmeric powder
- ½ teaspoon garam masala powder
- ½ teaspoon cumin, ground
- 1 teaspoon coriander powder
- 1 bay leaf
- ½ teaspoon caraway seeds
- ½ teaspoon fenugreek leaves, dried
- 1 and ½ cups water
- 2 tablespoons cream
- Salt to the taste

Directions:
Set the instant pot on Sauté mode, add the ghee, heat it up, add the onion, garlic, chili powder, turmeric powder, garam masala, cumin and coriander, stir and sauté for 5 minutes. Add the rest of the ingredients, toss, put the lid on and cook on High for 15 minutes. Release the pressure fast for 5 minutes, divide between plates and serve as a side dish.

Nutrition: calories 232, fat 5.4, fiber 3, carbs 6, protein 4.5

Spicy Gobi Mix

Preparation time: 5 minutes | Cooking time: 20 minutes | Servings: 4

Ingredients:
- 1 pound cauliflower florets
- ¼ teaspoon red chili powder
- ½ teaspoon smoked paprika
- 1 teaspoon soy sauce
- 1 cup chicken stock
- Salt and black pepper to the taste
- 3 tablespoons vegetable oil

Directions:
Set the instant pot on Sauté mode, add the oil, heat it up, add the cauliflower, chili powder and the paprika and brown for 5 minutes. Add the rest of the ingredients, put the lid on and cook on High for 15 minutes. Release the pressure fast for 5 minutes, divide the mix between plates and serve.

Nutrition: calories 142, fat 7, fiber 4, carbs 6, protein 3.4

Creamy Cauliflower Mix

Preparation time: 10 minutes | Cooking time: 20 minutes | Servings: 4

Ingredients:
- ½ pound cauliflower florets
- Salt to the taste
- ½ cup coconut, grated
- 2 green chilies, chopped
- 1 teaspoon ginger, grated
- 4 garlic cloves, minced
- 1 tablespoon chana dal
- 1 teaspoon poppy seeds
- ½ teaspoon fennel seeds
- 10 cashews, chopped
- ½ cup water
- 2 tablespoons coconut oil
- 2 cloves
- 1 yellow onion, chopped
- 1 teaspoon turmeric powder

Directions:
Set the instant pot on Sauté mode, add the oil, heat it up, add the coconut, chilies, ginger, garlic, chana dal, poppy seeds, fennel seeds and the onions, stir and sauté for 5 minutes. Add the cauliflower and the other ingredients, put the lid on and cook on High for 15 minutes. Release the pressure naturally for 10 minutes, divide the mix between plates and serve as a side dish.

Nutrition: calories 152, fat 7, fiber 2, carbs 7, protein 5

Brussels Sprouts Subzi

Preparation time: 10 minutes | Cooking time: 20 minutes | Servings: 2

Ingredients:
- 1 teaspoon coconut oil
- ½ teaspoon cumin seeds
- ½ teaspoon black mustard seeds
- 8 curry leaves, chopped
- 1 green chili, chopped
- 2 cups Brussels sprouts, halved
- 3 garlic cloves, minced
- 2 teaspoons sesame seeds
- ½ teaspoon coriander powder
- ½ teaspoon garam masala
- ½ teaspoon turmeric powder
- ¼ cup water
- Salt to the taste

Directions:
Set the instant pot on Sauté mode, add the oil, heat it up, add the cumin, mustard sees, curry leaves, chili, garlic, sesame seeds, coriander and garam masala, stir and cook for 5 minutes. Add the other ingredients, toss, put the lid on and cook on High for 15 minutes. Release the pressure naturally for 10 minutes, divide the mix between plates and serve.

Nutrition: calories 152, fat 4, fiber 3, carbs 4.4, protein 3

Spiced Brussels Sprouts

Preparation time: 10 minutes | Cooking time: 20 minutes | Servings: 4

Ingredients:
- 2 tablespoons sunflower oil
- 2 garlic cloves, minced
- ½ teaspoon brown mustard seeds
- 2 red chilies, chopped
- 3 curry leaves
- 1 pound Brussels sprouts, halved
- ½ teaspoon garam masala
- ¼ teaspoon turmeric powder
- Salt to the taste
- 2 teaspoons lemon juice
- 1 tablespoon coriander, chopped

Directions:
Set the instant pot on Sauté mode, add the oil, heat it up, add the garlic, chilies, mustard seeds, curry leaves, garam masala and turmeric, stir and cook for 4 minutes. Add the other ingredients, put the lid on and cook on High for 15 minutes. Release the pressure naturally for 10 minutes, divide the mix between plates and serve as a side dish.

Nutrition: calories 187, fat 7, fiber 3, carbs 5, protein 5

Curried Brussels Sprouts
Preparation time: 10 minutes | Cooking time: 20 minutes | Servings: 4

Ingredients:
- ½ pound Brussels sprouts, halved
- 1 cup yellow onion, chopped
- 1 tomato, chopped
- 1 green chili, chopped
- 1 and ½ tablespoons coconut oil
- 2 garlic cloves, minced
- ½ teaspoon cumin, ground
- ½ teaspoon turmeric powder
- ½ teaspoon chili powder
- 1 teaspoon coriander powder
- 1 cup green peas
- 1 teaspoon fennel seeds, ground
- ½ cup veggie stock

Directions:
Set the instant pot on Sauté mode, add the oil, heat it up, add the onion, chili and the garlic, stir and cook for 2 minutes. Add the cumin, turmeric, chili powder, coriander and fennel seeds, stir and cook for 3 minutes more. Add the remaining ingredients, toss, put the lid on and cook on High for 15 minutes. Release the pressure naturally for 10 minutes, divide everything between plates and serve.

Nutrition: calories 120, fat 4, fiber 3.4, carbs 8, protein 4

Kale Salad
Preparation time: 5 minutes | Cooking time: 15 minutes | Servings: 4

Ingredients:
- 2 bunches kale, torn
- 1 yellow onion, chopped
- 5 dates, chopped
- 2 tablespoons pistachios, chopped
- 2 tablespoons olive oil
- Juice of 1 lemon
- ¼ cup veggie stock
- Salt to the taste
- ½ teaspoon cumin, ground
- ½ teaspoon garam masala

Directions:
Set the instant pot on Sauté mode, add the oil, heat it up, add the onion, cumin and garam masala, toss and sauté for 5 minutes. Add the rest of the ingredients, toss, put the lid on and cook on High for 10 minutes. Release the pressure fast for 5 minutes, divide everything between plates and serve.

Nutrition: calories 165, fat 4, fiber 3, carbs 5.7, protein 6

Spiced Greens

Preparation time: 5 minutes | Cooking time: 15 minutes | Servings: 4

Ingredients:
- 1 tablespoon vegetable oil
- ½ teaspoon mustard seeds
- 1 teaspoon cumin seeds
- 4 green chilies, chopped
- 1 teaspoon ginger, grated
- ½ teaspoon turmeric powder
- 1 pound greens (kale, and Brussels sprouts), shredded
- Juice of 1 lemon
- ¼ cup veggie stock
- ½ teaspoon coriander, ground
- 1 tablespoon coriander, chopped

Directions:

In your instant pot, the greens with the oil, mustard sees, cumin and the other ingredients, put the lid on and cook on High for 15 minutes. Release the pressure fast for 5 minutes, divide the mix between plates and serve.

Nutrition: calories 173, fat 4.5, fiber 2, carbs 5, protein 6

Mango and Kale Mix

Preparation time: 5 minutes | Cooking time: 15 minutes | Servings: 4

Ingredients:
- 1 bunch kale, torn
- Juice of 1 lemon
- 3 tablespoons vegetable oil
- 2 teaspoons honey
- Salt to the taste
- 1 mango, peeled and cubed
- 1 tablespoon pepitas
- ¼ cup chicken stock

Directions:

In your instant pot, combine the kale with the lemon juice and the other ingredients, toss, put the lid on and cook on High for 15 minutes. Release the pressure fast for 5 minutes, divide between plates and serve as a side dish.

Nutrition: calories 173, fat 8, fiber 4.2, carbs 6, protein

Turmeric Broccoli Mix

Preparation time: 10 minutes | Cooking time: 15 minutes | Servings: 2

Ingredients:
- 1 broccoli head, florets separated
- ¼ cup chicken stock
- 1 teaspoon turmeric powder
- ½ teaspoon chili powder
- ½ teaspoon garam masala
- A pinch of salt and black pepper
- ¼ cup pine nuts, toasted
- 1 tablespoon olive oil

Directions:
In your instant pot, combine the broccoli with the stock and the other ingredients, put the lid on and cook on High for 15 minutes. Release the pressure naturally for 10 minutes, divide the mix between plates and serve as a side dish.

Nutrition: calories 190, fat 5, fiber 3, carbs 4.5, protein 4.23

Citrus Cauliflower Mix

Preparation time: 10 minutes | Cooking time: 15 minutes | Servings: 4

Ingredients:
- 1 pound cauliflower florets
- ½ teaspoon garam masala
- ½ teaspoon cumin, ground
- ½ teaspoon coriander, ground
- Zest of 1 orange, grated
- Juice of 1 orange
- ¼ cup chicken stock
- 1 red chili pepper, chopped
- A pinch of salt and black pepper
- 2 tablespoons coconut oil

Directions:
In your instant pot, combine the cauliflower with the garam masala and the other ingredients, toss, put the lid on and cook on High for 15 minutes. Release the pressure naturally for 10 minutes, divide everything between plates and serve as a side salad.

Nutrition: calories 242, fat 4, fiber 2.2, carbs 4, protein 5

Orange Pulao

Preparation time: 10 minutes | *Cooking time:* 20 minutes | *Servings:* 4

Ingredients:
- 1 cup basmati rice
- 4 carrots, chopped
- 1 cup orange juice
- 2 tablespoons vegetable oil
- Salt to the taste
- 1 yellow onion, chopped
- 1 teaspoon ginger garlic paste
- ½ teaspoon aniseed
- 2 curry leaves, chopped
- 1 cardamom

Directions:
Set the instant pot on Sauté mode, add the oil, heat it up, add the onion, ginger paste, aniseed, curry and cardamom, stir and cook for 5 minutes. Add the rest of the ingredients, put the lid on and cook on High for 15 minutes. Release the pressure naturally for 10 minutes, divide the mix between plates and serve.

Nutrition: calories 190, fat 6, fiber 2, carbs 6, protein 3.4

Narangi Pulao

Preparation time: 10 minutes | *Cooking time:* 20 minutes | *Servings:* 4

Ingredients:
- 1 cup basmati rice
- 1 tablespoon ghee, melted
- 1-inch cinnamon stick
- 1 star anise
- 2 cloves
- 1 cardamom
- 2 cups orange juice
- 1 tablespoon milk
- ½ teaspoon saffron powder
- 2 tablespoons sugar
- Salt to the taste

Directions:
Set the instant pot on Sauté mode, add the ghee, heat it up, add the cinnamon, star anise, cloves, cardamom and the saffron mixed with the milk, whisk and cook for 3 minutes. Add the rest of the ingredients, put the lid on and cook on High for 17 minutes. Release the pressure naturally for 10 minutes, divide the mix between plates and serve.

Nutrition: calories 181, fat 6, fiber 5, carbs 3.7, protein 7

Rice and Kale

Preparation time: 5 minutes | Cooking time: 20 minutes | Servings: 4

Ingredients:
- 2 cups basmati rice
- 3 cups chicken stock
- 2 cups kale, torn
- ½ teaspoon turmeric powder
- 1 teaspoon cumin seeds
- 2 tablespoons ghee, melted
- 3 garlic cloves, minced

Directions:
Set the instant pot on Sauté mode, add the ghee, heat it up, add the garlic, cumin and the turmeric, stir and cook for 3 minutes. Add the rest of the ingredients, put the lid on and cook on High for 17 minutes. Release the pressure fast for 5 minutes, divide the mix between plates and serve.

Nutrition: calories 181, fat 5, fiber 4, carbs 6, protein 3.6

Garlic Rice Mix

Preparation time: 10 minutes | Cooking time: 20 minutes | Servings: 6

Ingredients:
- 2 tablespoons butter
- 4 garlic cloves, minced
- Salt to the taste
- 1 and ½ cups rice
- 2 and ½ cups chicken stock
- 1/3 cup almonds, chopped
- 1 tablespoon cilantro, chopped

Directions:
Set your instant pot on Sauté mode, add the butter, heat it up, add the garlic and sauté for 2 minutes. Add the rest of the ingredients, put the lid on and cook on High for 18 minutes Release the pressure fast for 10 minutes, divide between plates and serve.

Nutrition: calories 182, fat 4, fiber 3, carbs 3.4, protein 4

Asparagus Rice Mix

Preparation time: 5 minutes | Cooking time: 20 minutes | Servings: 4

Ingredients:
- 1 cup basmati rice
- 1 cup chicken stock
- 1 cup water
- Salt to the taste
- 2 garlic cloves, minced
- ½ teaspoon sweet paprika
- ½ teaspoon turmeric powder
- ½ teaspoon orange zest, grated
- 1 pound asparagus, trimmed and chopped

Directions:
In the instant pot, combine the rice with the stock, water and the other ingredients, toss, put the lid on and cook on High for 20 minutes. Release the pressure fast for 5 minutes, divide the mix between plates and serve as a side dish.

Nutrition: calories 218, fat 20, fiber 3.4, carbs 41.6, protein 7.3

Spicy Eggplant Mix

***Preparation time:** 10 minutes | **Cooking time:** 15 minutes | **Servings:** 4*

Ingredients:
- 2 eggplants, roughly cubed
- ½ cup chicken stock
- ½ teaspoon cumin, ground
- ½ teaspoon coriander powder
- ½ teaspoon ginger, grated
- 2 teaspoons turmeric powder
- A pinch of salt and black pepper
- 2 tablespoons coconut oil, melted
- 2 garlic cloves, minced
- 1 teaspoon hot pepper flakes

Directions:

Set your instant pot on Sauté mode, add the oil, heat it up, add the garlic, cumin, coriander, ginger, and turmeric, stir and cook for 2 minutes. Add the rest of the ingredients, put the lid on and cook on High for 13 minutes. Release the pressure naturally for 10 minutes, divide between plates and serve.

Nutrition: calories 233, fat 4, fiber 4, carbs 4.7, protein 2.4

Ginger Broccoli and Orange Mix

***Preparation time:** 5 minutes | **Cooking time:** 20 minutes | **Servings:** 4*

Ingredients:
- 1 pound broccoli florets
- 1 orange, peeled and cut into segments
- ½ teaspoon turmeric powder
- ½ teaspoon garam masala
- ½ teaspoon ginger powder
- ½ teaspoon dry mango powder
- ¼ cup veggie stock
- 2 teaspoons ginger, grated
- 2 garlic cloves, minced
- Salt and white pepper to the taste

Directions:

In your instant pot, combine the broccoli with the orange and the other ingredients, put the lid on and cook on High for 20 minutes. Release the pressure fast for 5 minutes, divide the mix between plates and serve.

Nutrition: calories 230, fat 4.4, fiber 3, carbs 7, protein 4

Saffron Red Cabbage

Preparation time: 10 minutes | Cooking time: 15 minutes | Servings: 4

Ingredients:

- 1 pound red cabbage, shredded
- 2 tablespoons coconut oil
- ½ teaspoon saffron powder mixed with 1 tablespoon milk
- ½ cup yellow onion, chopped
- 1 teaspoon hot paprika
- ½ teaspoon chili powder
- 2 green chilies, chopped
- Salt and black pepper to the taste
- 1 tablespoon apple cider vinegar

Directions:

Set your instant pot on Sauté mode, add the oil, heat it up, add the onion, paprika, chilies and green chilies, stir and cook for 2 minutes. Add the saffron, stir and cook for 3 minutes more. Add the rest of the ingredients, toss, put the lid on and cook on High for 10 minutes. Release the pressure naturally for 10 minutes, divide the mix between plates and serve as a side dish.

Nutrition: calories 232, fat 3.7, fiber 3, carbs 6, protein 2.4

Cabbage Rice

Preparation time: 10 minutes | Cooking time: 20 minutes | Servings: 8

Ingredients:

- 2 cups basmati rice
- 3 and ½ cups water
- Salt to the taste
- ¼ teaspoon asafetida powder
- 2 tablespoons coconut oil
- ½ cup peanuts
- 1 teaspoon mustard seeds
- ½ teaspoon turmeric powder
- 15 curry leaves
- 2 tablespoons ginger, grated
- 4 green chilies, chopped
- 8 cups green cabbage, shredded
- 2 tablespoons lemon juice
- 2 tablespoons cilantro, chopped

Directions:

Set the instant pot on Sauté mode, add the oil, heat it up, add the mustard seeds, turmeric, curry leaves, ginger and the chilies, stir and cook for 3 minutes. Add the rice, water and the rest of the ingredients, put the lid on and cook on High for 17 minutes. Release the pressure naturally for 10 minutes, divide the mix between plates and serve.

Nutrition: calories 263, fat 4.6, fiber 4, carbs 8, protein 6

Creamy Beans and Rice

Preparation time: 10 minutes | Cooking time: 20 minutes | Servings: 4

Ingredients:
- 1 pound green beans, trimmed
- 1 cup basmati rice
- 1 and ½ cups coconut cream
- 5 garlic cloves, minced
- ½ teaspoon chili powder
- ½ teaspoon garam masala
- ½ teaspoon coriander powder
- A pinch of salt and black pepper
- 1 teaspoon sweet paprika

Directions:

In your instant pot, mix the beans with the rice, cream and the other ingredients, put the lid on and cook on High for 20 minutes. Release the pressure naturally for 10 minutes, divide the mix between plates and serve as a side dish.

Nutrition: calories 251, fat 11.7, fiber 4, carbs 6.9, protein 11

Tomato Salad

Preparation time: 10 minutes | Cooking time: 15 minutes | Servings: 4

Ingredients:
- 3 tomatoes, cut into wedges
- ½ teaspoon garam masala
- ½ red onion, chopped
- 1 cup curd
- 1 tablespoon lemon juice
- 1 cup mint leaves
- Salt to the taste
- 1 tablespoon water

Directions:

In a blender, combine the curd with the other ingredients except the tomatoes, garam masala and the onion and pulse well. In your instant pot, combine the tomatoes with the onion, garam masala and the mint mix, toss, put the lid on and cook on High for 15 minutes. Release the pressure naturally for 10 minutes, divide the mix between plates and serve.

Nutrition: calories 182, fat 4, fiber 4, carbs 4.5, protein 8

Beets and Almonds

Preparation time: 10 minutes | Cooking time: 20 minutes | Servings: 4

Ingredients:
- ½ cup chicken stock
- ½ cup almonds, chopped
- ½ teaspoon red chili powder
- ½ teaspoon cumin, ground
- ½ teaspoon mustard seeds
- ½ teaspoon turmeric powder
- 1 red onion, sliced
- 4 beets, peeled and cut into cubes
- 2 tablespoons coconut oil
- A pinch of salt and black pepper
- 2 tablespoons coriander, chopped

Directions:
In your instant pot, combine the beets with the stock, almonds and the other ingredients, toss, put the lid on and cook on High for 20 minutes. Release the pressure naturally for 10 minutes, divide the mix between plates and serve as a side dish.

Nutrition: calories 142, fat 5, fiber 3, carbs 8, protein 6

Spicy Artichokes and Rice

Preparation time: 10 minutes | Cooking time: 20 minutes | Servings: 4

Ingredients:
- 1 cup canned artichoke hearts, drained and roughly chopped
- 1 cup basmati rice
- 2 cups chicken stock
- 1 tablespoon coconut oil
- ½ teaspoon cumin, ground
- ½ teaspoon turmeric powder
- ½ teaspoon garam masala
- 2 tablespoons lemon juice
- A pinch of cayenne pepper
- ½ teaspoon red pepper flakes

Directions:
Set the instant pot on Sauté mode, add the oil, heat it up, add the cumin, turmeric, garam masala, cayenne and pepper flakes, stir and cook for 5 minutes. Add the rest of the ingredients, put the lid on and cook on High for 15 minutes. Release the pressure naturally for 10 minutes, divide the mix between plates and serve.

Nutrition: calories 152, fat 4, fiber 4, carbs 8, protein 6

Spicy Tomatoes

Preparation time: 5 minutes | Cooking time: 12 minutes | Servings: 4

Ingredients:
- 2 tomatoes, cut into wedges
- ½ tablespoon coconut oil
- 1 yellow onion, chopped
- 2 tablespoons lemon juice
- Salt to the taste
- ½ teaspoon cayenne pepper
- ½ teaspoon cumin, ground
- ½ teaspoon dry mango powder

Directions:

In your instant pot, combine the tomatoes with the oil and the other ingredients, put the lid on and cook on High for 12 minutes. Release the pressure fast for 5 minutes, divide the mix between plates and serve.

Nutrition: calories 140, fat 4, fiber 4, carbs 8, protein 4

Endives and Tomatoes Mix

Preparation time: 5 minutes | Cooking time: 15 minutes | Servings: 4

Ingredients:
- 2 endives, trimmed and shredded
- 1 pound tomatoes, cut into wedges
- 2 tablespoons coconut oil
- ½ teaspoon cumin, ground
- ½ teaspoon sweet paprika
- ½ teaspoon chili powder
- Salt and black pepper to the taste
- Juice of 1 lime
- ¼ cup veggie stock
- 2 tablespoons parsley, chopped

Directions:

In your instant pot, combine the endives with the tomatoes and the other ingredients except the parsley, put the lid on and cook on High for 15 minutes. Release the pressure fast for 5 minutes, divide the mix between plates and serve with the parsley sprinkled on top.

Nutrition: calories 140, fat 4, fiber 4, carbs 8, protein 5

Endives and Walnuts Mix

Preparation time: 10 minutes | Cooking time: 15 minutes | Servings: 2

Ingredients:

- 4 endives, trimmed and shredded
- 1 cup walnuts, chopped
- 2 tablespoons coconut oil, melted
- 2 shallots, chopped
- ½ teaspoon turmeric powder
- ½ teaspoon chili powder
- ½ teaspoon cumin, ground
- ½ teaspoon dry mango powder
- ½ cup chicken stock

Directions:

Set your instant pot on Sauté mode, add the oil, heat it up, add the shallots, walnuts, turmeric, chili powder, cumin and mango powder, stir and cook for 3 minutes. Add the rest of the ingredients, put the lid on and cook on High for 12 minutes. Release the pressure naturally for 10 minutes, divide the mix between plates and serve as a side dish.

Nutrition: calories 180, fat 4, fiber 5, carbs 9, protein 6

Endives with Orange Mix

Preparation time: 10 minutes | Cooking time: 15 minutes | Servings: 4

Ingredients:

- 2 endives, trimmed and shredded
- 2 oranges, peeled and cut into wedges
- 1 tablespoon coconut oil
- 1 yellow onion, chopped
- ½ cup chicken stock
- 6 garlic cloves, chopped
- Salt and black pepper to the taste
- 2 tablespoons coriander, chopped
- 1 teaspoon turmeric powder
- ½ teaspoon garam masala

Directions:

Set your instant pot on Sauté mode, add the oil, heat up, add the onion and garlic cloves, stir and cook for 3 minutes. Add the rest of the ingredients, put the lid on and cook on High for 12 minutes. Release the pressure naturally for 10 minutes, divide the mix between plates and serve.

Nutrition: calories 183, fat 4, fiber 4, carbs 8, protein 6

Indian Cumin Asparagus

Preparation time: 5 minutes | *Cooking time:* 12 minutes | *Servings:* 4

Ingredients:
- 1 pound fresh asparagus, trimmed and halved
- 1-inch ginger, grated
- 1 teaspoon cumin seeds
- 2 tablespoons lemon juice
- 1 tablespoon vegetable oil
- Salt to the taste
- ½ cup chicken stock
- ½ teaspoon turmeric powder
- ½ teaspoon chili powder
- ½ teaspoon garam masala

Directions:
Set your instant pot on Sauté mode, add the oil, heat it up, add the ginger, cumin, turmeric, chili powder and garam masala, stir and cook for 2 minutes. Add the rest of the ingredients, toss, put the lid on and cook on High for 10 minutes. Release the pressure fast for 5 minutes, divide the mix between plates and serve.

Nutrition: calories 169, fat 5.4, fiber 4, carbs 6.8, protein 6

Turmeric Fennel and Rice

Preparation time: 5 minutes | *Cooking time:* 20 minutes | *Servings:* 4

Ingredients:
- 1 fennel bulb, sliced
- 2 teaspoons turmeric powder
- 1 cup basmati rice
- ½ cup chicken stock
- ½ teaspoon chili powder
- ½ teaspoon garam masala
- 1 cup coconut cream
- A pinch of salt and black pepper

Directions:
In your instant pot, combine the rice with the stock, the fennel and the other ingredients, put the lid on and cook on High for 20 minutes. Release the pressure fast for 5 minutes, divide the mix between plates and serve as a side dish.

Nutrition: calories 152, fat 5, fiber 4, carbs 8, protein 7

Peas and Fennel Mix

Preparation time: 10 minutes | *Cooking time:* 15 minutes | *Servings:* 4

Ingredients:
- 1 pound fresh peas
- 1 fennel bulb, shredded
- Salt to the taste
- 1 yellow onion, chopped
- 1 tablespoon mint, chopped
- ½ cup coconut cream
- ½ teaspoon chili powder
- ½ teaspoon smoked paprika

Directions:
In your instant pot, combine the peas with the fennel and the other ingredients, put the lid on and cook on High for 15 minutes. Release the pressure naturally for 10 minutes, divide the mix between plates and serve.

Nutrition: calories 182, fat 5, fiber 5, carbs 4.9, protein 7

Indian Instant Pot Snack and Appetizer Recipes

Chili Paneer

Preparation time: 10 minutes | Cooking time: 20 minutes | Servings: 3

Ingredients:
- ½ green bell pepper, cubed
- ½ red bell pepper, cubed
- ½ yellow bell pepper, cubed
- 1 cup paneer, cubed
- ½ teaspoon cayenne pepper
- 2 teaspoons soy sauce
- ¼ teaspoon sugar
- ¼ cup spring onions, chopped
- 2 tablespoons vegetable oil
- Salt to the taste

Directions:
In your instant pot, combine the bell peppers with the other ingredients, put the lid on and cook on High for 15 minutes. Divide the mix into bowls and serve as an appetizer.

Nutrition: calories 207, fat 13.2, fiber 1.8, carbs 17.4, protein 5.8

Okra Bowls

Preparation time: 5 minutes | Cooking time: 15 minutes | Servings: 3

Ingredients:
- 20 okra
- 2 tablespoons gram flour
- ½ teaspoon turmeric powder
- ½ teaspoon turmeric powder
- 2 tablespoons vegetable oil
- 1 cup water

Directions:
In a bowl, combine the okra with the flour and the other ingredients except the water and toss. Put the water into the instant pot, add the trivet inside, put the bowls into the pot and cook on High for 15 minutes. Release the pressure fast for 5 minutes, divide everything into smaller bowls and serve as a snack.

Nutrition: calories 124, fat 9.5, fiber 2.7, carbs 7.7, protein 2.2

Khara Biscuits

Preparation time: 10 minutes | Cooking time: 15 minutes | Servings: 10

Ingredients:
- 1 and ½ cups whole wheat flour
- ½ cup butter
- 1 tablespoon milk powder
- 3 tablespoons curd
- 2 tablespoons sugar
- ½ cup cilantro, chopped
- 20 curry leaves, chopped
- 7 green chilies, chopped
- Salt to the taste
- 1 cup water

Directions:

In a bowl, combine the flour with the milk powder, butter and the other ingredients except the water and stir well until you obtain a dough. Transfer the dough to a baking sheet that fits the instant pot and press well on the bottom. Add the water to the instant pot, add the trivet and the baking sheet inside, and cook on High for 15 minutes. Release the pressure naturally for 10 minutes, cool the mix down, cut into biscuits and serve.

Nutrition: calories 194, fat 9.8, fiber 1.2, carbs 23, protein 3.7

Pyaaz Chutney

Preparation time: 10 minutes | Cooking time: 10 minutes | Servings: 10

Ingredients:
- 3 yellow onions, chopped
- 2 green chilies, chopped
- 1 tablespoon ginger, grated
- 2 tablespoons sunflower oil
- Salt to the taste
- 3 red chilies, chopped
- 1 teaspoon cumin seeds

Directions:

Set the instant pot on Sauté mode, add the oil, heat it up, add the onions and sauté for 4 minutes. Add the rest of the ingredients, put the lid on and cook on High for 6 minutes. Release the pressure naturally for 10 minutes, transfer the mix to a blender, pulse well, divide into bowls and serve.

Nutrition: calories 70, fat 2.9, fiber 0.8, carbs 3.6, protein 0.5

Tomato Chutney

Preparation time: 10 minutes | Cooking time: 20 minutes | Servings: 6

Ingredients:
- 1 pound red onions, chopped
- 2 pounds tomatoes, chopped
- 1 red chili, minced
- 2 garlic cloves, minced
- 1 tablespoon ginger, grated
- 1 tablespoon sugar
- 2 tablespoons red wine vinegar
- Salt to the taste
- 4 cardamom pods
- ½ teaspoon paprika

Directions:
In your instant pot, combine the onions with the tomatoes and the other ingredients, put the lid on and cook on High for 20 minutes. Release the pressure naturally for 10 minutes, whisk the mix, divide into jars and serve as a party dip.

Nutrition: calories 221, fat 2.4, fiber 4.5, carbs 9.4, protein 3.4

Garlic Dip

Preparation time: 10 minutes | Cooking time: 10 minutes | Servings: 4

Ingredients:
- 4 tablespoons chana daal
- 3 tablespoons urad daal
- 5 red chilies, minced
- 1 tablespoon cumin seeds
- 3 tablespoons garlic, minced
- 1 tablespoon vegetable oil
- 1 teaspoon sugar
- Salt to the taste

Directions:
In your instant pot, combine the urad dal with the chilies and the other ingredients, put the lid on and cook on High for 10 minutes. Release the pressure naturally for 10 minutes, transfer this to a blender, pulse, divide into bowls and serve.

Nutrition: calories 200, fat 3.4, fiber 3.4, carbs 9.7, protein 5.6

Minty Dip

Preparation time: 5 minutes | Cooking time: 5 minutes | Servings: 4

Ingredients:
- 2 cup yogurt
- ½ cup mint leaves, chopped
- 1 cucumber, grated
- 1 teaspoon cumin powder
- ½ teaspoon red chili powder
- ½ teaspoon sugar
- Salt to the taste

Directions:
In your instant pot, combine the yogurt with the mint and the other ingredients, put the lid on and cook on High for 5 minutes. Release the pressure fast for 5 minutes, divide the mix into bowls and serve.

Nutrition: calories 200, fat 6.7, fiber 3.5, carbs 5.6, protein 6.7

Garam Masala Hummus

Preparation time: 5 minutes | *Cooking time:* 15 minutes | *Servings:* 6

Ingredients:
- 15 ounces canned chickpeas, drained and rinsed
- ¼ cup lemon juice
- 3 garlic cloves, minced
- ½ cup tahini paste
- Salt to the taste
- ½ teaspoon sweet paprika
- 3 tablespoons olive oil
- 1 teaspoon garam masala

Directions:
In your instant pot, combine the chickpeas with the lemon juice and the other ingredients, toss, put the lid on and cook on High for 15 minutes. Release the pressure fast for 5 minutes, blend the mix using an immersion blender, divide into bowls and serve as an appetizer.

Nutrition: calories 300, fat 3.4, fiber 6.5, carbs 11, protein 4.5

Avocado Raita

Preparation time: 5 minutes | *Cooking time:* 5 minutes | *Servings:* 4

Ingredients:
- 1 yellow onion, chopped
- 2 avocados, peeled, pitted and chopped
- 2 tomatoes, chopped
- ½ teaspoon red chili powder
- 1 green chili, chopped
- 1 teaspoon cumin powder
- ½ cup coriander, chopped
- 1 tablespoon lemon juice
- 1 cup yogurt
- Salt to the taste

Directions:
In your instant pot, combine the avocado with the chili powder and the other ingredients, toss, put the lid on and cook on High for 5 minutes. Release the pressure fast for 5 minutes, transfer the mix to a blender, pulse well, divide into bowls and serve.

Nutrition: calories 299, fat 4.5, fiber 5.4, carbs 11.3, protein 5.6

Tamarind Dip

Preparation time: 10 minutes | Cooking time: 20 minutes | Servings: 4

Ingredients:
- 2 cups yogurt
- 2 red onions, chopped
- 2 tablespoons coconut oil, melted
- 1 cup tamarind chutney
- 1 cup mint, chopped
- 2 tomatoes, chopped
- 2 teaspoons red chili powder
- 2 tablespoons cumin seeds

Directions:
In your instant pot, combine the yogurt with the onions and other ingredients, put the lid on and cook on High for 20 minutes. Release the pressure naturally for 10 minutes, whisk the mix, divide into bowls and serve as a party dip.

Nutrition: calories 244, fat 4.4, fiber 3.4, carbs 11, protein 2.5

Cashew Dip

Preparation time: 5 minutes | Cooking time: 10 minutes | Servings: 4

Ingredients:
- 8 ounces paneer, cubed
- 1 cup cashews, chopped
- 8 tablespoons water
- 2 tablespoons vinegar
- ½ teaspoon turmeric powder
- A pinch of salt and black pepper
- 1 and ½ teaspoons sweet paprika
- 1 tablespoon lime juice
- 1 cup water

Directions:
In a bowl, combine all the ingredients except the water, whisk well and transfer to a ramekin. Put the water in the instant pot, add the trivet inside, put the ramekin inside, put the lid on and cook on High for 10 minutes. Release the pressure fast for 5 minutes and serve as a dip.

Nutrition: calories 232, fat 11.1, fiber 2, carbs 6.6, protein 5

Capsicum Masala

Preparation time: 10 minutes | Cooking time: 15 minutes | Servings: 4

Ingredients:
- 1 pound green bell peppers, deseeded and roughly cubed
- 2 tablespoons vegetable oil
- ½ teaspoon cumin seeds
- 1 tablespoon coconut powder
- 1 and ½ tablespoon sesame seed powder
- 2 teaspoons coriander powder
- 2 teaspoons fennel seed powder
- ½ teaspoon chili powder
- ¼ teaspoon turmeric powder
- 1 teaspoon lemon juice
- ¼ cup veggie stock

Directions:
In your instant pot, combine the bell peppers with the oil, cumin seeds and the rest of the ingredients, put the lid on and cook on High for 15 minutes. Release the pressure naturally for 10 minutes, transfer the mix to small bowls and serve cold as an appetizer.

Nutrition: calories 240, fat 4.6, fiber 3, carbs 7.6, protein 6

Peppers Dip

Preparation time: 5 minutes | Cooking time: 20 minutes | Servings: 4

Ingredients:
- 2 red bell peppers, chopped
- 4 tomatoes, chopped
- 12 garlic cloves, minced
- 20 almonds, chopped
- 1 tablespoon white wine vinegar
- 2 tablespoons vegetable oil
- Salt and black pepper to the taste

Directions:
Set the instant pot on Sauté mode, add the oil, heat it up, add the garlic and the almonds and sauté for 5 minutes. Add the bell peppers and the other ingredients, put the lid on and cook on High for 15 minutes. Release the pressure fast for 5 minutes, blend the mix using an immersion blender, divide into bowls and serve.

Nutrition: calories 160, fat 9, fiber 4, carbs 7.6, protein 7

Marinated Shrimp Bowls

Preparation time: 30 minutes | Cooking time: 6 minutes | Servings: 4

Ingredients:

- 1 pound shrimp, peeled and deveined
- 1 tablespoon vegetable oil
- Juice of 1 lime
- ½ tablespoon cilantro, chopped
- ¼ cup curd
- 1 teaspoon garlic, minced
- ½ teaspoon garam masala
- ¼ teaspoon chili powder
- Salt to the taste
- ¼ teaspoon turmeric powder

Directions:

In a bowl, combine the shrimp with the oil, lime juice and the other ingredients, toss and keep in the fridge for 25 minutes. Transfer everything to your instant pot, put the lid on and cook on High for 6 minutes. Release the pressure fast for 5 minutes, transfer the shrimp mixture to small bowls and serve as an appetizer.

Nutrition: calories 170, fat 11.9, fiber 4, carbs 9.5, protein 6

Spicy Shrimp Mix

Preparation time: 10 minutes | Cooking time: 6 minutes | Servings: 4

Ingredients:

- 1 pound shrimp, peeled and deveined
- 2 teaspoons red pepper flakes
- ½ teaspoon cumin, ground
- ½ teaspoon turmeric powder
- Salt to the taste
- ½ teaspoon turmeric powder
- 1 tablespoon vegetable oil

Directions:

In your instant pot, combine the shrimp with the pepper flakes and the other ingredients, put the lid on and cook on High for 6 minutes. Release the pressure naturally for 10 minutes, divide the shrimp into bowls and serve as an appetizer.

Nutrition: calories 280, fat 13.4, fiber 3, carbs 7, protein 9

Cumin Eggplant and Tomato Bowls
Preparation time: 5 minutes | *Cooking time:* 15 minutes | *Servings:* 4

Ingredients:
- 2 eggplants, roughly cubed
- 2 tomatoes, cubed
- Juice of 1 lime
- ½ teaspoon turmeric powder
- ½ teaspoon garam masala
- 2 teaspoons cumin, ground
- 2 tablespoons sunflower oil
- 2 tablespoons garlic, minced
- 1 chili pepper, chopped
- ¼ cup cilantro, chopped

Directions:
Set the instant pot on Sauté mode, add the oil, heat it up, add the turmeric, garam masala, cumin, garlic and the chili pepper, stir and cook for 5 minutes. Add the rest of the ingredients, put the lid on and cook on High for 10 minutes. Release the pressure fast for 5 minutes, divide the salad into cups and serve.

Nutrition: calories 250, fat 9, fiber 2.5, carbs 6, protein 6

Hot Shrimp and Peppers Salad
Preparation time: 5 minutes | *Cooking time:* 6 minutes | *Servings:* 4

Ingredients:
- 2 tablespoons lemon juice
- 1 yellow onion, chopped
- 1 tablespoon coconut oil
- ½ teaspoon hot paprika
- 2 red bell peppers, cut into strips
- 1 teaspoon turmeric powder
- ½ teaspoon coriander powder
- ½ teaspoon dry mango powder
- 2 pounds shrimp, peeled and deveined
- 2 tablespoons basil, chopped

Directions:
Set the instant pot on Sauté mode, add the oil, heat it up, add the onion, paprika, turmeric, coriander powder and mango powder and cook for 2 minutes. Add the rest of the ingredients, put the lid on and cook on High for 4 minutes. Release the pressure fast for 5 minutes, divide the shrimp mix into small bowls and serve.

Nutrition: calories 273, fat 9, fiber 3, carbs 5.5, protein 8

Spinach and Avocado Dip

Preparation time: 5 minutes | Cooking time: 5 minutes | Servings: 4

Ingredients:
- 4 cups spinach
- 1 avocado, peeled, pitted and chopped
- ¼ cup coconut cream
- 1 tablespoon lemon juice
- Salt to the taste
- ¼ teaspoon curry powder
- 1 garlic clove, minced
- 1 teaspoon ginger, grated

Directions:
In your instant pot, combine the spinach with the avocado and the other ingredients, put the lid on and cook on High for 5 minutes. Release the pressure fast for 5 minutes, blend the mix using an immersion blender, divide into bowls and serve.

Nutrition: calories 242, fat 8.4, fiber 5, carbs 11.8, protein 2.5

Spinach Spread

Preparation time: 5 minutes | Cooking time: 20 minutes | Servings: 4

Ingredients:
- 2 tablespoons ghee, melted
- 2 garlic cloves, minced
- 1 yellow onion, chopped
- 10 ounces spinach, chopped
- 1 tablespoon ginger, grated
- 2 teaspoons garam masala
- 2 teaspoons cumin
- 1 cup evaporated milk

Directions:
Set the instant pot on Sauté mode, add the ghee, heat it up, add the onion and the garlic and sauté for 5 minutes Add the rest of the ingredients, put the lid on and cook on High for 15 minutes Release the pressure fast for 5 minutes, blend the mix with an immersion blender, divide into bowls and serve as a spread.

Nutrition: calories 280, fat 9, fiber 2.5, carbs 7.6, protein 9

Beans Dip

***Preparation time:** 10 minutes | **Cooking time:** 20 minutes | **Servings:** 8*

Ingredients:

- ¼ teaspoon cumin, ground
- ½ teaspoon allspice, ground
- 16 ounces canned navy beans, drained and rinsed
- ¼ teaspoon ginger, grated
- 1 teaspoon curry powder
- 1 cup yellow bell pepper, chopped
- 1 zucchini, chopped
- 1 red onion, chopped
- 2 garlic cloves, minced
- ¼ cup mango chutney
- Salt to the taste
- 2 tablespoons yogurt

Directions:

In your instant pot, combine the beans with the cumin, allspice, ginger and the other ingredients, stir, put the lid on and cook on High for 20 minutes. Release the pressure naturally for 10 minutes, divide everything into bowls and serve as an appetizer.

Nutrition: calories 25, fat 0.1, fiber 0.8, carbs 5.1, protein 1.1

White Beans Spread

***Preparation time:** 10 minutes | **Cooking time:** 20 minutes | **Servings:** 4*

Ingredients:

- 10 ounces canned white beans, drained and rinsed
- ½ teaspoon garam masala
- ¼ teaspoon turmeric powder
- 2 garlic cloves, minced
- Salt to the taste
- 1 tablespoon lemon juice
- ¼ cup olive oil

Directions:

Set the instant pot on Sauté mode, add the oil, heat it up, add the garlic and cook for 2 minutes. Add the rest of the ingredients, put the lid on and cook on High for 18 minutes. Release the pressure naturally for 10 minutes, blend the mix using an immersion blender, divide into bowls and serve.

Nutrition: calories 180, fat 9, fiber 4, carbs 11.2, protein 8

Turmeric Shrimp Salad
Preparation time: 5 minutes | Cooking time: 8 minutes | Servings: 4

Ingredients:
- 2 pounds shrimp, peeled and deveined
- 2 tablespoons turmeric powder
- 1 teaspoon smoked paprika
- 2 tablespoons curd
- 2 teaspoons lime juice
- 1 tablespoon coconut oil
- A pinch of salt and black pepper

Directions:
In your instant pot, combine the shrimp with the turmeric and the other ingredients, toss, put the lid on and cook on High for 8 minutes. Release the pressure fast for 5 minutes, transfer the mix to small bowls and serve as an appetizer.

Nutrition: calories 177, fat 8, fiber 2, carbs 6.5, protein 7

Curd Chicken Salad
Preparation time: 10 minutes | Cooking time: 20 minutes | Servings: 4

Ingredients:
- 1 pound chicken breast, skinless, boneless and cubed
- 1 cup curd
- 1 cup spinach, torn
- 1 teaspoon turmeric powder
- ½ teaspoon chili powder
- ½ teaspoon garam masala
- 2 tablespoons ghee, melted
- 1 red onion, chopped
- 2 tablespoons garlic, chopped
- 1 cup tomatoes, cubed
- 1 tablespoon coriander, chopped

Directions:
Set your instant pot on Sauté mode, add the ghee, heat it up, add the chicken, turmeric, chili powder and the garam masala, stir and brown for 5 minutes. Add the rest of the ingredients except the coriander, put the lid on and cook on High for 15 minutes. Release the pressure naturally for 10 minutes, divide the mix into bowls, sprinkle the coriander on top and serve as an appetizer.

Nutrition: calories 221, fat 12, fiber 4, carbs 7, protein 11

Chicken Chutney Salad

***Preparation time:** 10 minutes | **Cooking time:** 20 minutes | **Servings:** 4*

Ingredients:
- 2 tablespoons mango chutney
- 1 tablespoon ghee, melted
- 1 teaspoon nigella seeds
- 1 red bell pepper, cut into strips
- 1 cup baby arugula
- 1 cup basmati rice
- 2 cup chicken stock
- 1 teaspoon turmeric powder
- 1 carrot, sliced
- 1 tablespoon curry powder
- Juice of 1 lime
- 1 tablespoon coriander, chopped
- 1 chicken breast, skinless, boneless and cubed
- Salt to the taste

Directions:
Set instant pot on Sauté mode, add the ghee, heat it up, add the chicken and brown for 5 minutes. Add the rest of the ingredients, put the lid on and cook on High for 15 minutes. Release the pressure naturally for 10 minutes, divide the mix into small bowls and serve as an appetizer.

Nutrition: calories 180, fat 9, fiber 3, carbs 5, protein 7

Mango Salad

***Preparation time:** 5 minutes | **Cooking time:** 7 minutes | **Servings:** 4*

Ingredients:
- 1 cup mango, peeled and cubed
- ½ cup coconut cream
- ¼ cup yellow onion, chopped
- ½ teaspoon chili powder
- 2 teaspoons jaggery powder
- Salt to the taste
- ½ teaspoon cumin seeds, roasted and crushed
- 1 tablespoon coriander, chopped

Directions:
In your instant pot, combine the mangoes with the cream and the other ingredients, put the lid on and cook on High for 7 minutes. Release the pressure fast for 5 minutes, divide into cups and serve.

Nutrition: calories 140, fat 4.4, fiber 3, carbs 5, protein 4

Cucumber and Mango Salad

Preparation time: 6 minutes | Cooking time: 6 minutes | Servings: 4

Ingredients:
- 2 tablespoons sesame oil
- Juice of 2 limes
- 1-inch ginger, grated
- 2 garlic cloves, minced
- 2 green chilies, chopped
- 2 mangoes, peeled and cubed
- 2 cucumbers, cubed
- 1 tomato, cubed
- 20 peanuts, chopped
- 1 tablespoon mint, chopped
- 1 tablespoon coriander, chopped
- Salt to the taste

Directions:
In your instant pot, combine the mangoes with the cucumbers and the other ingredients, put the lid on and cook on High for 6 minutes. Release the pressure fast for 6 minutes, divide the mix into small bowls and serve as an appetizer.

Nutrition: calories 176, fat 4, fiber 3.3, carbs 6, protein 7

Turkey Bowls

Preparation time: 10 minutes | Cooking time: 20 minutes | Servings: 4

Ingredients:
- 1 pound turkey breast, skinless, boneless and cubed
- 2 tomatoes, cubed
- 1 tablespoon coconut oil, melted
- 1 yellow onion, chopped
- ½ teaspoon sweet paprika
- ½ teaspoon chili powder
- ½ teaspoon turmeric powder
- ½ teaspoon garam masala
- ½ cup parsley, chopped
- ½ cup chicken stock
- Salt to the taste
- ½ cup spinach, torn

Directions:
Set your instant pot on Sauté mode, add the oil, heat it up, add the onion, paprika, chili powder, turmeric and the garam masala, stir and cook for 5 minutes. Add the meat and brown for 5 minutes more. Add the rest of the ingredients, put the lid on and cook on High for 10 minutes. Release the pressure naturally for 10 minutes, transfer the mix bowls and serve as an appetizer.

Nutrition: calories 281, fat 4.4, fiber 3, carbs 7, protein 15

Potato Dip

Preparation time: 10 *minutes* | *Cooking time:* 20 *minutes* | *Servings:* 4

Ingredients:
- 1 pound sweet potatoes, peeled and chopped
- ¼ cup coconut cream
- 2 tablespoons raisins
- ½ teaspoon turmeric powder
- 2 garlic cloves, minced
- ½ teaspoon chili powder
- 1 teaspoon ginger, grated
- 1 teaspoon cumin, ground
- ½ teaspoon sugar
- 2 tablespoons red vinegar
- ¼ cup sunflower oil

Directions:
Set your instant pot on Sauté mode, add the oil, heat it up, add the garlic, turmeric, chili powder, cumin and the ginger and sauté for 5 minutes. Add the potatoes and the rest of the ingredients, put the lid on and cook on High for 15 minutes. Release the pressure naturally for 10 minutes, blend the mix in your blender, divide into bowls and serve.

Nutrition: calories 201, fat 9, fiber 4, carbs 7, protein 7.6

Cheese Dip

Preparation time: 10 *minutes* | *Cooking time:* 10 *minutes* | *Servings:* 6

Ingredients:
- 8 ounces cream cheese, soft
- ½ cup milk
- 1 tablespoon almond milk
- 2 tablespoons red bell pepper, chopped
- 2 teaspoons corn flour
- ¼ teaspoon mustard powder

Directions:
In your instant pot, combine the cream cheese with the corn flour and the other ingredients, toss, put the lid on and cook on High for 10 minutes. Release the pressure naturally for 10 minutes, whisk the mix, divide into bowls and serve as a party dip.

Nutrition: calories 200, fat 8, fiber 2.5, carbs 6, protein 8

Endives Dip

Preparation time: 5 minutes | Cooking time: 12 minutes | Servings: 4

Ingredients:
- 4 endives, roughly shredded
- ¼ cup coconut cream
- 1 teaspoon turmeric powder
- ½ teaspoon chili powder
- ½ teaspoon garam masala
- A pinch of salt and black pepper
- 2 garlic cloves, chopped
- 2 tablespoons coconut oil, melted
- 2 tablespoons lemon juice

Directions:
Set the instant pot on Sauté mode, add the oil, heat it up, add the turmeric, chili powder, garam masala and the garlic, stir and sauté for 2 minutes. Add the rest of the ingredients, put the lid on and cook on High for 10 minutes. Release the pressure fast for 5 minutes, divide into bowls and serve as a party dip.

Nutrition: calories 171, fat 3.4, fiber 4, carbs 7, protein 5

Saffron Shrimp

Preparation time: 5 minutes | Cooking time: 5 minutes | Servings: 4

Ingredients:
- 1 pound shrimp, peeled and deveined
- ¼ cup coconut cream
- 1 teaspoon saffron powder mixed with 1 tablespoon milk
- 1 tablespoon ghee, melted
- 1 teaspoon cumin, ground
- 1 teaspoon mustard seeds
- 1 teaspoon chili powder
- A pinch of salt and black pepper

Directions:
Set the instant pot on Sauté mode, add the shrimp, the cream and the other ingredients, toss, put the lid on and cook on High for 5 minutes. Release the pressure fast for 5 minutes, arrange the shrimp into bowls and serve.

Nutrition: calories 242, fat 5.6, fiber 4, carbs 7, protein 6

Lentils Dip

Preparation time: 10 minutes | Cooking time: 20 minutes | Servings: 8

Ingredients:
- 1 and ½ cups red lentils, canned, drained and rinsed
- 2 teaspoons ginger, grated
- 2 tablespoons coconut oil
- 1 teaspoon coriander seeds
- 2 garlic cloves, minced
- 1 chili pepper, chopped
- 1 teaspoon garam masala
- 1 teaspoon turmeric powder
- Salt to the taste
- 2 and ½ cups tomatoes, chopped
- 2 tablespoons lemon juice
- ¼ cup scallions, chopped

Directions:
In your instant pot, mix the lentils with the oil, ginger and the other ingredients, toss, put the lid on and cook on High for 20 minutes. Release the pressure naturally for 10 minutes, transfer the mix to a food processor, pulse well, divide into small bowls, and serve.

Nutrition: calories 217, fat 5.4, fiber 3, carbs 8, protein 6

Chickpea Dip

Preparation time: 10 minutes | Cooking time: 20 minutes | Servings: 4

Ingredients:
- 2 teaspoons cumin seeds
- ½ teaspoon coriander seeds
- ¼ teaspoon mustard seeds
- ¼ teaspoon red pepper flakes
- ¼ teaspoon turmeric powder
- 16 ounces canned chickpeas, drained and rinsed
- ½ cup cilantro, chopped
- Salt to the taste
- 4 tablespoons lemon juice
- 2 garlic cloves, minced
- 3 tablespoons tahini paste

Directions:
In your instant pot, combine the cumin seeds with the coriander seeds and the other ingredients, put the lid on and cook on High for 20 minutes. Release the pressure naturally for 10 minutes, blend the mix using an immersion blender, divide into bowls and serve as a dip.

Nutrition: calories 241, fat 7.2, fiber 4, carbs 5, protein 4

Turmeric Onion Dip

Preparation time: *5 minutes* | ***Cooking time:*** *10 minutes.* | ***Servings:*** *4*

Ingredients:
- 1 cup coconut cream
- ½ teaspoon turmeric powder
- ½ teaspoon chili powder
- A pinch of salt and black pepper
- 1 tablespoon coconut oil
- 2 yellow onion, chopped
- Juice of 1 orange

Directions:
In your instant pot, combine the cream with the turmeric, onion and the other ingredients, whisk, put the lid on and cook on High for 10 minutes. Release the pressure fast for 5 minutes, divide the mix into bowls and serve as a party dip.

Nutrition: calories 220, fat 6.2, fiber 3.6, carbs 5, protein 4

Zucchini Salad

Preparation time: *10 minutes* | ***Cooking time:*** *15 minutes* | ***Servings:*** *4*

Ingredients:
- 1 teaspoon vegetable oil
- 1 teaspoon mustard seeds
- 1 yellow onion, chopped
- 2 tablespoons peanuts, chopped
- 1 teaspoon ginger, grated
- 2 garlic cloves, minced
- 3 zucchinis, cut into medium cubes
- 1 red bell pepper, cut into strips
- 1 green chili, chopped
- Juice of 1 lime
- ¼ cup cilantro, chopped

Directions:
Set your instant pot on Sauté mode, add the oil, heat it up, add the onion, ginger, garlic and the chili, stir and sauté for 2 minutes. Add the rest of the ingredients, toss gently, put the lid on and cook on High for 13 minutes. Release the pressure naturally for 10 minutes, divide into bowls and serve as an appetizer.

Nutrition: calories 200, fat 5, fiber 3, carbs 7.5, protein 6

Spiced Broccoli Spread

Preparation time: 10 minutes | Cooking time: 15 minutes | Servings: 4

Ingredients:
- 1 yellow onion, chopped
- 1 tablespoon coconut oil
- 1 pound broccoli florets
- 1 teaspoon chili powder
- ½ teaspoon coriander powder
- ½ teaspoon dry mango powder
- A pinch of salt and black pepper
- 3 garlic cloves, minced
- 1 cup coconut cream
- 1 tablespoons coriander, chopped

Directions:
Set your instant pot on Sauté mode, add the oil, heat it up, add the onion, chili powder, coriander and mango powder, stir and cook for 2 minutes. Add the rest of the ingredients, put the lid on and cook on High for 13 minutes. Release the pressure naturally for 10 minutes, blend the mix using an immersion blender, divide into bowls, and serve.

Nutrition: calories 270, fat 12.2, fiber 2, carbs 6, protein 7

Hot Cauliflower Dip

Preparation time: 10 minutes | Cooking time: 15 minutes | Servings: 4

Ingredients:
- 2 tablespoons ghee, melted
- 1 pound cauliflower florets
- 8 garlic cloves, minced
- ½ teaspoon garam masala
- 1 teaspoon red chili powder
- ½ teaspoon smoked paprika
- 1 red chili pepper, chopped
- ½ cup coconut cream

Directions:
Set your instant pot on Sauté mode, add the ghee, heat it up, add the garlic, chili powder, paprika, garam masala and the chili pepper, stir and cook for 2 minutes. Add the rest of the ingredients, put the lid on and cook on High for 13 minutes. Release the pressure naturally for 10 minutes, transfer the mix to a blender, pulse, divide into bowls and serve as a party dip.

Nutrition: calories 178, fat 3, fiber 3, carbs 5, protein 8

Zucchini Dip

Preparation time: 5 *minutes* | *Cooking time:* 15 *minutes* | *Servings:* 4

Ingredients:
- 2 tablespoons coconut oil
- 2 tablespoons lemon juice
- 2 tablespoons mint, chopped
- Salt to the taste
- 2 zucchinis, chopped
- 2 garlic cloves, minced
- ½ cup curd
- ½ teaspoon chili powder
- ½ teaspoon cumin, ground

Directions:
Set the instant pot on Sauté mode, add the oil, heat it up, add the garlic, chili powder and the cumin, stir and cook for 2 minutes. Add the rest of the ingredients, put the lid on, and cook on High for 13 minutes. Release the pressure fast for 5 minutes, blend the mix using an immersion blender and serve the dip

Nutrition: calories 170, fat 2, fiber 3, carbs 6, protein 8

Corn and Leeks Bowls

Preparation time: 10 *minutes* | *Cooking time:* 15 *minutes* | *Servings:* 4

Ingredients:
- 1 tablespoon ghee, melted
- ½ teaspoon cumin seeds
- 1 leek, sliced
- 4 cups corn
- Salt and black pepper to the taste
- 1 tablespoon lemon juice
- ½ cup corn
- 2 tablespoons basil, chopped

Directions:
In your instant pot, combine the corn with the cumin, leek and the other ingredients, toss, put the lid on and cook on High for 15 minutes. Release the pressure naturally for 10 minutes, divide the mix into small bowls and serve as an appetizer.

Nutrition: calories 180, fat 4, fiber 3, carbs 7, protein 9

Warm Cucumber Salad

Preparation time: 5 minutes | *Cooking time:* 5 minutes | *Servings:* 4

Ingredients:

- 2 cucumbers, sliced
- 1 carrot, grated
- 1 red onion, chopped
- 2 cups cherry tomatoes, halved
- 4 radishes, chopped
- 1 red chili pepper, minced
- ¼ cup cilantro, chopped
- 2 tablespoons lemon juice
- Salt and black pepper to the taste
- ¼ teaspoon cumin, ground
- ¼ cup veggie stock

Directions:

In your instant pot, combine the cucumbers with the carrot and the other ingredients, toss gently, put the lid on and cook on High for 5 minutes. Release the pressure fast for 5 minutes, divide into small bowls and serve as an appetizer.

Nutrition: calories 224, fat 12, fiber 4, carbs 7, protein 12

Barley and Turmeric Salad

Preparation time: 10 minutes | *Cooking time:* 20 minutes | *Servings:* 4

Ingredients:

- 1 cup barley, cooked
- 1 cup chickpeas, canned, drained and rinsed
- ¼ cup cherry tomatoes, halved
- ½ cup red cabbage, shredded
- ½ cup carrots, grated
- ¼ cup red onion, sliced
- 1 cup baby spinach
- 4 tablespoons peanuts, toasted
- 1 cup curd
- 1 teaspoon turmeric powder
- ½ teaspoon cumin powder
- 2 garlic cloves, minced
- Salt to the taste

Directions:

In your instant pot, combine the barley with the chickpeas, tomatoes and the other ingredients, toss, put the lid on and cook on High for 20 minutes. Release the pressure naturally for 10 minutes, divide into bowls and serve as an appetizer.

Nutrition: calories 372, fat 11.4, fiber 4, carbs 7, protein 9.4

Barley and Olives Salad

Preparation time: 5 minutes | Cooking time: 15 minutes | Servings: 4

Ingredients:
- 1 cup barley, cooked
- ½ cup curd
- 1 tablespoon ghee, melted
- 1 cup black olives, pitted and halved
- 1 cup cherry tomatoes, halved
- ½ teaspoon turmeric powder
- ½ teaspoon garam masala
- 1 handful coriander leaves, chopped

Directions:
Set your instant pot on Sauté mode, add the ghee, heat it up, add the barley, turmeric and garam masala, stir and cook for 5 minutes Add the rest of the ingredients, toss, put the lid on and cook on High for 10 minutes Release the pressure fast for 5 minutes, divide the salad bowls and serve cold as an appetizer.

Nutrition: calories 252, fat 12.2, fiber 3, carbs 6.6, protein 7

Broccoli Bites

Preparation time: 10 minutes | Cooking time: 15 minutes | Servings: 4

Ingredients:
- 1 cup chicken stock
- 1 pound broccoli florets
- A pinch of salt and black pepper
- ¼ teaspoon mustard seeds
- ¼ teaspoon cumin, ground
- 1 teaspoon ginger, grated
- 1 tablespoon chana dal
- 2 garlic cloves, minced
- 2 teaspoons sunflower oil
- ¼ teaspoon garam masala
- ¼ teaspoon turmeric powder

Directions:
Set your instant pot on Sauté mode, add the oil, heat it up, add mustard seeds, cumin, ginger, garlic, turmeric and garam masala, toss and cook for 5 minutes. Add the broccoli and the other ingredients, put the lid on and cook on High for 10 minutes. Release the pressure naturally for 10 minutes, divide the broccoli into bowls and serve as a snack.

Nutrition: calories 154, fat 2.89, fiber 3, carbs 4, protein 4

Quinoa, Almonds and Avocado Salad

Preparation time: 5 minutes | Cooking time: 15 minutes | Servings: 4

Ingredients:
- 1 cup red quinoa, cooked
- ½ cup almonds, toasted and chopped
- ½ cup coconut cream
- 1 avocado, peeled, pitted and cubed
- 1 tablespoon cilantro, chopped
- ½ teaspoon chana masala
- ½ teaspoon sweet paprika
- ½ teaspoon turmeric powder
- 1 cup mango, peeled and cubed
- A pinch of salt and black pepper

Directions:
In your instant pot, combine the quinoa with the almonds, the cream and the other ingredients, toss, put the lid on and cook on High for 15 minutes. Release the pressure fast for 5 minutes, divide the mix into small bowls and serve as an appetizer.

Nutrition: calories 242, fat 8.2, fiber 3, carbs 5, protein 7

Barley and Chickpea Bowls

Preparation time: 10 minutes | Cooking time: 15 minutes | Servings: 4

Ingredients:
- 1 cup barley, cooked
- 1 cup canned chickpeas, drained and rinsed
- 2 tablespoons ghee, melted
- Juice of 1 orange
- 2 garlic cloves, minced
- 2 tablespoons ginger, grated
- 1 yellow onion, chopped
- ½ teaspoon garam masala
- A pinch of salt and black pepper
- ½ cup coconut cream

Directions:
Set your instant pot on Sauté mode, add the ghee, heat it up, add the ginger, garlic, onion and the garam masala, stir and cook for 5 minutes. Add the barley and the rest of the ingredients, put the lid on and cook on High for 10 minutes. Release the pressure naturally for 10 minutes, divide everything into bowls and serve.

Nutrition: calories 342, fat 15.2, fiber 3, carbs 11.5, protein 8

Thyme Lentils and Tomatoes Bowls

Preparation time: 10 minutes | Cooking time: 15 minutes | Servings: 4

Ingredients:
- ½ cup coconut cream
- 1 cup canned lentils, drained and rinsed
- ½ teaspoon thyme, dried
- 1 yellow onion, chopped
- 2 tablespoons ghee, melted
- ½ teaspoon turmeric powder
- ¼ teaspoon chili powder
- 1 cup cherry tomatoes, cubed
- 1 tablespoon garlic, minced
- Juice of 1 lime
- 2 tablespoons parsley, chopped
- Salt and black pepper to the taste

Directions:
Set the instant pot on Sauté mode, add the ghee, heat it up, add the onion, turmeric, chili powder and the garlic, stir and cook for 5 minutes. Add the rest of the ingredients, toss gently, put the lid on and cook on High for 10 minutes. Release the pressure naturally for 10 minutes, divide the mix into bowls and serve as an appetizer.

Nutrition: calories 312, fat 4.5, fiber 3, carbs 5.9, protein 7

Mushroom Dip

Preparation time: 10 minutes | Cooking time: 25 minutes | Servings: 4

Ingredients:
- 1 pound mushrooms, sliced
- 2 garlic cloves, minced
- 1 tablespoon ghee, melted
- Salt to the taste
- 1 tablespoon parsley, chopped
- 1 cup curd
- 1 tablespoon lemon juice
- 1 teaspoon coriander powder
- ½ teaspoon turmeric powder
- 1 teaspoon cayenne pepper

Directions:
Set the instant pot on Sauté mode, add the ghee, heat it up, add the mushrooms and the garlic and sauté for 5 minutes. Add the rest of the ingredients, toss, put the lid on and cook on High for 20 minutes. Release the pressure naturally for 10 minutes, whisk the dip, divide it into bowls and serve.

Nutrition: calories 152, fat 3, fiber 4, carbs 5, protein 9

Mushroom and Broccoli Dip

Preparation time: *5 minutes* | **Cooking time:** *20 minutes* | **Servings:** *4*

Ingredients:
- ½ cup broccoli florets, chopped
- 2 tablespoons butter
- ½ cup mushrooms, chopped
- ¼ cup yellow onion, chopped
- ½ teaspoon garlic paste
- ¼ teaspoon green chili paste
- 1 and ¼ cups milk
- 1 cup paneer, cubed
- Salt to the taste
- 1 tablespoon lime juice
- Zest of 1 lime, grated

Directions:
Set your instant pot on Sauté mode, add the butter, heat it up, add the onion, garlic paste, chili paste and the mushrooms, stir and cook for 5 minutes. Add the rest of the ingredients, put the lid on and cook on High for 15 minutes. Release the pressure fast for 5 minutes, blend the mix using an immersion blender, divide into bowls and serve.

Nutrition: calories 210, fat 12.2, fiber 3, carbs 5.9, protein 4

Creamy Mushroom Spread

Preparation time: *10 minutes* | **Cooking time:** *20 minutes* | **Servings:** *4*

Ingredients:
- 1 cup mushrooms, sliced
- 1 tablespoon butter
- ½ cup yellow onion, chopped
- ½ teaspoon green chilies, minced
- Salt to the taste
- 1 cup coconut cream
- ½ teaspoon smoked paprika
- ½ teaspoon cumin, ground
- ½ teaspoon mustard seeds, toasted and crushed

Directions:
Set your instant pot on Sauté mode, add the butter, heat it up, add the onion, chilies and the mushrooms, stir and cook for 5 minutes. Add the rest of the ingredients, put the lid on and cook on High for 15 minutes. Release the pressure naturally for 10 minutes, blend the mix using an immersion blender, divide into bowls and serve as a party spread.

Nutrition: calories 232, fat 7.2, fiber 3, carbs 4, protein 4

Shrimp and Green Beans Bowls

Preparation time: 5 minutes | Cooking time: 8 minutes | Servings: 4

Ingredients:

- 1 pound shrimp, peeled and deveined
- 1 tablespoon coconut oil
- 1 cup green beans, trimmed and halved
- 2 red onions, chopped
- ½ cup coconut cream
- 2 teaspoons turmeric powder
- ½ teaspoon coriander, ground
- ½ teaspoon cumin, ground
- ½ teaspoon sweet paprika
- 2 tablespoons cilantro, chopped

Directions:

Set your instant pot on Sauté mode, add the oil, heat it up, add the onions, turmeric, coriander, cumin and the paprika, stir and cook for 2 minutes. Add the shrimp and the rest of the ingredients, put the lid on and cook on High for 6 minutes. Release the pressure fast for 5 minutes, divide the mix into small bowls and serve as an appetizer.

Nutrition: calories 200, fat 5, fiber 2, carbs 5, protein 7

Indian Instant Pot Fish and Seafood Recipes

Fish Tikka
Preparation time: 10 minutes | Cooking time: 15 minutes | Servings: 3

Ingredients:
- 1 pound cod fillets, boneless, skinless and cubed
- 1 and ½ teaspoon ginger garlic paste
- A pinch of salt and black pepper
- 2 teaspoons red chili powder
- 1 cup yogurt
- ½ teaspoon turmeric powder
- ½ teaspoon fenugreek leaves, dried
- 2 tablespoons lemon juice
- ¼ teaspoon garam masala
- ½ teaspoon coriander powder
- 1 tablespoon vegetable oil

Directions:
Set the instant pot on Sauté mode, add the oil, heat it up, add the ginger paste chili powder, turmeric, fenugreek, coriander and garam masala, stir and cook for 4 minutes. Add the fish and the rest of the ingredients, toss, put the lid on and cook on High for 11 minutes. Release the pressure naturally for 10 minutes, divide the mix into bowls and serve.

Nutrition: calories 173, fat 5.5, fiber 0.7, carbs 5.7, protein 24.1

Fish Pulusu
Preparation time: 10 minutes | Cooking time: 20 minutes | Servings: 4

Ingredients:
- 2 pounds white fish, skinless, boneless and cubed
- 3 green chilies, chopped
- 1 cup yellow onion, chopped
- 1 tablespoon ginger garlic paste
- 3 tablespoons sunflower oil
- 2 tablespoons poppy seeds
- 2 teaspoons garam masala
- 1 teaspoon red chili powder
- 1 tablespoon coriander, chopped
- 2 tablespoons tamarind paste
- 1 bay leaf
- 1 teaspoon cumin, ground

Directions:
Set the instant pot on Sauté mode, add the oil, heat it up, add the onion, ginger and the chilies, stir and cook for 4 minutes. Add the fish and the rest of the ingredients, toss, put the lid on and cook on High for 16 minutes. Release the pressure naturally for 10 minutes, divide the mix into bowls and serve.

Nutrition: calories 331, fat 13.4, fiber 1.5, carbs 6.7, protein 47.7

Chili Fish Mix

Preparation time: 10 minutes | Cooking time: 20 minutes | Servings: 2

Ingredients:

- 4 garlic cloves, minced
- 2 tablespoons spring onions, chopped
- ¼ cup green bell pepper, cubed
- ¼ cup red bell pepper, cubed
- 1 teaspoon soy sauce
- 1 teaspoon white vinegar
- 2 teaspoons red chili sauce
- ½ teaspoon sugar
- Salt to the taste
- ¼ cup coconut cream
- 1 pound white fish fillets, boneless, skinless and cubed

Directions:

In your instant pot, combine the fish with the garlic, onions and the other ingredients, toss gently, put the lid on and cook on High for 20 minutes. Release the pressure naturally for 10 minutes, divide everything into bowls and serve.

Nutrition: calories 486, fat 24.3, fiber 1.4, carbs 7.6, protein 57.2

Salmon Curry

Preparation time: 5 minutes | Cooking time: 20 minutes | Servings: 4

Ingredients:

- 4 salmon fillets, boneless and cubed
- ¼ teaspoon mustard seeds
- ¼ teaspoon fenugreek leaves, dried
- 4 shallots, chopped
- 2 curry leaves, chopped
- 2 teaspoons ginger, grated
- 1 tablespoon chili powder
- 3 garlic cloves, minced
- ½ teaspoon turmeric powder
- ½ tablespoon coriander powder
- 1 cup water
- 2 tablespoons vegetable oil
- Salt to the taste

Directions:

Set the instant pot on sauté mode, add the oil, heat it up, add the mustard seeds, fenugreek leaves, shallots, curry leaves, ginger and the garlic, stir and cook for 5 minutes. Add the salmon fillets and the rest of the ingredients, put the lid on and cook on High for 15 minutes. Release the pressure fast for 5 minutes, divide the mix into bowls and serve.

Nutrition: calories 318, fat 18.3, fiber 1, carbs 4.5, protein 35.4

Cod and Tomato Bowls

Preparation time: 5 minutes | Cooking time: 15 minutes | Servings: 4

Ingredients:

- 1 pound cod fillets, boneless, skinless and cubed
- ½ teaspoon chili powder
- ½ teaspoon smoked paprika
- ½ teaspoon turmeric powder
- 1 pound cherry tomatoes, halved
- 2 garlic cloves, minced
- 1 tablespoon coconut oil, melted
- Salt and black pepper to the taste
- 1 tablespoon coriander, chopped
- ½ teaspoon cumin, ground

Directions:

Set the instant pot on Sauté mode, add the oil, heat it up, add the chili powder, paprika, turmeric, cumin and the garlic and sauté for 2 minutes. Add the rest of the ingredients, put the lid on and cook on High for 13 minutes. Release the pressure fast for 5 minutes, divide everything into bowls and serve.

Nutrition: calories 332, fat 9, fiber 2, carbs 7.5, protein 11

Cod Curry

Preparation time: 10 minutes | Cooking time: 15 minutes | Servings: 4

Ingredients:

- 1 pound cod fillets, boneless, skinless and cubed
- 1 cup coconut milk
- 2 red onions, sliced
- 2 garlic cloves, minced
- 1 tablespoons cumin, ground
- 1 tablespoon ginger, grated
- ½ teaspoon turmeric powder
- A pinch of salt and black pepper
- 2 tablespoons lime juice

Directions:

Set your instant pot on Sauté mode, add the oil, heat it up, add the onions, garlic and the ginger and sauté for 2 minutes. Add the fish and the rest of the ingredients, put the lid on and cook on High for 13 minutes. Release the pressure naturally for 10 minutes, divide the curry into bowls and serve.

Nutrition: calories 310, fat 12, fiber 2.6, carbs 6, protein 11

Salmon and Broccoli

Preparation time: 10 minutes | Cooking time: 12 minutes | Servings: 4

Ingredients:

- 4 salmon fillets, boneless and cubed
- 1 cup broccoli florets
- 2 tablespoons ghee
- ½ teaspoon turmeric powder
- ½ teaspoon garam masala
- 2 garlic cloves, minced
- Salt and black pepper to the taste
- ½ cup veggie stock

Directions:
Set the instant pot on Sauté mode, add the ghee, heat it up, add the garlic, turmeric and garam masala, toss and cook for 2 minutes. Add the rest of the ingredients, put the lid on and cook on High for 10 minutes. Release the pressure naturally for 10 minutes, divide the mix between plates and serve.

Nutrition: calories 356, fat 12, fiber 2, carbs 15.,6, protein 9

Charred Salmon

Preparation time: 10 minutes | Cooking time: 15 minutes | Servings: 4

Ingredients:

- 4 salmon fillets, boneless
- 1 tablespoon ginger, grated
- 1 cup yogurt
- 1 red chili pepper, chopped
- 2 garlic cloves, minced
- 2 teaspoons garam masala
- 1 tablespoon vegetable oil
- 1 bunch asparagus, trimmed and chopped
- 1 tablespoon cilantro, chopped

Directions:
In your instant pot, combine the salmon with the yogurt, oil, chili pepper and the other ingredients, toss gently, put the lid on and cook on High for 15 minutes. Release the pressure naturally for 10 minutes, divide the salmon mix between plates and serve.

Nutrition: calories 311, fat 13, fiber 2, carbs 7.7, protein 11

Lemon Cod and Rice

Preparation time: 10 minutes | Cooking time: 20 minutes | Servings: 4

Ingredients:
- 4 cod fillets, boneless, skinless and cubed
- 1 cup basmati rice
- 2 cups chicken stock
- ½ teaspoon cumin, ground
- ½ teaspoon fenugreek leaves, dried
- Salt to the taste
- Zest of 1 lemon, grated
- Juice of ½ lemon
- 1 yellow onion, chopped
- 1 tablespoon ghee, melted
- ¼ cup parsley, chopped

Directions:
Set the instant pot on Sauté mode, add the ghee, heat it up, add the cumin, fenugreek, and the onion, stir and cook for 5 minutes. Add the fish and the other ingredients, toss, put the lid on and cook on High for 15 minutes. Release the pressure naturally for 10 minutes, divide the mix between plates and serve.

Nutrition: calories 320, fat 12, fiber 4, carbs 11.6, protein 8

Shrimp and Lime Rice

Preparation time: 5 minutes | Cooking time: 15 minutes | Servings: 4

Ingredients:
- 1 pound shrimp, peeled and deveined
- 1 tablespoon lime juice
- 1 tablespoon lime zest, grated
- 1 cup white rice
- 2 cups chicken stock
- ½ teaspoon turmeric powder
- ½ teaspoon dried mango powder
- 1 yellow onion, chopped
- 2 tomatoes, cubed
- A pinch of salt and black pepper
- 1 tablespoon parsley, chopped
- ½ tablespoon sweet paprika, chopped
- 2 garlic cloves, minced

Directions:
In your instant pot, combine the shrimp with the lime juice, lime zest, rice and the rest of the ingredients, put the lid on and cook on High for 15 minutes. Release the pressure fast for 5 minutes, divide the mix into bowls and serve.

Nutrition: calories 232, fat 7, fiber 3, carbs 11.7, protein 9

Spiced Cod

Preparation time: 5 minutes | Cooking time: 15 minutes | Servings: 4

Ingredients:
- 4 cod fillets, boneless
- A pinch of salt and black pepper
- 2 teaspoons cumin, ground
- 1 teaspoon coriander, ground
- ½ teaspoon ginger, grated
- 4 tablespoons lemon juice
- ½ cup chicken stock
- ½ teaspoon garam masala
- ½ teaspoon chili powder

Directions:
In your instant pot, combine the fish with the cumin, coriander and the other ingredients, put the lid on and cook on High for 15 minutes. Release the pressure fast for 5 minutes, divide the fish mix between plates and serve.

Nutrition: calories 332, fat 9.6, fiber 2, carbs 13.6, protein 8

Seafood Salad

Preparation time: 10 minutes | Cooking time: 15 minutes | Servings: 4

Ingredients:
- ¼ pound shrimp, peeled and deveined
- 2 shallots, chopped
- ¼ pound squid rings
- 1 cup crab meat, drained
- 3 tablespoons yogurt
- ½ cup chicken stock
- 1 teaspoon fennel seeds
- 1 teaspoon black mustard seeds
- 1 tablespoon lime juice
- 1 tablespoon coriander, chopped

Directions:
In your instant pot, combine the shrimp with the shallots and the other ingredients, toss, put the lid on and cook on High for 15 minutes. Release the pressure naturally for 10 minutes, divide the mix into bowls and serve.

Nutrition: calories 356, fat 13, fiber 3, carbs 11.6, protein 11

Trout and Sauce

Preparation time: 5 minutes | Cooking time: 20 minutes | Servings: 4

Ingredients:
- 2 trout, cut into chunks
- Salt and black pepper to the taste
- 1 teaspoon turmeric powder
- 2 yellow onions, chopped
- 10 ounces canned tomatoes, chopped
- 2 bay leaves
- 2 green cardamom pods
- 1 teaspoon chili powder
- ½ teaspoon garam masala
- 1 teaspoon cinnamon powder
- 2 teaspoon coriander, ground

Directions:
In your instant pot, mix the trout chunks with the turmeric, salt, pepper and the other ingredients, toss gently, put the lid on and cook on High for 20 minutes. Release the pressure fast for 5 minutes, divide everything into bowls and serve.

Nutrition: calories 290, fat 14.3, fiber 2, carbs 11.6, protein 9

Cod and Cauliflower

Preparation time: 10 minutes | Cooking time: 20 minutes | Servings: 4

Ingredients:
- 4 cod fillets, boneless
- 1 tablespoon sunflower oil
- 1 cup cauliflower florets
- 1 red onion, chopped
- 1 teaspoon turmeric powder
- ½ teaspoon chana masala
- ½ teaspoon dry mango powder
- 2 tablespoons coriander, chopped
- 3 tablespoons coconut oil, melted
- A pinch of salt and black pepper
- ½ cup coconut cream

Directions:
Set the instant pot on Sauté mode, add the oil, heat it up, add the onion, turmeric and chana masala, stir and cook for 5 minutes. Add the cod and the rest of the ingredients, put the lid on and cook on High for 15 minutes. Release the pressure naturally for 10 minutes, divide the whole mix into bowls and serve.

Nutrition: calories 280, fat 12, fiber 2, carbs 5.5, protein 6

Salmon and Chili Sauce

Preparation time: 10 minutes | Cooking time: 15 minutes | Servings: 4

Ingredients:

- 1 tablespoon sunflower oil
- 1 pound salmon meat, skinless, boneless and cubed
- 1 teaspoon red chili powder
- ½ teaspoon fenugreek leaves, dried
- ½ teaspoon turmeric powder
- ½ cup spring onions, chopped
- 1 cup coconut cream
- 2 tablespoons lemon zest, grated
- 1 teaspoon lemon juice
- A pinch of salt and black pepper

Directions:

Set the instant pot on Sauté mode, add the oil, heat it up, add the chili powder, fenugreek, turmeric and the onions, stir and cook for 3 minutes. Add the salmon and the other ingredients, put the lid on and cook on High for 12 minutes. Release the pressure naturally for 10 minutes, divide the mix into bowls and serve.

Nutrition: calories 392, fat 14.5, fiber 2, carbs 22.4, protein 7

Indian Salmon and Asparagus

Preparation time: 10 minutes | Cooking time: 20 minutes | Servings: 4

Ingredients:

- 1 pound salmon fillets, skinless, boneless and cubed
- 1 yellow onion, chopped
- 1 bunch asparagus, trimmed and halved
- ½ teaspoon saffron powder mixed with 1 tablespoon oil
- ½ tablespoon sweet paprika
- ½ teaspoon cumin, ground
- ½ teaspoon chana masala
- 1 and ½ cups coconut cream
- A pinch of salt and black pepper
- 1 tablespoon cilantro, chopped

Directions:

In your instant pot, combine the salmon with the onion and the rest of the ingredients except the cilantro, put the lid on and cook on High for 20 minutes. Release the pressure naturally for 10 minutes, divide the mix into bowls, sprinkle the cilantro on top and serve.

Nutrition: calories 340, fat 9.1, fiber 2, carbs 15.6, protein 7

Cod and Butter Sauce

Preparation time: 5 minutes | Cooking time: 20 minutes | Servings: 4

Ingredients:
- 4 cod fillets, boneless
- 2 tablespoons butter
- 2 yellow onions, chopped
- 2 garlic cloves, minced
- 1 teaspoon turmeric powder
- ½ teaspoon garam masala
- 2 tablespoons lemon juice
- A pinch of salt and black pepper
- 2 tablespoons coriander leaves, chopped

Directions:
Set the instant pot on Sauté mode, add the butter, heat it up, add the onion, garlic, turmeric and garam masala, stir and cook for 5 minutes. Add the fish and the other ingredients, toss, put the lid on and cook on High for 15 minutes. Release the pressure fast for 5 minutes, divide the mix between plates and serve.

Nutrition: calories 300, fat 10, fiber 2, carbs 11.5, protein 9

Turmeric Salmon and Lime Sauce

Preparation time: 5 minutes | Cooking time: 20 minutes | Servings: 4

Ingredients:
- 1 pound salmon fillets, boneless and cubed
- 2 tablespoons ghee, melted
- 1 teaspoon turmeric powder
- 2 tablespoons lime juice
- 1 teaspoon lime zest, grated
- 2 garlic cloves, minced
- ½ cup chicken stock
- A pinch of salt and black pepper

Directions:
Set the instant pot on Sauté mode, add the ghee, heat it up, add the garlic and turmeric, stir and cook for 3 minutes. Add the fish and the remaining ingredients, put the lid on and cook on Low for 17 minutes. Release the pressure fast for 5 minutes, divide everything between plates and serve.

Nutrition: calories 310, fat 13, fiber 3, carbs 8.6, protein 11

Indian Halibut

Preparation time: 5 minutes | Cooking time: 15 minutes | Servings: 4

Ingredients:
- 2 teaspoons cumin seeds
- 2 teaspoons fennel seeds
- 2 teaspoons coriander seeds
- 1 teaspoon turmeric powder
- 4 cloves
- ½ teaspoon chili powder
- 4 halibut fillets, boneless
- 3 tablespoons mustard oil
- ¼ cup chicken stock

Directions:
Set your instant pot on Sauté mode, add the oil, heat it up, add the cumin, fennel and the coriander, stir and cook for 2 minutes. Add the halibut and the rest of the ingredients, put the lid on and cook on High for 13 minutes. Release the pressure fast for 5 minutes, divide the mix between plates and serve.

Nutrition: calories 291, fat 12, fiber 3, carbs 11.6, protein 7

Simple Masala

Preparation time: 10 minutes | Cooking time: 15 minutes | Servings: 2

Ingredients:
- 1 pound cod fillet, boneless, skinless and cubed
- 2 tablespoons ghee, melted
- ¼ cup coconut cream
- 2 garlic cloves, minced
- 1 yellow onion, chopped
- 1 teaspoon ginger, grated
- 3 tablespoons coriander, chopped
- ½ teaspoon chili powder
- 1 tablespoon lemon juice

Directions:
Set your instant pot on Sauté mode, add the ghee, heat it up, add the garlic, onion and ginger and sauté for 3 minutes. Add the fish and the other ingredients, put the lid on and cook on High for 12 minutes. Release the pressure naturally for 10 minutes, divide the mix between plates and serve.

Nutrition: calories 320, fat 12, fiber 2, carbs 14.6, protein 13

Spicy Tuna

Preparation time: 5 minutes | Cooking time: 15 minutes | Servings: 4

Ingredients:
- 3 garlic cloves, minced
- 1 yellow onion, chopped
- 2 green chilies, chopped
- ½ tablespoon turmeric powder
- 2 teaspoons chili powder
- 14 ounces canned tuna, drained and flaked
- 1 tablespoon ghee, melted
- 1 cup white rice, cooked

Directions:

In your instant pot, combine the tuna with the onion, ghee and the rest of the ingredients, put the lid on and cook on High for 15 minutes. Release the pressure fast for 5 minutes, divide the mix into bowls and serve.

Nutrition: calories 370, fat 13.9, fiber 3, carbs 23.5, protein 10

Turmeric Tuna

Preparation time: 5 minutes | Cooking time: 15 minutes | Servings: 4

Ingredients:
- 4 tuna fillets, boneless
- 3 garlic cloves, minced
- ½ teaspoon garam masala
- ½ teaspoon dry mango powder
- 1 teaspoon ginger, grayed
- 1 teaspoon turmeric powder
- 1 tablespoon chili paste
- 2 lemongrass sticks, chopped
- 1 tablespoon ginger, grated
- 2 tablespoons olive oil
- 1 cup coconut cream

Directions:

Set the instant pot on Sauté mode, add the oil, heat it up, add the garlic, garam masala, mango powder, ginger, and chili paste, stir and cook for 3 minutes. Add the fish and the rest of the ingredients, toss gently, put the lid on and cook on High for 12 minutes. Release the pressure fast for 5 minutes, divide the mix between plates and serve.

Nutrition: calories 311, fat 13, fiber 4, carbs 16.7, protein 10

Ginger Trout and Tomatoes

Preparation time: 10 minutes | Cooking time: 15 minutes | Servings: 4

Ingredients:

- 1 pound trout fillets, boneless, skinless and cut into chunks
- 2 tablespoons ghee, melted
- 1 cup tomatoes, cubed
- 2 garlic cloves, minced
- 1 yellow onion, chopped
- 2 tablespoons ginger, grated
- 1 teaspoon turmeric powder
- ½ teaspoon chili powder
- ½ teaspoon fenugreek leaves, dried
- A pinch of salt and black pepper
- 1 tablespoon coriander, chopped

Directions:

Set your instant pot on Sauté mode, add the ghee, heat it up, add the garlic, onion, ginger, turmeric and chili powder, stir and cook for 3 minutes. Add the rest of the ingredients, toss, put the lid on and cook on Low for 12 minutes Release the pressure naturally for 10 minutes, divide the mix into bowls and serve.

Nutrition: calories 344, fat 12, fiber 3, carbs 33.6, protein 13

Chives Tuna Curry

Preparation time: 5 minutes | Cooking time: 20 minutes | Servings: 4

Ingredients:

- 1 pound tuna, boneless, skinless and cubed
- 1 teaspoon curry powder
- ½ teaspoon turmeric powder
- 2 garlic cloves, minced
- ½ teaspoon chili powder
- ½ teaspoon smoked paprika
- Juice of 1 lemon
- 2 tablespoons chives, chopped
- A pinch of salt and black pepper
- 1 tablespoon coconut oil
- 1 cup chicken stock

Directions:

Set the instant pot on Sauté mode, add the oil, heat it up, add the curry powder, turmeric, chili powder, the paprika and the garlic, stir and cook for 2 minutes. Add the tuna and the rest of the ingredients, put the lid on and cook on High for 18 minutes. Release the pressure fast for 5 minutes, divide the mix between plates and serve.

Nutrition: calories 300, fat 12, fiber 3, carbs 7.6, protein 11

Salmon, Spinach and Coconut Mix

Preparation time: 5 minutes | Cooking time: 20 minutes | Servings: 4

Ingredients:

- 1 pound salmon, skinless, boneless and cubed
- 1 cup spinach, torn
- ½ tablespoon coconut, grated
- 1 tablespoon coconut oil
- 1 cup radishes, cubed
- 1 white onion, chopped
- ½ cup chicken stock
- 2 garlic cloves, minced
- 1 teaspoon turmeric powder
- ½ teaspoon garam masala

Directions:

Set instant pot on Sauté mode, add the oil, heat it up, add the onion, garlic, turmeric and the garam masala, stir and cook for 5 minutes. Add the salmon and the rest of the ingredients, put the lid on and cook on High for 15 minutes. Release the pressure fast for 5 minutes, divide the mix into bowls and serve.

Nutrition: calories 282, fat 10, fiber 2.6, carbs 7.6, protein 6

Tilapia, Tomatoes and Radish Saad

Preparation time: 10 minutes | Cooking time: 15 minutes | Servings: 4

Ingredients:

- 1 cup cherry tomatoes, halved
- 1 pound tilapia fillets, boneless, skinless and cubed
- 1 cup radishes, halved
- 2 tablespoons coconut oil
- 1 teaspoon dry mango powder
- ½ teaspoon turmeric powder
- 1 red onion, chopped
- 2 chili peppers, chopped
- 2 teaspoons red pepper flakes
- A pinch of salt and black pepper
- ½ cup chicken stock

Directions:

Set your instant pot on Sauté mode, add the oil, heat it up, add the onion, chili pepper, pepper flakes, mango and turmeric powder, stir and cook for 3 minutes. Add the fish and the rest of the ingredients, put the lid on and cook on High for 12 minutes. Release the pressure naturally for 10 minutes, divide the mix between plates and serve.

Nutrition: calories 292, fat 11, fiber 3, carbs 8.6, protein 9

Sea Bass with Fennel

Preparation time: 10 minutes | Cooking time: 20 minutes | Servings: 6

Ingredients:

- 1 fennel, shredded
- 1 cucumber, sliced
- 1 cup radishes, sliced
- 1 tablespoon sherry vinegar
- 2 tablespoons coconut oil
- 1 tablespoon chives, chopped
- 2 garlic cloves, minced
- 1 pound sea bass fillets, boneless and cubed
- Juice of 1 lemon
- ½ cup coconut cream

Directions:

Set your instant pot on Sauté mode, add the oil, heat it up, add the garlic, and the fennel and sauté for 5 minutes. Add the cucumber, the fish and the rest of the ingredients, put the lid on and cook on High for 15 minutes. Release the pressure naturally for 10 minutes, divide the mix between plates and serve.

Nutrition: calories 432, fat 15.5, fiber 3, carbs 33.6, protein 6

Shrimp and Radish Curry

Preparation time: 5 minutes | Cooking time: 15 minutes | Servings: 4

Ingredients:

- 1 and ½ pound shrimp, peeled and deveined
- 1 cup radishes, sliced
- 1 cup coconut, grated
- ½ cup red onion, chopped
- ¼ teaspoon turmeric powder
- 1 tablespoon coconut oil
- ¼ teaspoon coriander seeds
- ½ tablespoon tamarind paste
- 1 cup water
- Salt to the taste

Directions:

Set your instant pot on Sauté mode, add the oil, heat it up, add the onion, turmeric, coriander and the tamarind, stir and cook for 5 minutes. Add the shrimp and the rest of the ingredients, put the lid on and cook on High for 10 minutes. Release the pressure fast for 5 minutes, divide everything into bowls and serve.

Nutrition: calories 242, fat 6, fiber 1, carbs 7.6, protein 8

Shrimp and Okra

Preparation time: 10 minutes | Cooking time: 15 minutes | Servings: 4

Ingredients:
- 1 and ½ pounds shrimp, peeled and deveined
- 1 cup okra, sliced
- 1 red onion, chopped
- 1 tablespoon coconut oil
- 3 garlic cloves, minced
- ½ tablespoon sweet paprika
- ½ teaspoon garam masala
- 1 cup chicken stock
- ½ teaspoon marjoram, dried
- A pinch of salt and black pepper
- 1 tablespoon cilantro, chopped

Directions:
Set your instant pot on Sauté mode, add the oil, heat it up, add the onion, garlic, paprika and garam masala, stir and cook for 3 minutes. Add the shrimp and the rest of the ingredients, put the lid on and cook on High for 12 minutes. Release the pressure naturally for 10 minutes, divide the mix into bowls and serve warm.

Nutrition: calories 270, fat 14, fiber 3, carbs 8, protein 10

Shrimp and Spiced Potatoes

Preparation time: 10 minutes | Cooking time: 20 minutes | Servings: 4

Ingredients:
- 1 pound shrimp, peeled and deveined
- 1 pound sweet potatoes, peeled and cubed
- 2 tablespoons ghee, melted
- ½ cup chicken stock
- 1 yellow onion, chopped
- 1 cup tomatoes, cubed
- ½ teaspoon turmeric powder
- ½ teaspoon garam masala
- ½ teaspoon coriander powder
- ½ teaspoon dry mango powder
- 2 tablespoons parsley, chopped
- 1 tablespoon lemon juice

Directions:
Set your instant pot on Sauté mode, add the ghee, heat it up, add the onion, turmeric, garam masala, coriander, and mango powder and cook for 5 minutes. Add the shrimp and the rest of the ingredients, put the lid on and cook on High for 15 minutes. Release the pressure naturally for 10 minutes, divide the mix between plates and serve.

Nutrition: calories 348, fat 8.8, fiber 5.9, carbs 38.1, protein 28.5

Tuna and Avocado Mix

Preparation time: 5 minutes | Cooking time: 20 minutes | Servings: 4

Ingredients:

- 1 pound tuna fillets, boneless, skinless and cubed
- 2 tablespoons ghee melted
- 1 avocado, pitted, peeled and cubed
- ½ cup celery, chopped
- ¼ cup red onion, chopped
- 2 teaspoons lemon juice
- 1 teaspoon lemon zest, grated
- 2 tablespoons cilantro, chopped
- Salt and black pepper to the taste
- ½ teaspoon turmeric powder
- ½ teaspoon dried fenugreek leaves

Directions:

Set your instant pot on Sauté mode, add the ghee, heat it up, add the onion, celery, turmeric and fenugreek leaves, stir and cook for 5 minutes. Add the tuna and the rest of the ingredients, put the lid on and cook on High for 15 minutes. Release the pressure fast for 5 minutes, divide everything into bowls and serve.

Nutrition: calories 400, fat 13.2, fiber 2, carbs 14.5, protein 11

Tuna and Turmeric Green Beans Mix

Preparation time: 5 minutes | Cooking time: 20 minutes | Servings: 4

Ingredients:

- 1 pound tuna fillets, boneless, skinless and roughly cubed
- ½ pound green beans, trimmed and halved
- ½ teaspoon turmeric powder
- ½ teaspoon dry mango powder
- ½ teaspoon garam masala
- 2 tablespoons butter, melted
- Salt and black pepper to the taste
- 2 shallots, chopped
- 1 tablespoon parsley, chopped
- Juice of 1 lemon
- ½ cup chicken stock

Directions:

Set the instant pot on Sauté mode, add the butter, heat it up, add the shallots and the green beans and sauté for 5 minutes. Add the tuna and sear it for 3 minutes more. Add the rest of the ingredients, put the lid on and cook on High for 12 minutes. Release the pressure fast for 5 minutes, divide everything between plates and serve.

Nutrition: calories 411, fat 14, fiber 3, fiber 15.6, carbs 11

Lemongrass Shrimp and Corn
Preparation time: 10 minutes | Cooking time: 15 minutes | Servings: 4

Ingredients:
- 2 pounds shrimp, peeled and deveined
- 2 tablespoons lemongrass past
- 10 curry leaves, chopped
- 1 bunch cilantro, chopped
- 1 chili pepper, chopped
- 2 tablespoons vegetable oil
- 1 teaspoon cumin seeds
- 24 ounces coconut milk
- ½ cup heavy cream
- 3 cups corn

Directions:
Ina blender, combine the curry leaves with the lemongrass, cilantro and chili and pulse well. Set the instant pot on Sauté mode, add the oil, heat it up, add the lemongrass paste and cook for 2 minutes. Add the shrimp and the other ingredients, put the lid on and cook on Low for 13 minutes. Release the pressure naturally for 10 minutes, divide the mix into bowls and serve.

Nutrition: calories 260, fat 11, fiber 5.5, carbs 11.5, protein 8

Cardamom Shrimp and Zucchinis
Preparation time: 10 minutes | Cooking time: 15 minutes | Servings: 4

Ingredients:
- 2 tablespoons ghee, melted
- 3 cardamom pods
- Juice of 1 lime
- 2 zucchinis, cubed
- ½ teaspoon cumin, ground
- 1 tablespoon cilantro, chopped
- ½ teaspoon mustard seeds
- ½ teaspoon turmeric powder
- 1 teaspoon garam masala
- ½ cup corn
- 1 shallot, chopped
- 1 pound shrimp, peeled and deveined
- 2 cups coconut milk
- 2 tablespoons almonds, chopped
- 1 red chili, chopped
- Salt and black pepper to the taste

Directions:
Set the instant pot on Sauté mode, add the ghee, heat it up, add the cardamom, cumin, mustard seeds, turmeric, garam masala, the chili and the shallots, stir and cook for 5 minutes. Add the shrimp and the other ingredients, toss, put the lid on and cook on High for 10 minutes. Release the pressure naturally for 10 minutes, divide the mix into bowls and serve.

Nutrition: calories 224, fat 13, fiber 3, carbs 7, protein 11

Fenugreek Tuna and Mushroom Curry

Preparation time: 10 minutes | Cooking time: 15 minutes | Servings: 4

Ingredients:

- 1 pound tuna fillets, boneless, skinless and cubed
- ½ teaspoon dry fenugreek leaves
- ½ teaspoon dried mango leaves
- ½ teaspoon turmeric powder
- ½ teaspoon chana masala
- 1 cup tomato puree
- 1 tablespoon lime juice
- A pinch of salt and black pepper
- ½ teaspoon curry powder
- 2 cups mushrooms, sliced
- 1 yellow onion, chopped
- 2 tablespoons ghee, melted

Directions:

Set your instant pot on Sauté mode, add the ghee, heat it up, add the onion, mushrooms and the other ingredients except the tuna, tomato puree and the lime juice, stir and sauté for 5 minutes. Add the remaining ingredients, put the lid on and cook on High for 10 minutes. Release the pressure naturally for 10 minutes, divide the mix into bowls and serve.

Nutrition: calories 321, fat 12, fiber 3, carbs 6, protein 8

Tilapia Masala

Preparation time: 10 minutes | Cooking time: 15 minutes | Servings: 4

Ingredients:

- 1 pound tilapia, boneless, skinless and cubed
- 2 tablespoons sunflower oil
- Juice of 1 lemon
- 1 bay leaf
- 1 tablespoon coriander, ground
- 1 tablespoon cumin, ground
- 1 teaspoon cinnamon powder
- 1 teaspoon ginger, grated
- 1 teaspoon cardamom, ground
- ½ teaspoon nutmeg, ground
- ½ teaspoon allspice
- 1 cup chicken stock

Directions:

Set your instant pot on Sauté mode, add the oil, heat it up, add the tilapia and cook for 3 minutes. Add the rest of the ingredients, put the lid on and cook on High for 12 minutes. Release the pressure naturally for 10 minutes, divide the mix into bowls and serve.

Nutrition: calories 331, fat 11, fiber 3, carbs 10.6, protein 9

Spicy Tilapia

Preparation time: 10 minutes | Cooking time: 15 minutes | Servings: 4

Ingredients:
- 4 tilapia fillets, boneless
- 2 tablespoons ghee, melted
- 1 yellow onion, chopped
- 1 tablespoon garlic, minced
- 1 teaspoon ginger, grated
- 1 green chili, chopped
- 1 teaspoon turmeric powder
- 1 teaspoon red chili powder
- ½ teaspoon garam masala
- 4 tablespoons mustard
- ½ teaspoon cumin seeds, ground
- ½ cup coconut cream

Directions:
Set the instant pot on Sauté mode, add the ghee, heat it up, add the fish and sear it for 2 minutes on each side. Add the rest of the ingredients, put the lid on and cook on High for 11 minutes. Release the pressure naturally for 10 minutes, divide the mix between plates and serve.

Nutrition: calories 292, fat 9, fiber 4, carbs 11.7, protein 9

Tilapia Curry

Preparation time: 10 minutes | Cooking time: 20 minutes | Servings: 4

Ingredients:
- 1 pound tilapia, skinless, boneless and cubed
- ½ red onion, chopped
- 2 teaspoons red chili powder
- 2 teaspoons turmeric powder
- ¼ cup coconut, grated
- Salt and black pepper to the taste
- 1 cup coconut milk
- A pinch of asafetida powder
- 2 tablespoons vegetable oil

Directions:
Set the pot on Sauté mode, add the oil, heat it up, add the onion and sauté for 2 minutes Add the fish and the rest of the ingredients, put the lid on and cook on High for 18 minutes. Release the pressure naturally for 10 minutes, divide the curry into bowls and serve.

Nutrition: calories 332, fat 8, fiber 2, carbs 6, protein 11

Classic Indian Sea Bass Mix

Preparation time: 5 minutes | *Cooking time:* 20 minutes | *Servings:* 4

Ingredients:
- 4 sea bass fillets, boneless
- 2 tablespoons chili powder
- ½ teaspoon turmeric powder
- 1 teaspoon ginger paste
- 1 teaspoon garlic, minced
- 1 tablespoon white vinegar
- Salt and black pepper to the taste
- ¼ cup water
- 2 tomatoes, cubed
- 1 tablespoon sunflower oil

Directions:
Set the instant pot on Sauté mode, add the oil, heat it up, add the fish and sear it for 2 minutes on each side. Add the rest of the ingredients, put the lid on and cook on High for 18 minutes. Release the pressure fast for 5 minutes, divide everything between plates and serve.

Nutrition: calories 302, fat 11.5, fiber 1, carbs 5, protein 8

Sea Bass and Lentils

Preparation time: 5 minutes | *Cooking time:* 20 minutes | *Servings:* 4

Ingredients:
- 2 tablespoons vegetable oil
- 1 yellow onion, chopped
- 1 carrot, chopped
- 1 red bell pepper, chopped
- 4 garlic cloves, minced
- 1 tablespoon ginger, grated
- 1 tablespoon curry powder
- 2 tomatoes, cubed
- 2 cups veggie stock
- 1 cup red lentils
- Salt and black pepper to the taste
- 1 pound sea bass fillets, boneless, skinless and roughly cubed
- Salt and black pepper to the taste
- 1 teaspoon turmeric powder
- 1 teaspoon coriander, ground
- 1 teaspoon cumin, ground

Directions:
Set the instant pot on Sauté mode, add the oil, heat it up, add the onion, carrots, bell pepper, garlic and ginger, stir and cook for 5 minutes. Add the rest of the ingredients, toss, put the lid on and cook on High for 15 minutes. Release the pressure fast for 5 minutes, divide the mix between plates and serve.

Nutrition: calories 322, fat 9, fiber 2, carbs 17.6, protein 7

Tandoori Sea Bass

***Preparation time:** 10 minutes | **Cooking time:** 20 minutes | **Servings:** 4*

Ingredients:
- 4 sea bass fillets, boneless
- 5 tablespoons yogurt
- 1 tablespoon vegetable oil
- Salt and black pepper to the taste
- Juice of 1 lemon
- 2 garlic cloves, minced
- 1 tablespoon ginger, grated
- 1 green chili, chopped
- 1 tablespoon tandoori powder
- 1 tablespoon coriander, chopped
- ½ cup heavy cream

Directions:
Set your instant pot on Sauté mode, add the oil, heat it up, add the garlic, ginger, chili and tandoori powder, stir and cook for 3 minutes. Add the fish and the rest of the ingredients, put the lid on and cook on High for 17 minutes. Release the pressure naturally for 10 minutes, divide the mix between plates and serve.

Nutrition: calories 340, fat 7, fiber 3, carbs 16.6, protein 8

Spiced Mussels

***Preparation time:** 10 minutes | **Cooking time:** 12 minutes | **Servings:** 4*

Ingredients:
- 2 tablespoons vegetable oil
- 2 tablespoons ginger, grated
- 2 yellow onions, chopped
- Salt and black pepper to the taste
- 1 teaspoon turmeric powder
- 1 tablespoon coriander, ground
- 1 cup fish stock
- ¼ teaspoon cayenne pepper
- ½ cup coconut milk
- 2 pounds mussels, scrubbed
- 2 tablespoons lemon juice
- ¼ cup cilantro, chopped

Directions:
Set the instant pot on Sauté mode, add the oil, heat it up, add the ginger, onion, turmeric, coriander and cayenne, stir and cook for 2 minutes. Add the mussels and the other ingredients, put the lid on and cook on High for 10 minutes. Release the pressure naturally for 10 minutes, divide the mix into bowls and serve.

Nutrition: calories 310, fat 22, fiber 2, carbs 7, protein 24

Curry Clams

Preparation time: 10 minutes | Cooking time: 15 minutes | Servings: 4

Ingredients:

- 2 pounds clams
- 1 and ½ tablespoons vegetable oil
- Salt and black pepper to the taste
- 1 tablespoon ginger, grated
- 1 yellow onion, chopped
- 2 teaspoons sweet paprika
- ½ teaspoon cumin, ground
- 1 teaspoon coriander, ground
- ½ teaspoon cayenne pepper
- ½ cup coconut milk
- 1 tablespoon lime juice

Directions:

Set your instant pot on Sauté mode, add the oil, heat it up, add the ginger, onion, paprika, cumin, coriander and the cayenne pepper, stir and cook for 2 minutes. Add the rest of the ingredients, put the lid on and cook on High for 13 minutes. Release the pressure naturally for 10 minutes, divide the mix into bowls and serve.

Nutrition: calories 221, fat 8, fiber 3, carbs 6, protein 7

Spicy Tamarind Clams

Preparation time: 10 minutes | Cooking time: 15 minutes | Servings: 4

Ingredients:

- 1 and ½ pounds clams, scrubbed
- 2 tablespoons vegetable oil
- 1 teaspoon mustard seeds
- 3 garlic cloves, minced
- 1 tablespoon turmeric powder
- 1 yellow onion, chopped
- 1 teaspoon tamarind paste
- 1/3 cup coconut, grated
- ½ teaspoon red pepper flakes, crushed
- ½ teaspoon hot paprika
- ½ teaspoon coriander, ground
- ½ cup chicken stock

Directions:

Set the instant pot on Sauté mode, add the oil, heat it up, add the garlic, onion, turmeric, mustard seeds, and tamarind paste, stir and cook for 2 minutes. Add the clams and the rest of the ingredients, put the lid on and cook on High for 13 minutes. Release the pressure naturally for 10 minutes, divide the mix into bowls and serve.

Nutrition: calories 235, fat 8, fiber 4, carbs 7, protein 9

Crab Curry

Preparation time: 10 minutes | Cooking time: 15 minutes | Servings: 4

Ingredients:
- 2 cups crab meat
- 1 teaspoon tamarind paste
- ½ cup chicken stock
- 2 yellow onions, chopped
- 2 tomatoes, cubed
- 2 red chilies, chopped
- 2 tablespoons garlic paste
- 1 tablespoon ginger paste
- 2 tablespoons coriander powder
- 2 tablespoons cumin powder
- 1 cup coconut, grated
- ½ teaspoon red chili powder

Directions:
In your instant pot, combine the crab meat with the tamarind paste and the other ingredients, toss, put the lid on and cook on High for 15 minutes. Release the pressure naturally for 10 minutes, divide everything into bowls and serve.

Nutrition: calories 211, fat 8, fiber 4, carbs 8, protein 8

Spicy Crab and Eggplant Mix

Preparation time: 10 minutes | Cooking time: 20 minutes | Servings: 4

Ingredients:
- 1 pound crab meat
- 1 cup chicken stock
- 2 tablespoons vegetable oil
- 4 tablespoons coconut, shredded
- 3 garlic cloves, minced
- 1 teaspoon ginger, grated
- Salt and black pepper to the taste
- 1 eggplant, cubed
- 1 yellow onion, chopped
- 1 tablespoon curry powder
- 8 curry leaves, chopped
- 2 pandan leaves, dried
- 1 tablespoon tamarind paste

Directions:
Set the instant pot on Sauté mode, add the oil, heat it up, add the coconut, garlic, ginger, onion, curry powder, stir and cook for 5 minutes. Add the crab and the rest of the ingredients, put the lid on and cook on High for 15 minutes. Release the pressure naturally for 10 minutes, divide the mix between plates and serve.

Nutrition: calories 293, fat 6.7, fiber 3, carbs 9.6, protein 6

Mustard Seed Mahi Mahi

Preparation time: 10 minutes | Cooking time: 17 minutes | Servings: 4

Ingredients:
- 2 pounds mahi mahi, skinless, boneless and cubed
- ¼ teaspoon sweet paprika
- ¼ teaspoon turmeric powder
- Salt and black pepper to the taste
- 1 tablespoon lime juice
- ½ cup chicken stock
- 2 tablespoons vegetable oil
- 1 tablespoon garlic, minced
- 1 teaspoon mustard seeds
- ½ teaspoons mustard powder
- 1 cup tomatoes, cubed
- 1 tablespoon coriander, chopped

Directions:
Set the instant pot on Sauté mode, add the oil, heat it up, add the garlic, mustard seeds, mustard powder, paprika and turmeric and cook for 2 minutes. Add the fish and the other ingredients, toss, put the lid on and cook on High for 15 minutes. Release the pressure naturally for 10 minutes, divide the mix between plates and serve.

Nutrition: calories 280, fat 11, fiber 4, carbs 9.5, protein 12

Mahi Mahi Tikka

Preparation time: 10 minutes | Cooking time: 20 minutes | Servings: 4

Ingredients:
- 1 pound mahi mahi, boneless, skinless and cubed
- Salt to the taste
- 1 tablespoon ghee, melted
- 1 teaspoon red chili powder
- 1 cup yogurt
- 3 tablespoons garlic, minced

Directions:
In your instant pot, mix the fish with salt and the other ingredients, toss, put the lid on and cook on High for 20 minutes. Release the pressure naturally for 10 minutes, divide the mix into bowls, and serve.

Nutrition: calories 290, fat 12, fiber 3, carbs 7, protein 9

Fish and Onions Paste

Preparation time: 5 minutes | Cooking time: 15 minutes | Servings: 4

Ingredients:
- 1 pound cod fillets, boneless
- 4 pearl onions, peeled
- 2 tablespoons coconut oil, melted
- ½ teaspoon turmeric powder
- 3 garlic cloves, minced
- 1 teaspoon chili powder
- 1 teaspoon black peppercorns
- ½ teaspoon garam masala
- Juice of ½ lime
- Salt to the taste
- ½ cup fish stock

Directions:
In a blender, combine the pearl onions with the oil and the other ingredients except the fish, pulse well and transfer this to your instant pot. Add the trout as well, put the lid on and cook on High for 15 minutes. Release the pressure fast for 5 minutes, divide the mix into bowls and serve.

Nutrition: calories 275, fat 14.3, fiber 2, carbs 11, protein 33

Cod and Cilantro Chutney

Preparation time: 10 minutes | Cooking time: 15 minutes | Servings: 4

Ingredients:
- 4 cod fillets, boneless
- 1 tablespoon olive oil
- Juice of 1 lemon
- ½ teaspoon cumin, ground
- 2 garlic cloves, minced
- 1-inch ginger, grated
- 1 cup cilantro leaves
- ½ cup mint, chopped

Directions:
In a blender, combine the oil with the lemon juice, cilantro and the other ingredients except the fish and pulse well. Put the fish in the instant pot, add the chutney mix, toss gently, put the lid on and cook on High for 15 minutes. Release the pressure naturally for 10 minutes, divide the mix between plates and serve.

Nutrition: calories 282, fat 7.7, fiber 3, carbs 6, protein 9

Coriander Cod Mix

Preparation time: 10 minutes | Cooking time: 15 minutes | Servings: 4

Ingredients:

- 1 pound cod fillet, boneless, skinless and cubed
- 2 garlic cloves, minced
- 2 green chilies, chopped
- 1 tablespoon ghee, melted
- 1 cup cherry tomatoes, halved
- ½ teaspoon garam masala
- ½ tablespoon lime juice
- 1 tablespoon coriander powder
- A pinch of salt and black pepper
- ½ cup tomato sauce

Directions:

Set your instant pot on Sauté mode, add the ghee, heat it up, add the garlic, chilies, coriander and garam masala, stir and cook for 2 minutes. Add the fish and the rest of the ingredients, put the lid on and cook on High for 13 minutes. Release the pressure naturally for 10 minutes, divide the mix between plates and serve.

Nutrition: calories 270, fat 11.2, fiber 3, carbs 9.6, protein 14

Indian Instant Pot Poultry Recipes

Spiced Yogurt Turkey

Preparation time: 10 minutes | Cooking time: 25 minutes | Servings: 4

Ingredients:
- 1 bunch lemongrass, chopped
- 4 garlic cloves, minced
- 1 pound turkey breast, skinless, boneless and cubed
- Juice of ½ lemon
- 1 green chili pepper, chopped
- 1 teaspoon garam masala
- 2 teaspoons turmeric powder
- 5 ounces yogurt
- 1 tablespoon ginger, grated
- A pinch of salt and black pepper
- ¼ cup cilantro, chopped

Directions:
In your instant pot, combine the turkey with the lemongrass, garlic and the rest of the ingredients, toss, put the lid on and cook on High for 25 minutes. Release the pressure naturally for 10 minutes, divide everything between plates and serve.

Nutrition: calories 263, fat 12, fiber 3, carbs 6, protein 14

Cilantro Turkey and Lemon Mix

Preparation time: 10 minutes | Cooking time: 25 minutes | Servings: 4

Ingredients:
- 1 pound turkey breast, skinless, boneless and cubed
- 1 cup green onions, chopped
- ½ cup cashews, chopped
- 1 cup cilantro, chopped
- 1 teaspoon coriander seeds
- 1 teaspoon cumin seeds
- 1 tablespoon ghee, melted
- 2 tablespoons ginger, grated
- ½ cup yogurt
- ½ coconut cream
- 2 tablespoons lemon juice

Directions:
Set the instant pot on Sauté mode, add the ghee, heat it up, add the onion, coriander, cumin and the ginger, stir and cook for 2 minutes. Add the meat and brown it for 3 minutes more. Add the rest of the ingredients, put the lid on and cook on High for 20 minutes. Release the pressure naturally for 10 minutes, divide everything between plates and serve.

Nutrition: calories 262, fat 18,8, fiber 2, carbs 14.5, protein 9

Turkey Meatballs and Sauce

Preparation time: 10 minutes | Cooking time: 21 minutes | Servings: 4

Ingredients:
- 2 tablespoons ghee, melted
- 1 big turkey breast, skinless, boneless and minced
- ½ cup chicken stock
- ½ cup tomato sauce
- 1 yellow onion, chopped
- 1 tablespoon lime juice
- Salt and black pepper to the taste
- 3 tablespoons Dijon mustard
- 2 tablespoons sweet paprika
- 1 teaspoon turmeric powder
- ½ teaspoon cumin powder
- ½ teaspoon garam masala
- 1 tablespoon cilantro, chopped

Directions:
In a bowl, combine the meat with the lime juice, salt, pepper, turmeric, cumin, garam masala and the cilantro, stir and shape medium meatballs out of this mix. Set the instant pot on Sauté mode, add the ghee, melt it, add the meatballs and brown them for 3 minutes on each side. Add the rest of the ingredients, toss, put the lid on and cook on High for 15 minutes. Release the pressure naturally for 10 minutes, divide the mix between plates, and serve.

Nutrition: calories 280, fat 11.9, fiber 2, carbs 9.5, protein 10

Citrus Turkey and Spiced Broccoli

Preparation time: 10 minutes | Cooking time: 25 minutes | Servings: 4

Ingredients:
- 1 pound turkey breast, skinless, boneless and cubed
- 1 cup orange juice
- 1 cup broccoli florets
- ½ teaspoon nutmeg, ground
- ½ teaspoon chana masala
- ½ teaspoon dried fenugreek powder
- ½ teaspoon dried mango powder
- 1 tablespoon oregano, chopped
- A pinch of salt and black pepper
- 1 teaspoon chili powder

Directions:
In your instant pot, combine the turkey with the broccoli and the other ingredients, toss gently, put the lid on and cook on High for 25 minutes. Release the pressure naturally for 10 minutes, divide the mix between plates and serve.

Nutrition: calories 320, fat 14.4, fiber 2, carbs 15.6, protein 11

Cinnamon Turkey and Cauliflower

Preparation time: 10 minutes | Cooking time: 25 minutes | Servings: 4

Ingredients:
- 1 pound turkey breast, skinless, boneless and cubed
- 1 cup cauliflower florets
- 2 tablespoons ghee, melted
- ½ teaspoon turmeric, ground
- ½ teaspoon cinnamon powder
- ½ teaspoon garam masala
- ½ teaspoon chili powder
- 1 yellow onion, chopped
- 1 cup chicken stock
- ½ cup cilantro, chopped

Directions:
Set your instant pot on Sauté mode, add the ghee, heat it up, add the onion and the turkey and cook for 5 minutes. Add the rest of the ingredients, toss, put the lid on and cook on High for 20 minutes. Release the pressure naturally for 10 minutes, divide mix between plates and serve.

Nutrition: calories 310, fat 13.8, fiber 2, carbs 5.6, protein 11

Curry Chicken Thighs

Preparation time: 10 minutes | Cooking time: 25 minutes | Servings: 4

Ingredients:
- 4 chicken thighs, bone-in and skinless
- 1 yellow onion, chopped
- 2 tablespoons canola oil
- 2 carrots, sliced
- ½ teaspoon cayenne pepper
- Salt and black pepper to the taste
- 1 tablespoon curry powder
- 4 garlic cloves, minced
- 14 ounces canned tomatoes, chopped
- 1 cup chicken stock
- ½ cup heavy cream
- ¼ cup cilantro, chopped

Directions:
Set your instant pot on Sauté mode, add the oil, heat it up, add the onion and the chicken thighs and brown for 5 minutes Add the rest of the ingredients, put the lid on and cook on High for 20 minutes Release the pressure naturally for 10 minutes, divide everything between plates and serve.

Nutrition: calories 290, fat 8, fiber 2, carbs 15.3, protein 11

Ginger Chicken Mix

Preparation time: 10 minutes | Cooking time: 25 minutes | Servings: 4

Ingredients:
- 2 chicken breasts, skinless, boneless and halved
- 1 teaspoon garlic powder
- 1 teaspoon ginger, grated
- ½ cup chicken stock
- ¼ teaspoon cardamom, ground
- 2 tablespoons vegetable oil
- 1 teaspoon sweet paprika

Directions:
Set the instant pot on Sauté mode, add the oil, heat it up, add the meat and brown for 5 minutes Add the rest of the ingredients, toss, put the lid on and cook on High for 20 minutes Release the pressure naturally for 10 minutes, divide the mix between plates and serve.

Nutrition: calories 292, fat 12, fiber 3, carbs 13.5, protein 12

Masala Chicken and Peppers

Preparation time: 10 minutes | Cooking time: 20 minutes | Servings: 4

Ingredients:
- 2 chicken breasts, skinless, boneless and cubed
- 1 cup chicken stock
- 2 tablespoons ghee, melted
- 2 red chilies, minced
- 1 teaspoon garam masala
- ½ teaspoon turmeric powder
- 2 red bell pepper, cut into strips
- 1 teaspoon ginger, grated
- 2 teaspoons cilantro, chopped

Directions:
Set the instant pot on Sauté mode, add the ghee, heat it up, add the chilies, masala, turmeric, peppers and the ginger, stir and cook for 2 minutes. Add the meat and brown for 3 minutes more. Add the rest of the ingredients, put the lid on and cook on High for 15 minutes. Release the pressure naturally for 10 minutes, divide the mix between plates and serve.

Nutrition: calories 450, fat 15.7, fiber 1, carbs 22.5, protein 12

Cumin Chicken and Artichokes

Preparation time: 10 minutes | Cooking time: 20 minutes | Servings: 4

Ingredients:

- 1 pound chicken breast, skinless, boneless and cubed
- 2 artichokes, trimmed and halved
- A pinch of salt and black pepper
- 1 cup chicken stock
- 1 red onion, chopped
- 1 tablespoon ginger, grated
- 1 and ½ teaspoons cumin, ground
- ½ teaspoon dried fenugreek leaves
- ½ teaspoon turmeric powder
- 1 teaspoon cardamom, ground

Directions:

In your instant pot, combine the chicken with the stock, onion and the other ingredients, put the lid on and cook on High for 20 minutes. Release the pressure naturally for 10 minutes, divide the mix between plates and serve.

Nutrition: calories 291, fat 7, fiber 2, carbs 6, protein 12

Curry Chicken and Eggplants

Preparation time: 10 minutes | Cooking time: 20 minutes | Servings: 4

Ingredients:

- 1 pound chicken breast, skinless, boneless and cubed
- 2 eggplants, cubed
- ½ cup chicken stock
- A pinch of salt and black pepper
- 2 tablespoons sunflower oil
- 2 shallots, chopped
- 1 tablespoon red curry paste
- ½ cup tomato sauce
- 1 tablespoon oregano, dried
- 1 teaspoon turmeric powder
- ½ teaspoon garam masala

Directions:

Set your instant pot on Sauté mode, add the oil, heat it up, shallots, meat and the curry paste, stir and brown for 5 minutes. Add the eggplants and the rest of the ingredients, put the lid on and cook on High for 15 minutes. Release the pressure naturally for 10 minutes, divide everything between plates and serve.

Nutrition: calories 252, fat 12, fiber 4, carbs 7, protein 13.6

Cardamom Turkey Mix

Preparation time: 10 minutes | *Cooking time:* 20 minutes | *Servings:* 4

Ingredients:

- 1 turkey breast, skinless, boneless and cubed
- 2 tablespoons ghee, melted
- ½ cup chicken stock
- 1 yellow onion, chopped
- A pinch of salt and black pepper
- 2 cardamom pods, crushed
- 2 black peppercorns, crushed
- ½ teaspoon cumin, ground
- 4 garlic cloves, minced
- 1 tablespoon cilantro, chopped

Directions:

In your instant pot, mix the turkey with the ghee and the other ingredients, toss, put the lid on and cook on High for 20 minutes. Release the pressure naturally for 10 minutes, divide everything between plates and serve.

Nutrition: calories 271, fat 14, fiber 5.3, carbs 7, protein 14

Cinnamon Chicken and Rice Mix

Preparation time: 10 minutes | *Cooking time:* 25 minutes | *Servings:* 4

Ingredients:

- 1 pound chicken breast, skinless, boneless and cubed
- 2 tablespoons coconut oil, melted
- 1 cup white rice
- 2 cups chicken stock
- 1 yellow onion, chopped
- 1 tablespoon curry powder
- ½ teaspoon chili powder
- ½ teaspoon cumin, ground
- ½ teaspoon garam masala
- A handful cilantro, chopped
- Salt and black pepper to the taste
- ½ pound cherry tomatoes, halved
- 1 tablespoon cinnamon powder

Directions:

Set your instant pot on Sauté mode, add the oil, heat it up, add the meat and brown for 5 minutes. Add the rest of the ingredients, put the lid on and cook on High for 20 minutes. Release the pressure naturally for 10 minutes, divide everything between plates, and serve.

Nutrition: calories 263, fat 14, fiber 1.6, carbs 8.8, protein 12

Ginger Chicken and Sweet Potatoes

Preparation time: 10 minutes | Cooking time: 25 minutes | Servings: 4

Ingredients:
- 1 pound chicken breast, skinless, boneless and halved
- 1 tablespoon canola oil
- 2 sweet potatoes, peeled and cut into wedges
- Salt and black pepper to the taste
- 1 tablespoon chili powder
- 1 tablespoon ginger, grated
- 1 teaspoon garam masala
- ½ teaspoon coriander powder
- 2 garlic cloves, minced
- ½ cup chicken stock
- 2 green onions, chopped
- 1 tablespoon cilantro, chopped

Directions:
Set your instant pot on Sauté mode, add the oil, heat it up, add the meat, ginger, chili powder, garlic and garam masala, stir and cook for 5 minutes. Add the rest of the ingredients, put the lid on and cook on High for 20 minutes. Release the pressure naturally for 10 minutes, divide everything between plates and serve.

Nutrition: calories 263, fat 12, fiber 3, carbs 11.6, protein 14

Turkey with Spiced Potatoes

Preparation time: 10 minutes | Cooking time: 25 minutes | Servings: 4

Ingredients:
- 1 big turkey breast, skinless, boneless and cubed
- 1 tablespoon ghee, melted
- 1 pound baby potatoes, peeled and halved
- 1 teaspoon chili powder
- 1 teaspoon garam masala
- ½ teaspoon dried mango powder
- ½ teaspoon nutmeg, ground
- ½ teaspoon cinnamon powder
- ½ teaspoon sweet paprika
- 1 cup chicken stock
- Salt and black pepper to the taste
- 1 tablespoon coriander, chopped

Directions:
Set the instant pot on Sauté mode, add the ghee, heat it up, add the meat, chili powder, and garam masala, toss and brown for 5 minutes. Add the potatoes and the rest of the ingredients, put the lid on and cook on High for 20 minutes. Release the pressure naturally for 10 minutes, divide the mix between plates and serve.

Nutrition: calories 353, fat 13, fiber 2, carbs 15.7, protein 16

Coconut Chicken and Tomatoes

Preparation time: 10 minutes | Cooking time: 25 minutes | Servings: 4

Ingredients:

- 1 pound chicken breast, skinless, boneless and cubed
- 1 yellow onion, chopped
- 2 garlic cloves, minced
- 1 tablespoon canola oil
- ½ cup chicken stock
- ½ cup coconut, shredded
- 2 tomatoes, cubed
- 1 teaspoon turmeric powder
- ½ teaspoon chana masala
- A pinch of salt and black pepper
- 1 teaspoon oregano, dried

Directions:

Set your instant pot on Sauté mode, add the oil, heat it up, add the onion, garlic and the meat and brown for 5 minutes Add the rest of the ingredients, toss, put the lid on and cook on High for 20 minutes. Release the pressure naturally for 10 minutes, divide everything between plates and serve.

Nutrition: calories 284, fat 14, fiber 4, carbs 11.7, protein 15

Sage Chicken and Mango

Preparation time: 10 minutes | Cooking time: 20 minutes | Servings: 4

Ingredients:

- 1 pound chicken breast, skinless, boneless and cubed
- 1 tablespoon ghee, melted
- 1 yellow onion, chopped
- 3 garlic cloves, minced
- 1 cup chicken stock
- 1 mango, peeled and cubed
- Salt and black pepper to the taste
- ½ teaspoon cumin, ground
- ½ teaspoon coriander, ground
- ½ teaspoon cardamom, crushed
- ½ teaspoon dry mango powder
- 1 tablespoon sage, chopped
- 1 tablespoon coriander, chopped

Directions:

Set pot on Sauté mode, add the ghee, heat it up, add the onion, garlic, the meat, salt and pepper, stir and brown for 5 minutes. Add the rest of the ingredients, put the lid on and cook on High for 15 minutes. Release the pressure naturally for 10 minutes, divide the mix between plates and serve.

Nutrition: calories 263, fat 13, fiber 2, carbs 8.7, protein 15

Curry Turkey, Asparagus and Tomatoes

Preparation time: 10 minutes | Cooking time: 25 minutes | Servings: 4

Ingredients:
- 1 pound turkey breast, skinless, boneless and cubed
- 1 asparagus bunch, trimmed and halved
- 1 cup cherry tomatoes, cubed
- 1 tablespoon red curry paste
- ½ teaspoon smoked paprika
- ½ teaspoon garam masala
- ½ teaspoon cumin, ground
- 1 cup chicken stock
- ½ teaspoon chili powder
- A pinch of salt and black pepper

Directions:
In your instant pot, mix the chicken with the tomatoes and the other ingredients, toss, put the lid on and cook on High for 25 minutes. Release the pressure naturally for 10 minutes, divide everything between plates and serve.

Nutrition: calories 290, fat 13, fiber 2, carbs 9.5, protein 16

Creamy Chicken Mix

Preparation time: 10 minutes | Cooking time: 25 minutes | Servings: 4

Ingredients:
- 1 pound chicken breast, skinless, boneless and cubed
- ½ cup coconut, shredded
- ½ cup coconut cream
- 1 tablespoon ghee, melted
- 1 red bell pepper, chopped
- 1 green bell pepper, chopped
- 1 tomato, cubed
- ¼ cup chicken stock
- A pinch of salt and black pepper
- 1 tablespoon mustard
- 3 garlic cloves, minced

Directions:
Set the instant pot on Sauté mode, add the ghee, heat it up, add the meat, garlic and bell peppers and brown for 5 minutes Add the coconut and the rest of the ingredients, put the lid on and cook on High for 20 minutes. Release the pressure naturally for 10 minutes, divide the mix between plates and serve.

Nutrition: calories 290, fat 12, fiber 2, carbs 6,6, protein 15

Chicken, Avocado and Turmeric Rice

Preparation time: 10 minutes | Cooking time: 25 minutes | Servings: 4

Ingredients:

- 1 pound chicken breast, skinless, boneless and sliced
- 1 red onion, sliced
- 1 tablespoon sunflower oil
- 1 avocado, peeled, pitted and cubed
- 3 garlic cloves, minced
- A pinch of salt and black pepper
- 2 cups chicken stock
- 1 cup basmati rice
- 1 tablespoon ginger, grated
- 1 teaspoon turmeric powder
- ½ teaspoon garam masala
- 1 tablespoon cilantro, chopped

Directions:

Set the instant pot on Sauté mode, add the oil, heat it up, add the onion, garlic, the meat, ginger, turmeric and garam masala, stir and brown for 5 minutes. Add the rest of the ingredients, put the lid on and cook on High for 20 minutes. Release the pressure naturally for 10 minutes, divide the mix between plates and serve.

Nutrition: calories 253, fat 14, fiber 2, carbs 13.7, protein 16

Cinnamon Turkey and Green Beans

Preparation time: 10 minutes | Cooking time: 25 minutes | Servings: 4

Ingredients:

- 1 turkey breast, skinless, boneless and cubed
- ½ pound green beans, trimmed and halved
- 2 tablespoons vegetable oil
- 2 garlic cloves, minced
- ½ tablespoon cinnamon powder
- ½ teaspoon sweet paprika
- ½ teaspoon garam masala
- ½ teaspoon turmeric powder
- ½ teaspoon cumin, ground
- 1 yellow onion, sliced
- 1 cup chicken stock
- A pinch of salt and black pepper

Directions:

In your instant pot, combine the meat with the green beans and the rest of the ingredients, put the lid on and cook on High for 25 minutes. Release the pressure naturally for 10 minutes, divide the mix between plates and serve.

Nutrition: calories 273, fat 13, fiber 3, carbs 11.7, protein 17

Chicken and Masala Fennel

***Preparation time:** 10 minutes | **Cooking time:** 20 minutes | **Servings:** 4*

Ingredients:
- 1 pound chicken breast, skinless, boneless and sliced
- 2 fennel bulbs, sliced
- ½ teaspoon garam masala
- ½ teaspoon coriander, ground
- ½ teaspoon cumin, ground
- 1 cup chicken stock
- 2 shallots, chopped
- Juice of 1 lime
- 1 tablespoon vegetable oil
- 1 cup tomatoes, cubed
- 1 tablespoon cilantro, chopped

Directions:
Set the instant pot on Sauté mode, add the oil, heat it up, add the shallots, fennel and the meat and brown for 5 minutes Add the rest of the ingredients except the cilantro, put the lid on and cook on High for 15 minutes. Release the pressure naturally for 10 minutes, divide the mix between plates and serve with the cilantro sprinkled on top.

Nutrition: calories 276, fat 15, fiber 3, carbs 6.7, protein 16

Turkey and Lime Sauce

***Preparation time:** 10 minutes | **Cooking time:** 25 minutes | **Servings:** 4*

Ingredients:
- 1 pound turkey breast, skinless, boneless and sliced
- 2 tablespoons ghee, melted
- ½ teaspoon chili powder
- 2 green chilies, chopped
- ½ teaspoon garam masala
- 1 cup chicken stock
- A pinch of salt and black pepper
- 1 tablespoon cilantro, chopped
- 1 cup lime juice

Directions:
Set your instant pot on Sauté mode, add the ghee, heat it up, add the meat, chili powder, chilies and garam masala, stir and brown for 5 minutes. Add the rest of the ingredients, put the lid on and cook on High for 20 minutes. Release the pressure naturally for 10 minutes, divide the mix between plates and serve.

Nutrition: calories 282, fat 15, fiber 2, carbs 11.6, protein 1

Cumin Chicken with Tomato Chutney

Preparation time: 10 minutes | Cooking time: 25 minutes | Servings: 4

Ingredients:
- 2 chicken breasts, skinless, boneless and cubed
- ½ cup tomato chutney
- 2 green chilies, chopped
- ½ cup chicken stock
- ½ teaspoon sweet paprika
- ½ teaspoon garam masala
- ½ teaspoon cumin, ground
- 6 curry leaves, chopped
- 1 tablespoon sunflower oil
- 1 tablespoon lemon juice
- A pinch of salt and black pepper
- 1 tablespoon parsley, chopped

Directions:

Set the instant pot on Sauté mode, add the oil, heat it up, add the meat, chilies, cumin, paprika and garam masala, stir and brown for 5 minutes. Add the rest of the ingredients, put the lid on and cook on High for 20 minutes. Release the pressure naturally for 10 minutes, divide everything between plates and serve.

Nutrition: calories 334, fat 12, fiber 3, carbs 15.5, protein 7

Hot Chicken and Pineapple Mix

Preparation time: 10 minutes | Cooking time: 25 minutes | Servings: 4

Ingredients:
- 1 pound chicken breast, skinless, boneless and sliced
- 1 tablespoon chili powder
- ½ teaspoon hot paprika
- ½ teaspoon garam masala
- ½ teaspoon dried fenugreek leaves
- 1 cup pineapple, peeled and cubed
- 1 cup chicken stock
- 2 tablespoons tomato sauce
- 1 tablespoon parsley, chopped

Directions:

In your instant pot, combine the chicken with the pineapple, chili powder and the other ingredients, toss, put the lid on and cook on High for 25 minutes. Release the pressure naturally for 10 minutes, divide everything between plates and serve.

Nutrition: calories 263, fat 14, fiber 3, carbs 5.7, protein 16

Chicken and Turmeric Zucchini Mix

Preparation time: 10 minutes | Cooking time: 25 minutes | Servings: 4

Ingredients:

- 1 pound chicken breast, skinless, boneless and cubed
- 2 zucchinis, cubed
- 1 tablespoon canola oil
- ½ teaspoon turmeric powder
- ½ teaspoon garam masala
- ½ teaspoon cumin, ground
- ½ teaspoon chili powder
- A pinch of salt and black pepper
- 2 tablespoons tomato paste
- 1 cup chicken stock
- 1 tablespoon parsley, chopped

Directions:

Set your instant pot on Sauté mode, add the oil, heat it up, add the meat, turmeric, garam masala, cumin and chili powder, stir and brown for 5 minutes Add the rest of the ingredients, put the lid on and cook on High for 20 minutes. Release the pressure naturally for 10 minutes, divide the mix between plates and serve.

Nutrition: calories 263, fat 12, fiber 2, carbs 11.7, protein 18

Fenugreek Chicken Mix

Preparation time: 10 minutes | Cooking time: 20 minutes | Servings: 4

Ingredients:

- 2 chicken breasts, skinless, boneless and cubed
- Salt and black pepper to the taste
- 1 teaspoon fenugreek, dried
- 1 tablespoon coconut oil, melted
- ½ cup heavy cream
- ½ teaspoon turmeric powder
- 1 tablespoon smoked paprika
- 1 cup chicken stock
- 1 tablespoon basil, chopped

Directions:

In your instant pot, combine the chicken with salt, pepper, fenugreek and the other ingredients, toss, put the lid on and cook on High for 20 minutes. Release the pressure naturally for 10 minutes, divide the mix between plates and serve.

Nutrition: calories 291, fat 11.7, fiber 3, carbs 6, protein 22.4

Turkey, Cauliflower and Rice Mix
Preparation time: 10 minutes | Cooking time: 30 minutes | Servings: 4

Ingredients:
- 1 pound turkey breast, skinless, boneless and cubed
- 1 cup cauliflower florets
- 1 cup basmati rice
- ½ teaspoon dried mango powder
- ½ teaspoon coriander, ground
- 2 cups chicken stock
- 1 yellow onion, chopped
- 2 garlic cloves, minced
- 1 tablespoon chili powder
- 1 cup tomato sauce
- A pinch of salt and black pepper
- 1 tablespoon cilantro, chopped

Directions:
In your instant pot, combine the meat with the cauliflower and the other ingredients, toss, put the lid on and cook on High for 30 minutes. Release the pressure naturally for 10 minutes, divide the mix between plates and serve.

Nutrition: calories 263, fat 12, fiber 3, carbs 11.7, protein 15

Cocoa Turkey and Beans
Preparation time: 10 minutes | Cooking time: 25 minutes | Servings: 4

Ingredients:
- 1 pound turkey breast, skinless, boneless and cubed
- 1 cup canned red kidney beans, drained
- 1 cup chicken stock
- ½ teaspoon garam masala
- 2 green chilies, chopped
- ½ teaspoon turmeric powder
- 1 tablespoon cocoa powder
- 1 tablespoon cumin, ground
- A pinch of salt and black pepper
- 1 tablespoon cilantro, chopped

Directions:
In your instant pot, combine the meat with the beans, stock and the other ingredients, toss, put the lid on and cook on High for 25 minutes. Release the pressure naturally for 10 minutes, divide everything between plates and serve.

Nutrition: calories 294, fat 14, fiber 2, carbs 9.6, protein 15

Chicken Meatballs Curry

Preparation time: 10 minutes | Cooking time: 25 minutes | Servings: 4

Ingredients:

- 1 pound chicken breast, skinless, boneless and minced
- 1 egg, whisked
- 2 tablespoons coconut flour
- Salt and black pepper to the taste
- 1 yellow onion, chopped
- 2 garlic cloves, minced
- 1 tablespoon cilantro, chopped
- 1 tablespoon canola oil
- 2 cups coconut cream
- 1 tablespoon green curry paste
- ½ bunch coriander, chopped

Directions:

In a bowl, combine the meat with the egg, flour, salt, pepper, onion, garlic and cilantro, stir and shape medium meatballs from this mix. Set your instant pot on Sauté mode, add the oil, heat it up, add the meatballs and brown them for 5 minutes. Add the rest of the ingredients, put the lid on and cook on High for 20 minutes. Release the pressure naturally for 10 minutes, divide the mix into bowls and serve.

Nutrition: calories 321, fat 12, fiber 6.4, carbs 11.7, protein 15

Paprika Turkey Mix

Preparation time: 10 minutes | Cooking time: 25 minutes | Servings: 4

Ingredients:

- 1 pound turkey breast, skinless, boneless and cubed
- 1 teaspoon smoked paprika
- ½ teaspoon hot paprika
- ½ teaspoon dried mango powder
- 1 cup tomatoes, cubed
- 2 tablespoons ghee, melted
- 2 shallots, chopped
- 2 garlic cloves, minced
- 1 cup chicken stock
- 1 tablespoon parsley, chopped

Directions:

Set your instant pot on Sauté mode, add the ghee, heat it up, add the meat, smoked and hot paprika, stir and brown for 5 minutes. Add the rest of the ingredients, put the lid on and cook on High for 20 minutes. Release the pressure naturally for 10 minutes, divide everything between plates and serve.

Nutrition: calories 363, fat 12, fiber 5, carbs 5.7, protein 16

Chicken and Lime Turmeric Carrots

Preparation time: 10 minutes | Cooking time: 25 minutes | Servings: 4

Ingredients:
- 1 tablespoon canola oil
- 1 pound chicken breasts, skinless, boneless and halved
- A pinch of salt and black pepper
- ½ pound baby carrots, peeled
- ½ teaspoon garam masala
- ½ teaspoon nutmeg, ground
- 1 tablespoon lime juice
- ½ teaspoon turmeric powder
- 1 cup chicken stock
- 1 yellow onion, chopped
- 1 tablespoon coriander, chopped

Directions:
Set your instant pot on Sauté mode, add the oil, heat it up, add the meat, onion, garam masala and the nutmeg, toss and brown for 5 minutes Add the carrots and the other ingredients, put the lid on and cook on High for 20 minutes Release the naturally for 10 minutes, divide between plates and serve.

Nutrition: calories 292, fat 14, fiber 3, carbs 15.7, protein 14

Chicken and Zucchini Rice Mix

Preparation time: 10 minutes | Cooking time: 25 minutes | Servings: 4

Ingredients:
- 2 pounds chicken breasts, skinless, boneless and cubed
- 1 cup basmati rice
- 2 cups chicken stock
- 2 zucchinis, cubed
- 1 tablespoon hot chili powder
- ½ teaspoon chana masala
- 10 curry leaves, chopped
- 1 tablespoon coriander, chopped
- A pinch of salt and black pepper

Directions:
In your instant pot, mix the rice with the meat and the other ingredients, toss, put the lid on and cook on High for 25 minutes. Release the pressure naturally for 10 minutes, divide everything between plates and serve.

Nutrition: calories 312, fat 12, fiber 6.2, carbs 11.6, protein 15

Cheesy Turkey and Rice

Preparation time: 10 minutes | Cooking time: 25 minutes | Servings: 4

Ingredients:
- 1 pound turkey breast, skinless, boneless and cubed
- ½ cup brown rice
- 1 cup chicken stock
- 1 and ½ cup cream cheese
- 1 tablespoon turmeric powder
- ½ teaspoon cumin, ground
- ½ teaspoon coriander, ground
- 1 tablespoon chili powder
- 1 tablespoon cilantro, chopped
- A pinch of salt and black pepper

Directions:
In your instant pot, combine the meat with the rice, stock and the other ingredients, toss, put the lid on and cook on High for 25 minutes. Release the pressure naturally for 10 minutes, divide between plates and serve.

Nutrition: calories 363, fat 14, fiber 4.5, carbs 15.6, protein 18

Chicken, Tomatoes and Mushrooms

Preparation time: 10 minutes | Cooking time: 25 minutes | Servings: 4

Ingredients:
- 1 pound chicken breast, skinless, boneless and cubed
- 1 cup cherry tomatoes, cubed
- 1 cup mushrooms, sliced
- 2 tablespoons ghee, melted
- ½ cup coconut cream
- 1 yellow onion, chopped
- ½ teaspoon turmeric powder
- ½ teaspoon dried fenugreek powder
- 5 curry leaves, chopped
- ¼ cup cilantro, chopped

Directions:
Set the instant pot on Sauté mode, add the ghee, heat it up, add the onion, the mushrooms and the meat and brown for 5 minutes Add the remaining ingredients, put the lid on and cook on High for 20 minutes Release the pressure naturally for 10 minutes, divide everything between plates and serve.

Nutrition: calories 362, fat 16, fiber 6.2, carbs 8, protein 16

Turkey and Masala Corn

Preparation time: 10 minutes | Cooking time: 25 minutes | Servings: 4

Ingredients:
- 1 pound turkey breast, skinless, boneless and cubed
- 1 cup corn
- 1 tablespoon vegetable oil
- 2 teaspoons garam masala
- ½ teaspoon turmeric powder
- 1 yellow onion, sliced
- 1 cup chicken stock
- A pinch of salt and black pepper

Directions:
Set the instant pot on Sauté mode, add the oil, heat it up, add the onion and the meat and brown for 5 minutes. Add the rest of the ingredients, put the lid on and cook on High for 20 minutes. Release the pressure naturally for 10 minutes, divide everything between plates and serve.

Nutrition: calories 343, fat 16, fiber 2.6, carbs 14.4, protein 17

Chicken and Chickpeas Mix

Preparation time: 10 minutes | Cooking time: 25 minutes | Servings: 4

Ingredients:
- 2 tablespoons vegetable oil
- 1 cup yellow onion, chopped
- 1 cup canned chickpeas, drained and rinsed
- A pinch of salt and black pepper
- 1 pound chicken breast, skinless, boneless and cubed
- 1 cup chicken stock
- ½ teaspoon turmeric powder
- ½ teaspoon cumin, ground
- ½ teaspoon chili powder
- 2 teaspoons coriander, ground

Directions:
Set your instant pot on Sauté mode, add the oil, heat it up, add the onion, the meat, turmeric, cumin, chili and coriander, stir and brown for 5 minutes. Add the rest of the ingredients, put the lid on and cook on High for 20 minutes. Release the pressure naturally for 10 minutes, divide the mix between plates and serve.

Nutrition: calories 291, fat 17, fiber 3, carbs 14.7, protein 16

Turkey and Curried Lentils

Preparation time: 10 minutes | Cooking time: 25 minutes | Servings: 4

Ingredients:
- 3 garlic cloves, minced
- 1 pound turkey breast, skinless, boneless and cubed
- 1 cup canned lentils, drained and rinsed
- 1 tablespoon yellow curry paste
- ½ teaspoon turmeric powder
- ½ teaspoon coriander, ground
- 2 black peppercorns, crushed
- 2 tablespoons vegetable oil
- 2 red chilies, chopped
- 1 cup chicken stock
- 2 tablespoons cilantro, chopped

Directions:
Set your instant pot on Sauté mode, add the oil, heat it up, add meat, turmeric, coriander, chilies and black peppercorns, stir and brown for 5 minutes. Add the rest of the ingredients, put the lid on and cook on High for 20 minutes. Release the pressure naturally for 10 minutes, divide everything between plates and serve.

Nutrition: calories 256, fat 9, fiber 1, carbs 14.5, protein 12

Turkey, Chickpeas and Zucchinis

Preparation time: 10 minutes | Cooking time: 25 minutes | Servings: 4

Ingredients:
- 1 yellow onion, chopped
- 2 zucchinis, cubed
- 1 pound turkey breast, skinless, boneless and cubed
- 1 cup canned chickpeas, drained and rinsed
- ½ teaspoon garam masala
- ½ teaspoon cumin, ground
- ½ teaspoon dry mango powder
- ½ teaspoon fenugreek leaves, dried
- 2 tablespoons ghee, melted
- 4 garlic cloves, minced
- 1 teaspoon hot paprika
- A pinch of salt and black pepper
- 1 cup chicken stock

Directions:
Set your instant pot on Sauté mode, add the ghee, heat it up, add the onion, the meat, garam masala, cumin , mango powder, garlic and fenugreek, stir and brown for 5 minutes. Add the rest of the ingredients, put the lid on and cook on High for 20 minutes. Release the pressure naturally for 10 minutes, divide the mix between plates and serve.

Nutrition: calories 283, fat 11, fiber 2, carbs 14.8, protein 15

Chicken with Turmeric Cabbage

Preparation time: 10 minutes | *Cooking time:* 25 minutes | *Servings:* 4

Ingredients:

- 1 pound chicken breasts, skinless, boneless and cubed
- 1 green cabbage head, shredded
- ½ teaspoon garam masala
- ½ teaspoon turmeric powder
- 1 tablespoon vegetable oil
- 1 yellow onion, chopped
- A pinch of salt and black pepper
- 1 teaspoon red pepper flakes
- 1 cup chicken stock

Directions:

Set your instant pot on Sauté mode, add the oil, heat it up, add the meat, garam masala, turmeric and the onion and brown for 5 minutes Add the rest of the ingredients, put the lid on and cook on High for 20 minutes. Release the pressure naturally for 10 minutes, divide everything between plates and serve.

Nutrition: calories 272, fat 14.7, fiber 3, carbs 11.7, protein 14

Coriander Chicken Masala

Preparation time: 10 minutes | *Cooking time:* 25 minutes | *Servings:* 4

Ingredients:

- 1 pound chicken breast, skinless, boneless and cubed
- ½ teaspoon garam masala
- 1 teaspoon cumin, ground
- 1 tablespoon ghee, melted
- ½ teaspoon sweet paprika
- 1 teaspoon turmeric powder
- 1 cup chicken stock
- A pinch of salt and black pepper

Directions:

Set your instant pot on Sauté mode, add the ghee, heat it up, add the meat and garam masala, stir and brown for 5 minutes Add the rest of the ingredients, put the lid on and cook on High for 20 minutes. Release the pressure naturally for 10 minutes, divide everything between plates and serve.

Nutrition: calories 211, fat 8.9, fiber 5, carbs 6, protein 12

Chives Chicken and Broccoli

Preparation time: 10 minutes | Cooking time: 25 minutes | Servings: 4

Ingredients:
- 1 pound chicken breast, boneless, skinless and cubed
- 1 cup broccoli florets
- 1 tablespoon canola oil
- ½ teaspoon garam masala
- ½ teaspoon cumin, ground
- ½ teaspoon coriander, ground
- 4 curry leaves, chopped
- 1 yellow onion, chopped
- 1 cup chicken stock
- A pinch of salt and black pepper
- 1 tablespoon chives, chopped

Directions:
Set the instant pot on Sauté mode, add the oil, heat it up, add the meat, garam masala, cumin, coriander, curry leaves and the onion and brown for 5 minutes. Add the rest of the ingredients except the chives, put the lid on and cook on High for 20 minutes. Release the pressure naturally for 10 minutes, divide everything between plates, sprinkle the chives on top and serve.

Nutrition: calories 293, fat 15, fiber 4, carbs 6, protein 14

Chicken with Turmeric Beets and Broccoli

Preparation time: 10 minutes | Cooking time: 20 minutes | Servings: 4

Ingredients:
- 2 chicken breasts, skinless, boneless and halved
- 1 beet, peeled and cubed
- 1 cup broccoli florets
- ½ teaspoon turmeric powder
- ½ teaspoon garlic powder
- ½ teaspoon garam masala
- 3 celery stalks, chopped
- 1 cup chicken stock
- 1 tablespoon tomato sauce
- A pinch of salt and black pepper
- 1 teaspoon chili powder
- 1 tablespoon cilantro, chopped

Directions:
In your instant pot, combine the meat with the beet, broccoli and the other ingredients, toss, put the lid on and cook on High for 20 minutes Release the pressure naturally for 10 minutes, divide between plates and serve.

Nutrition: calories 223, fat 9, fiber 2, carbs 4, protein 11

Chicken with Avocado and Cucumber Mix

Preparation time: 10 minutes | Cooking time: 20 minutes | Servings: 4

Ingredients:

- 2 chicken breasts, skinless, boneless and cubed
- 2 cucumbers, sliced
- 1 avocado, peeled, pitted and cubed
- 2 tablespoons coconut oil, melted
- 1 tablespoon sweet paprika
- ½ teaspoon turmeric powder
- ½ teaspoon cumin, ground
- 2 black peppercorns, crushed
- 1 cardamom pod, crushed
- 1 cup chicken stock
- 1 yellow onion, chopped
- ½ teaspoon cinnamon powder
- 1 tablespoon cilantro, chopped

Directions:

Set instant pot on Sauté mode, add the oil, heat it up, add the meat, paprika, turmeric, cumin, peppercorns, cardamom and the onion, stir and brown for 5 minutes. Add the rest of the ingredients, put the lid on and cook on High for 15 minutes. Release the pressure naturally for 10 minutes, divide the mix between plates and serve.

Nutrition: calories 290, fat 14.1, fiber 2, carbs 14.7, protein 14

Chicken with Cauliflower and Pomegranate Mix

Preparation time: 10 minutes | Cooking time: 25 minutes | Servings: 4

Ingredients:

- 1 pound chicken breast, skinless, boneless and sliced
- 1 cup pomegranate seeds
- 1 cup cauliflower florets
- 1 tablespoon sunflower oil
- 1 red onion, chopped
- 1 cup chicken stock
- 1 tablespoon sweet paprika
- 1 teaspoon red chili powder
- ½ teaspoon garam masala
- A pinch of salt and black pepper
- 1 tablespoon cilantro, chopped

Directions:

Set the instant pot on Sauté mode, add the oil, heat it up, add the meat, the onion paprika, chili powder, and garam masala, toss and brown for 5 minutes Add the rest of the ingredients, put the lid on and cook on High for 20 minutes. Release the pressure naturally for 10 minutes, divide everything between plates and serve.

Nutrition: calories 263, fat 8, fiber 2, carbs 7, protein 12

Garlic Turkey, Tomatoes and Rice

Preparation time: 10 minutes | Cooking time: 20 minutes | Servings: 4

Ingredients:
- 1 pound turkey breasts, skinless, boneless and cubed
- 1 cup cauliflower rice
- 1 cup cherry tomatoes
- ½ cup chicken stock
- 4 garlic cloves, minced
- ½ teaspoon garam masala
- ½ teaspoon curry powder
- 4 curry leaves, chopped
- 1 tablespoon basil, chopped

Directions:
In your instant pot, combine the turkey with the cauliflower rice and the other ingredients, toss, put the lid on and cook on High for 20 minutes. Release the pressure naturally for 10 minutes, divide everything between plates and serve.

Nutrition: calories 390, fat 11.8, fiber 2, carbs 7, protein 15

Hot Cayenne Chicken Mix

Preparation time: 10 minutes | Cooking time: 25 minutes | Servings: 4

Ingredients:
- 2 chicken breasts, skinless, boneless and cubed
- ½ teaspoon cayenne pepper
- ½ teaspoon hot chili powder
- ½ teaspoon garam masala
- 2 garlic cloves, minced
- ½ teaspoon cumin, ground
- 2 tablespoons ghee, melted
- 1 cup tomato, cubed
- 1 yellow onion, chopped
- 1 cup chicken stock

Directions:
Set the instant pot on Sauté mode, add the ghee, heat it up, add the meat, cayenne, chili powder, garam masala and the garlic and brown for 5 minutes. Add the other ingredients, put the lid on and cook on High for 20 minutes. Release the pressure naturally for 10 minutes, divide everything between plates and serve.

Nutrition: calories 282, fat 12.5, fiber 2, carbs 15.6, protein 18

Turkey with Turmeric Yogurt Mix

Preparation time: 10 minutes | Cooking time: 25 minutes | Servings: 4

Ingredients:

- 1 pound turkey breasts, skinless, boneless and cubed
- 1 teaspoon turmeric powder
- ½ teaspoon coriander, ground
- ½ teaspoon nutmeg, ground
- 1 cup yogurt
- 2 teaspoons cumin, ground
- A pinch of salt and black pepper
- ¾ cup coconut cream
- ¼ cup cilantro, chopped

Directions:

In your instant pot, mix the turkey with the turmeric, coriander and the rest of the ingredients, put the lid on and cook on High for 25 minutes. Release the pressure naturally for 10 minutes, divide everything into bowls and serve.

Nutrition: calories 285, fat 16, fiber 4, carbs 8, protein 18

Turkey with Chili Black Beans

Preparation time: 10 minutes | Cooking time: 25 minutes | Servings: 4

Ingredients:

- 1 pound turkey breasts, skinless, boneless and cubed
- 1 tablespoon coconut oil, melted
- ½ cup coconut, shredded
- 1 and ½ cups chicken stock
- A pinch of salt and black pepper
- 1 teaspoon red chili powder
- ½ teaspoon turmeric powder
- ½ teaspoon chana masala
- 2 green chilies, chopped
- 1 cup black beans, soaked overnight and drained
- 2 tablespoons tomato sauce

Directions:

Set your instant pot on Sauté mode, add the oil, heat it up, add the meat, chili powder, turmeric, masala and the chilies and brown for 5 minutes. Add the rest of the ingredients, put the lid on and cook on High for 20 minutes. Release the pressure naturally for 10 minutes, divide everything between plates and serve.

Nutrition: calories 292, fat 17, fiber 2, carbs 7, protein 16

Chicken Wings and Turmeric Sauce

Preparation time: 10 minutes | Cooking time: 25 minutes | Servings: 4

Ingredients:
- 1 pound chicken wings, halved
- 1 tablespoon canola oil
- 1 teaspoon turmeric powder
- 1 cup coconut cream
- A pinch of salt and black pepper
- 2 shallots, chopped
- ½ teaspoon garam masala
- ½ teaspoon garlic powder
- 1 tomato, chopped
- ¼ cup cilantro, chopped

Directions:
Set your instant pot on Sauté mode, add the oil, heat it up, add the meat, shallots, turmeric, garam masala and garlic powder, stir and brown for 5 minutes. Add the remaining ingredients, put the lid on and cook on High for 20 minutes. Release the pressure naturally for 10 minutes, divide everything between plates and serve.

Nutrition: calories 324, fat 14, fiber 2, carbs 15.9, protein 11

Turkey and Chili Asparagus

Preparation time: 10 minutes | Cooking time: 25 minutes | Servings: 4

Ingredients:
- 2 pounds turkey breast, skinless, boneless and cubed
- 1 asparagus bunch, trimmed and halved
- 1 tablespoon coconut oil, melted
- ½ teaspoon red chili powder
- 2 green chilies, chopped
- ½ teaspoon curry powder
- ½ teaspoon garam masala
- A pinch of salt and black pepper
- 1 teaspoon cayenne pepper
- 1 cup chicken stock
- 1 tablespoon cilantro, chopped

Directions:
Set your instant pot on Sauté mode, add the oil, heat it up, add the turkey, chili powder, chilies, curry powder and garam masala, stir and brown for 5 minutes Add the rest of the ingredients, put the lid on and cook on High for 20 minutes. Release the pressure naturally for 10 minutes, divide everything between plates and serve.

Nutrition: calories 329, fat 9, fiber 4, carbs 16.7, protein 16

Chicken with Coriander Broccoli Sauté
Preparation time: 10 minutes | Cooking time: 25 minutes | Servings: 4

Ingredients:
- 1 yellow onion, chopped
- 2 chicken breast, skinless, boneless and cubed
- 1 cup broccoli florets
- 1 cup coconut cream
- 2 tablespoons vegetable oil
- 1 tablespoon coriander, chopped
- ½ teaspoon turmeric powder
- ½ teaspoon garam masala
- 2 garlic cloves, minced
- A pinch of salt and black pepper

Directions:
Set your instant pot on Sauté mode, add the oil, heat it up, add the meat, onion, coriander, turmeric, garam masala and the garlic, toss and brown for 5 minutes. Add the rest of the ingredients, toss, put the lid on and cook on High for 20 minutes. Release the pressure naturally for 10 minutes, divide the mix between plates and serve.

Nutrition: calories 262, fat 12, fiber 4, carbs 7.7, protein 16

Chicken, Zucchini and Mushrooms Curry
Preparation time: 10 minutes | Cooking time: 30 minutes | Servings: 4

Ingredients:
- 1 pound chicken thighs, boneless and skinless
- 1 tablespoon coconut oil, melted
- 1 cup mushrooms, sliced
- 1 tablespoon green curry paste
- ½ teaspoon turmeric powder
- ½ teaspoon garam masala
- 1 zucchini, cubed
- 4 garlic cloves, minced
- 1 red onion, chopped
- ¼ cup parsley, chopped
- 1 cup chicken stock
- ½ cup heavy cream
- A pinch of salt and black pepper

Directions:
Set the instant pot on Sauté mode, add the oil, heat it up, add the meat, curry paste, turmeric, garam masala, garlic and the onion, stir and brown for 5 minutes. Add the rest of the ingredients, put the lid on and cook on High for 25 minutes. Release the pressure naturally for 10 minutes, divide everything into bowls and serve.

Nutrition: calories 361, fat 9, fiber 8, carbs 12, protein 8

Chicken and Endives Rice Mix

Preparation time: 10 minutes | Cooking time: 30 minutes | Servings: 4

Ingredients:
- 2 endives, trimmed and shredded
- 1 cup basmati rice
- 2 cups chicken stock
- 1 pound chicken breasts, skinless, boneless and cubed
- ½ teaspoon coriander, ground
- ½ teaspoon cumin, ground
- ½ teaspoon turmeric powder
- ½ teaspoon garam masala
- 1 tablespoon chives, chopped
- 2 tablespoons tomato paste

Directions:
In your instant pot, mix the chicken with the endives, rice and the rest of the ingredients, put the lid on and cook on High for 30 minutes. Release the pressure naturally for 10 minutes, divide everything between plates and serve.

Nutrition: calories 321, fat 12, fiber 2, carbs 15.6, protein 18

Lime Turmeric Chicken Wings

Preparation time: 10 minutes | Cooking time: 25 minutes | Servings: 4

Ingredients:
- 2 shallots, chopped
- 1 tablespoon lime zest, grated
- 2 tablespoons lime juice
- 1 pound chicken wings, halved
- 2 tablespoons ghee, melted
- 1 cup coconut cream
- 1 teaspoon turmeric powder
- ½ teaspoon dried fenugreek leaves
- ½ teaspoon garam masala
- 4 garlic cloves, minced
- A pinch of salt and black pepper

Directions:
Set your instant pot on sauté mode, add the ghee, heat it up, add the shallots, the meat and turmeric, toss and brown for 5 minutes. Add the rest of the ingredients, put the lid on and cook on High for 20 minutes. Release the pressure naturally for 10 minutes, divide everything between plates and serve.

Nutrition: calories 331, fat 11, fiber 3, carbs 14.7, protein 18

Turkey Bowls

Preparation time: 10 minutes | Cooking time: 25 minutes | Servings: 4

Ingredients:
- 2 tablespoons ghee, melted
- 1 eggplant, cubed
- 1 zucchini, cubed
- ½ cup chicken stock
- 2 tomatoes, cubed
- 1 big turkey breast, skinless, boneless and cubed
- A pinch of salt and black pepper
- 1 cup pomegranate seeds
- 1 tablespoon lemon juice
- ½ teaspoon chana masala
- ½ teaspoon coriander, ground
- ½ teaspoon cumin, ground
- 1 cup walnuts, chopped
- 1 bunch cilantro, chopped

Directions:
Set your instant pot on sauté mode, add the ghee, heat it up, add the meat, chana masala, coriander and the cumin, stir and brown for 5 minutes. Add the rest of the ingredients, put the lid on and cook on High for 20 minutes. Release the pressure naturally for 10 minutes, divide everything into bowls and serve.

Nutrition: calories 352, fat 12, fiber 2, carbs 7, protein 17

Turkey with Brussels Sprouts Rice

Preparation time: 10 minutes | Cooking time: 25 minutes | Servings: 4

Ingredients:
- 1 pound turkey breasts, skinless, boneless and cubed
- 1 cup Brussels sprouts, trimmed and halved
- 1 cup basmati rice
- 2 and ½ cups chicken stock
- 1 teaspoon turmeric powder
- ½ teaspoon red chili powder
- 1 teaspoon dried mango powder
- 1 tablespoon canola oil
- A pinch of salt and black pepper

Directions:
Set your instant pot on sauté mode, add the oil, heat it up, add the meat, turmeric, chili powder and mango powder, stir and brown for 5 minutes. Add the rest of the ingredients, put the lid on and cook on High for 20 minutes. Release the pressure naturally for 10 minutes, divide everything between plates and serve.

Nutrition: calories 287, fat 9, fiber 3, carbs 13.7, protein 16

Creamy Turkey and Peas Mix

Preparation time: 10 minutes | Cooking time: 30 minutes | Servings: 4

Ingredients:
- 1 pound turkey breast, skinless, boneless and cubed
- 2 tablespoons ghee, melted
- 1 cup peas
- 1 cup chicken stock
- ½ cup heavy cream
- A pinch of salt and black pepper
- 1 tablespoon sweet paprika
- 1 tablespoon chili powder
- ½ teaspoon turmeric powder
- ½ teaspoon cumin, ground
- ½ teaspoon coriander, ground
- 1 tablespoon cilantro, chopped

Directions:
Set the instant pot on Sauté mode, add the ghee, heat it up, add the meat, paprika, chili, turmeric, cumin and coriander, stir and brown for 5 minutes. Add the remaining ingredients, toss, put the lid on and cook on High for 25 minutes. Release the pressure naturally for 10 minutes, divide the mix between plates and serve.

Nutrition: calories 271, fat 11, fiber 2, carbs 15.7, protein 14

Chicken with Chili Onions

Preparation time: 10 minutes | Cooking time: 30 minutes | Servings: 4

Ingredients:
- 2 pounds turkey breast, skinless, boneless and cubed
- 1 cup chicken stock
- 2 red onions, sliced
- 2 shallots, chopped
- 2 tablespoons canola oil
- ½ cup coconut cream
- ½ tablespoon chili powder
- ½ teaspoon garam masala
- ½ teaspoon dried fenugreek leaves
- A pinch of salt and black pepper
- 2 tablespoons cilantro, chopped

Directions:
Set your instant pot on Sauté mode, add the oil, heat it up, add the onions, shallots, the meat, chili powder and garam masala, stir and brown for 5 minutes. Add the rest of the ingredients, put the lid on and cook on High for 25 minutes. Release the pressure naturally for 10 minutes, divide the mix between plates and serve.

Nutrition: calories 321, fat 12, fiber 6.2, carbs 11.5, protein 17

Masala Turkey with Nutmeg Potatoes

Preparation time: 10 minutes | *Cooking time:* 30 minutes | *Servings:* 4

Ingredients:

- 1 pound turkey breasts, skinless, boneless and cubed
- 2 teaspoons garam masala
- 2 tablespoons sunflower oil
- ½ pound gold potatoes, peeled and cut into wedges
- 1 teaspoon nutmeg, ground
- 2 tablespoons ginger, grated
- 2 teaspoons garlic, minced
- ½ teaspoon cumin, ground
- 1 tablespoon basil, chopped
- 1 cup chicken stock

Directions:

Set your instant pot on sauté mode, add the oil, heat it up, add the meat and the garam masala, stir and brown for 5 minutes Add the potatoes and the nutmeg, toss and cook for 5 minutes more. Add the rest of the ingredients, put the lid on and cook on High for 20 minutes. Release the pressure naturally for 10 minutes, divide everything between plates and serve.

Nutrition: calories 321, fat 11.6, fiber 3, carbs 22.8, protein 16

Chicken, Rice and Mango Mix

Preparation time: 10 minutes | *Cooking time:* 30 minutes | *Servings:* 4

Ingredients:

- 2 chicken breasts, skinless, boneless and cubed
- 1 mango, peeled, pitted and cubed
- 1 cup basmati rice
- 2 cups chicken stock
- 1 yellow onion, chopped
- 4 garlic cloves, minced
- A pinch of salt and black pepper
- 1 teaspoon red chili powder
- 2 red chilies, chopped
- 1 teaspoon turmeric powder

Directions:

In your instant pot, mix the chicken with the mango, the rice with and the rest of the ingredients, put the lid on and cook on High for 30 minutes. Release the pressure naturally for 10 minutes, divide everything into bowls and serve.

Nutrition: calories 291, fat 14, fiber 3, carbs 11.6, protein 13

Coconut Turkey and Carrots Rice

Preparation time: 10 minutes | Cooking time: 30 minutes | Servings: 4

Ingredients:
- 1 tablespoon canola oil
- 1 pound turkey breast, skinless, boneless and cubed
- ½ cup coconut, shredded
- 1 cup basmati rice
- 1 yellow onion, chopped
- 2 carrots, grated
- 4 garlic cloves, minced
- 1 cup coconut milk
- A pinch of salt and black pepper
- 1 tablespoon sweet paprika

Directions:
Set the instant pot on Sauté mode, add the oil, heat it up, add the meat, onion, garlic and the carrots, stir and cook for 10 minutes. Add the rest of the ingredients, put the lid on and cook on High for 20 minutes. Release the pressure naturally for 10 minutes, divide everything between plates and serve.

Nutrition: calories 291, fat 17, fiber 2, carbs 11.7, protein 14

Indian Instant Pot Meat Recipes

Beef Curry

Preparation time: 10 minutes | Cooking time: 30 minutes | Servings: 4

Ingredients:
- 2 pounds beef stew meat, cubed
- ¼ cup cilantro, chopped
- 1 yellow onion, chopped
- 3 garlic cloves, minced
- ½ cup tomatoes, crushed
- Salt and black pepper to the taste
- 1 tablespoon garam masala
- 1 teaspoon turmeric powder
- ½ teaspoon coriander, ground
- ½ teaspoon cumin, ground
- ½ teaspoon cayenne pepper
- 1 teaspoon brown sugar
- 1 tablespoon vegetable oil
- ½ teaspoon lemon zest, grated
- 1 cup beef stock

Directions:
Set the instant pot on Sauté mode, add the oil, heat it up, add the meat, onion, garlic, masala, turmeric and coriander, stir and brown for 10 minutes. Add the rest of the ingredients, toss, put the lid on and cook on High for 20 minutes. Release the pressure naturally for 10 minutes, divide the mix into bowls and serve.

Nutrition: calories 481, fat 17.9, fiber 1.2, carbs 5.7, protein 70.3

Ribs Curry

Preparation time: 10 minutes | Cooking time: 35 minutes | Servings: 4

Ingredients:
- 2 pounds beef ribs
- 1 yellow onion, chopped
- 1 teaspoon garam masala
- 2 tablespoons tomato paste
- 4 garlic cloves, minced
- 1 tablespoon red curry paste
- 14 ounces coconut cream
- 3 cups beef stock
- 1 tablespoon fish sauce
- 1 pound cauliflower florets
- ½ cup basil, chopped
- 2 bay leaves
- 1 tablespoon sunflower oil
- Salt and black pepper to the taste

Directions:
Set the instant pot on Sauté mode, add the oil, heat it up, add the ribs, onion, garlic, curry paste, and the garam masala, stir and brown for 5 minutes. Add the remaining ingredients, put the lid don and cook on High for 30 minutes. Release the pressure naturally for 10 minutes, divide everything into bowls and serve.

Nutrition: calories 761, fat 42, fiber 6.1, protein 17.6, protein 76.5

Coconut Pork Mix

Preparation time: 10 minutes | Cooking time: 30 minutes | Servings: 6

Ingredients:
- 2 pounds pork stew meat, cubed
- 2 cups beef stock
- 4 garlic cloves, minced
- 1 leek, sliced
- ½ cup coconut, shredded
- 1 teaspoon garam masala
- ½ teaspoon cumin, ground
- 1 teaspoon sage, dried
- ½ cup heavy cream
- 1 tablespoon coconut oil
- Salt and black pepper to the taste

Directions:
Set the instant pot on Sauté mode, add the oil, heat it up, add the meat, garlic and the leek and brown for 5 minutes. Add the rest of the ingredients, toss, put the lid on and cook on High for 25 minutes. Release the pressure naturally for 10 minutes, divide everything into bowls and serve.

Nutrition: calories 377, fat 15.7, fiber 6.7, carbs 22.3, protein 14.3

Madras Beef Mix

Preparation time: 10 minutes | Cooking time: 30 minutes | Servings: 4

Ingredients:
- 1 tablespoon cumin, ground
- 2 tablespoons coriander, ground
- 1 teaspoon turmeric powder
- 1 teaspoon chili powder
- Salt and black pepper to the taste
- 2 teaspoons ginger, grated
- 2 garlic cloves, minced
- 2 tablespoons lemon juice
- 2 pounds beef stew meat, cubed
- 2 tablespoons canola oil
- 1 cup beef stock
- 2 tablespoons tomato paste
- 1 tablespoon mint, chopped

Directions:
Set the instant pot on Sauté mode, add the oil, heat it up, add the meat, garlic, ginger, chili powder, turmeric, coriander and the cumin, stir and brown for 5 minutes. Add the rest of the ingredients, put the lid on and cook on High for 25 minutes. Release the pressure naturally for 10 minutes, divide the mix into bowls and serve.

Nutrition: calories 399, fat 16.6, fiber 7.7, carbs 26.5, protein 12.7

Ginger Beef Curry

Preparation time: 10 minutes | Cooking time: 35 minutes | Servings: 4

Ingredients:
- 2 tablespoons vegetable oil
- 1 yellow onion, chopped
- 12 curry leaves, chopped
- 6 garlic cloves, minced
- 4 teaspoons ginger, grated
- 1 tablespoon tomato paste
- 2 teaspoons coriander, ground
- 1 cup water
- 1 teaspoon garam masala
- ½ teaspoon turmeric powder
- 4 star anise
- Salt and black pepper to the taste
- 2 pounds beef short ribs, cut into medium pieces

Directions:
Set the instant pot on Sauté mode, add the oil, heat it up, add the onion, garlic, curry leaves, ginger and the meat and brown for 5 minutes. Add the rest of the ingredients, toss, put the lid on and cook on High for 30 minutes. Release the pressure naturally for 10 minutes, divide the mix into bowls and serve.

Nutrition: calories 353, fat 14.4, fiber 4.5, carbs 22.3, protein 46

Beef with Veggies Mix

Preparation time: 10 minutes | Cooking time: 25 minutes | Servings: 6

Ingredients:
- 2 pound beef stew meat, cut into strips
- 2 yellow onions, chopped
- 2 tomatoes, cubed
- 2 tablespoons ginger paste
- 2 tablespoons garlic paste
- 3 green chilies, chopped
- 2 tablespoons coriander seeds
- 4 tablespoons fennel seeds
- 8 cloves
- 6 cardamom pods
- 1 tablespoon black peppercorns, crushed
- 10 curry leaves, chopped
- 1 cup coconut, shredded
- 1 tablespoon mustard seeds
- 2 tablespoons sunflower oil

Directions:
Set the instant pot on Sauté mode, add the oil, heat it up, add the meat, onions, garlic and ginger paste, stir and brown for 5 minutes. Add the rest of the ingredients, put the lid on and cook on High for 20 minutes. Release the pressure naturally for 10 minutes, divide the mix into bowls and serve.

Nutrition: calories 344, fat 12.4. fiber 6.6, carbs 19.9, protein 25

Aromatic Beef

Preparation time: 10 minutes | Cooking time: 30 minutes | Servings: 4

Ingredients:
- 1 pound beef stew meat, cubed
- 4 garlic cloves, minced
- 2 cups yellow onion, chopped
- 1 tablespoon ginger, grated
- 1 cup yogurt
- 2 bay leaves
- 1 teaspoon sweet paprika
- 2 tablespoons curry powder
- 1 teaspoon garam masala
- 2 tablespoons lemon juice
- Salt and black pepper to the taste

Directions:
In your instant pot, combine the beef with the garlic and the other ingredients, toss, put the lid on and cook on High for 30 minutes. Release the pressure naturally for 10 minutes, divide the mix into bowls and serve.

Nutrition: calories 388, fat 15.5, fiber 5.67, carbs 25.5. protein 22

Lemony Beef Mix

Preparation time: 10 minutes | Cooking time: 30 minutes | Servings: 4

Ingredients:
- 2 pounds beef stew meat, cubed
- 1 tablespoon garlic, minced
- 1-inch ginger, grated
- 2 cups red onion, chopped
- 2 tablespoons lemon juice
- 2 teaspoons coriander powder
- 2 teaspoons meat masala
- 2 teaspoons chili powder
- 1 teaspoon turmeric powder
- ½ cup water
- Salt to the taste

Directions:
In your instant pot, combine the meat with the garlic, ginger and the other ingredients, toss, put the lid on and cook on High for 30 minutes. Release the pressure naturally for 10 minutes, divide everything into bowls and serve.

Nutrition: calories 388, fat 14.5, fiber 5.5, carbs 22, protein 17

Beef and Lentils Curry

Preparation time: 10 minutes | Cooking time: 35 minutes | Servings: 4

Ingredients:
- ¼ cup vegetable oil
- 1 tablespoon coriander, ground
- 1 teaspoon cumin seeds
- 1 yellow onion, chopped
- 4 garlic cloves, minced
- 1 tablespoon ginger, grated
- 2 pounds beef stew meat, cubed
- 14 ounces canned tomatoes, chopped
- 1 teaspoon turmeric powder
- 2 cups water
- ½ cup green lentils, rinsed
- 1 green chili, chopped
- Salt and black pepper to the taste

Directions:
Set the instant pot on Sauté mode, add the oil, heat it up, add the meat, ginger, garlic and onion, stir and brown for 5 minutes. Add the coriander, cumin and the other ingredients, toss, put the lid on and cook on High for 30 minutes. Release the pressure naturally for 10 minutes, divide the mix into bowls and serve.

Nutrition: calories 372, fat 15.5, fiber 6.6, carbs 19.8, protein 22

Pork with Red Lentils Mix

Preparation time: 10 minutes | Cooking time: 30 minutes | Servings: 4

Ingredients:
- 1 pound pork stew meat, cubed
- ½ cup curry paste
- 2 teaspoons vegetable oil
- 2 garlic cloves, minced
- 1 yellow onion, chopped
- 1 cup red lentils
- 2 teaspoons ginger, grated
- 1 and ½ cups beef stock
- 1 cup coconut milk
- 2 tablespoons coriander, chopped

Directions:
Set the instant pot on Sauté mode, add the oil, heat it up, add the meat, onion and the garlic and sauté for 5 minutes. Add the rest of the ingredients, put the lid on and cook on High for 25 minutes. Release the pressure naturally for 10 minutes, divide the mix into bowls and serve.

Nutrition: calories 356, fat 16.5, fiber 4.5, carbs 22, protein 4.65

Kheema Masala

Preparation time: 10 minutes | Cooking time: 20 minutes | Servings: 4

Ingredients:
- 2 pounds beef, ground
- 1 red onion, chopped
- 10 garlic cloves, minced
- 2 tablespoons cumin powder
- 2 green chilies, chopped
- 1 tablespoon coriander, ground
- 1 tomato, cubed
- ½ cup dill, chopped
- 1 potato, peeled and cubed
- Salt and black pepper to the taste
- ¼ cup beef stock

Directions:
In your instant pot, combine the beef with the onion, garlic and the other ingredients, toss, put the lid on and cook on High for 20 minutes. Release the pressure naturally for 10 minutes, divide the mix between plates and serve..

Nutrition: calories 254, fat 12, fiber 2, carbs 14.6, protein 16

Beef and Peas

Preparation time: 10 minutes | Cooking time: 20 minutes | Servings: 4

Ingredients:
- 2 pounds beef meat, ground
- 2 tablespoons canola oil
- 2 garlic cloves, minced
- 1-inch ginger, grated
- 1 chili pepper, minced
- 1 teaspoon garam masala
- 2 tomatoes, cubed
- Salt and black pepper to the taste
- ½ cup peas
- ¼ cup cilantro, chopped
- ¼ cup beef stock

Directions:
Set the instant pot on Sauté mode, add the oil, heat it up, add the garlic, chili pepper and the meat and brown for 5 minutes Add the rest of the ingredients, toss, put the lid on and cook on High for 15 minutes Release the pressure naturally for 10 minutes, divide the mix between plates and serve.

Nutrition: calories 343, fat 15, fiber 3, carbs 14.6, protein 20

Coconut Beef and Cilantro Mix

Preparation time: 10 minutes | Cooking time: 25 minutes | Servings: 4

Ingredients:
- 2 pounds beef stew meat, cubed
- 2 tablespoons canola oil
- 1 teaspoon garam masala
- ½ teaspoon coriander, ground
- 2 and ½ tablespoons curry powder
- 2 yellow onions, chopped
- Salt and black pepper to the taste
- 2 garlic cloves, minced
- 10 ounces coconut milk
- 2 tablespoons cilantro, chopped

Directions:
Set your instant pot on Sauté mode, add the oil, heat it up, add the meat, garam masala, coriander, onions and garlic and brown for 5 minutes Add the rest of the ingredients, put the lid on and cook on High for 20 minutes Release the pressure naturally for 10 minutes, divide everything between plates and serve.

Nutrition: calories 363, fat 16, fiber 3, carbs 15.6, protein 16

Saag Gosht

Preparation time: 10 minutes | Cooking time: 30 minutes | Servings: 4

Ingredients:
- 1 and ½ pound beef, cubed
- 2 tablespoons ghee, melted
- 1 yellow onion, chopped
- 1 tablespoon ginger, grated
- 1 teaspoon coriander, ground
- 1 teaspoon cumin, ground
- 1 teaspoon sweet paprika
- ½ teaspoon turmeric powder
- ½ teaspoon cloves, ground
- ½ teaspoon cinnamon powder
- ½ teaspoon garam masala
- 2 tomatoes, cubed
- 1 tablespoon tomato paste
- 2 cups beef stock
- 2 tablespoons yogurt
- 1 bay leaf
- 10 ounces spinach, torn

Directions:
Set your instant pot on Sauté mode, add the ghee, heat it up, add the meat, onion, ginger, coriander, cumin, paprika and turmeric, stir and brown for 5 minutes Add the rest of the ingredients except the cilantro, put the lid on and cook on High for 25 minutes Release the pressure naturally for 10 minutes, divide the mix between plates and serve.

Nutrition: calories 354, fat 14, fiber 4, carbs 15.6, protein 15

Spicy Beef

Preparation time: 10 minutes | Cooking time: 30 minutes | Servings: 4

Ingredients:
- 2 pounds beef stew meat, cubed
- 1 yellow onion, chopped
- 2 tablespoons canola oil
- A pinch of salt and black pepper
- 1 cup beef stock
- 6 garlic cloves, chopped
- 2 green chilies, minced
- 1 teaspoon coriander, ground
- ½ teaspoon cumin, ground
- ½ teaspoon allspice, ground
- 1 teaspoon chili powder
- ½ teaspoon hot paprika
- ½ cup beef stock
- 1 tablespoon parsley, chopped

Directions:
Set your instant pot on Sauté mode, add the oil, heat it up, add the meat, onion, garlic, and the chilies, stir and brown for 5 minutes Add the rest of the ingredients except the parsley, put the lid on and cook on High for 25 minutes Release the pressure naturally for 10 minutes, divide the mix between plates and serve with the parsley sprinkled on top,

Nutrition: calories 363, fat 12, fiber 4, carbs 22.6, protein 16

Beef and Veggies Curry

***Preparation time:** 10 minutes | **Cooking time:** 35 minutes | **Servings:** 4*

Ingredients:

- 1 and ½ pound beef, cubed
- 1 yellow onion, chopped
- 2 garlic cloves, minced
- 1 tablespoon ginger, grated
- 2 teaspoons cumin, ground
- 2 teaspoons coriander, ground
- 2 tablespoons canola oil
- 1 teaspoon turmeric powder
- ½ teaspoon cardamom powder
- 12 ounces canned tomatoes, cubed
- 1 and ½ cups beef stock
- 2 carrots, chopped
- Salt and black pepper to the taste
- 1 cup green beans, trimmed and halve d
- 1 cup cauliflower florets
- 1/3 cup yogurt

Directions:

Set your instant pot on Sauté mode, add the oil, heat it up, add the meat, onion, garlic , ginger, cumin, coriander, turmeric and cardamom, stir and brown for 5 minutes Add the rest of the ingredients, put the lid on and cook on High for 30 minutes Release the pressure naturally for 10 minutes, divide the mix between plates and serve.

Nutrition: calories 363, fat 14, fiber 6.4, carbs 22.6, protein 18

Beef with Squash Curry

***Preparation time:** 10 minutes | **Cooking time:** 35 minutes | **Servings:** 4*

Ingredients:

- 2 pounds beef roast, cubed
- 1 tablespoon ghee, melted
- 1 yellow onion, chopped
- 2 tablespoons cumin, ground
- 4 garlic cloves, minced
- 2 tablespoons mustard seeds
- 1 tablespoon turmeric powder
- 1 tablespoon garam masala
- 1 teaspoon chili powder
- 8 curry leaves, chopped
- 2 cups beef stock
- ½ pound butternut squash, peeled and cubed
- 1 eggplant, cubed
- ½ cup coriander, chopped
- ½ cup coconut cream

Directions:

Set the instant pot on Sauté mode, add the ghee, heat it up, add the meat, onion, cumin, garlic, mustard seeds, turmeric, garam masala and chili powder, stir and brown for 5 minutes Add the rest of the ingredients, put the lid on and cook on High for 30 minutes Release the pressure naturally for 10 minutes, divide the mix into bowls and serve.

Nutrition: calories 354, fat 14, fiber 4, carbs 32.6, protein 17

Indian Beef and Pumpkin Mix

Preparation time: 10 minutes | *Cooking time:* 30 minutes | *Servings:* 4

Ingredients:

- 2 tablespoons ghee, melted
- 2 pounds beef stew meat, cubed
- 1 teaspoon cinnamon powder
- ½ teaspoon ginger, grated
- Salt and black pepper to the taste
- ½ teaspoon red pepper, crushed
- 4 shallots, chopped
- ½ cup beef stock
- 4 garlic cloves, minced
- 14 ounces canned tomatoes, cubed
- 4 cups pumpkin, peeled and cubed
- ¼ cup cilantro, chopped

Directions:

Set the instant pot on Sauté mode, add the ghee, heat it up, add the meat, cinnamon, ginger, pepper, shallots and the garlic and brown for 5 minutes Add the rest of the ingredients, put the lid on and cook on High for 25 minutes Release the pressure naturally for 10 minutes, divide the mix into bowls and serve.

Nutrition: calories 283, fat 9.5, fiber 4.8, carbs 25.7, protein 25.6

Beef with Lemony Scallions

Preparation time: 10 minutes | *Cooking time:* 35 minutes | *Servings:* 4

Ingredients:

- 4 scallions, chopped
- 2 tablespoons ghee, melted
- 2 pounds beef stew meat, cubed
- 2 cups beef stock
- 2 garlic cloves, minced
- 1 tablespoon lemon zest, grated
- 1 tablespoon lemon juice
- ½ teaspoon cumin, ground
- ½ teaspoon coriander, ground
- ½ teaspoon garam masala
- A pinch of salt and black pepper
- 2 tablespoons cilantro, chopped

Directions:

Set your instant pot on Sauté mode, add the ghee, heat it up, add the scallions, meat, garlic, lemon juice and lemon zest, stir and brown for 5 minutes Add the rest of the ingredients, put the lid on and cook on High for 30 minutes. Release the pressure naturally for 10 minutes, divide the mix between plates and serve.

Nutrition: calories 263, fat 14, fiber 5, carbs 7.5, protein 15

Cheesy Beef and Rice

Preparation time: 10 minutes | Cooking time: 30 minutes | Servings: 4

Ingredients:
- 2 pounds beef stew meat, cubed
- ½ teaspoon turmeric powder
- ½ teaspoon garam masala
- 3 ounces cream cheese
- 1 tablespoon canola oil
- 1 red onion, chopped
- 1 cup basmati rice
- 1 and ½ cups beef stock
- 1 tablespoon parsley, chopped
- A pinch of salt and black pepper

Directions:
Set your instant pot on Sauté mode, add the oil, heat it up, add the meat, onion, turmeric and garam masala and brown for 5 minutes. Add the rest of the ingredients, toss, put the lid on and cook on High for 25 minutes. Release the pressure naturally for 10 minutes, divide everything into bowls and serve.

Nutrition: calories 283, fat 14, fiber 3, carbs 22.7, protein 17

Beef with Cinnamon Zucchini Mix

Preparation time: 10 minutes | Cooking time: 30 minutes | Servings: 4

Ingredients:
- 2 tablespoons chili paste
- 1 pound beef stew meat, cubed
- 1 cup beef stock
- 1 tablespoon ghee, melted
- ½ teaspoon turmeric powder
- ½ teaspoon garam masala
- ½ teaspoon allspice, ground
- ½ teaspoon cardamom, ground
- 1 tablespoon cinnamon powder
- ¼ teaspoon red pepper flakes
- A pinch of salt and black pepper
- 3 zucchinis, cubed

Directions:
Set your instant pot on Sauté mode, add the ghee, heat it up, add the meat, chili paste, turmeric, garam masala, allspice, cardamom and cinnamon, stir and brown for 5 minutes. Add the rest of the ingredients, toss. put the lid on and cook on High for 25 minutes. Release the pressure naturally for 10 minutes, divide the mix between plates and serve.

Nutrition: calories 276, fat 14, fiber 3, carbs 15.7, protein 20

Cumin Beef

Preparation time: 10 minutes | Cooking time: 30 minutes | Servings: 4

Ingredients:
- 2 pounds beef stew meat, cubed
- 1 tablespoon canola oil
- ½ cup lime juice
- 1 yellow onion, chopped
- ¼ cup beef stock
- 1 tablespoon cumin, ground
- ½ teaspoon garam masala
- 2 teaspoons sweet paprika
- 1 and ½ teaspoons cinnamon powder
- 1 tablespoon coriander, chopped

Directions:

Set your instant pot on Sauté mode, add the oil, heat it up, add the meat, onion, cumin, garam masala, paprika and cinnamon, stir and brown for 5 minutes. Add the rest of the ingredients, toss, put the lid on and cook on High for 25 minutes. Release the pressure naturally for 10 minutes, divide the mix between plates and serve.

Nutrition: calories 287, fat 16, fiber 4, carbs 15.6, protein 20

Beef and Beets Mix

Preparation time: 10 minutes | Cooking time: 40 minutes | Servings: 4

Ingredients:
- 2 pounds beef roast, cubed
- 1 cup beef stock
- 1 beet, peeled and cubed
- 1 yellow onion, chopped
- 3 garlic cloves, chopped
- Salt and black pepper to the taste
- ½ teaspoon turmeric powder
- ½ teaspoon cumin, ground
- ½ teaspoon allspice, ground
- 1 cup tomato puree
- 1 tablespoon coriander, chopped

Directions:

In your instant pot, mix the beef with the stock, the beet and the other ingredients, toss, put the lid on and cook on High for 40 minutes. Release the pressure naturally for 10 minutes, divide the mix into bowls and serve.

Nutrition: calories 284, fat 11.8, fiber 3, carbs 22.6, protein 17

Lamb Curry

Preparation time: 10 minutes | Cooking time: 30 minutes | Servings: 6

Ingredients:
- 2 pounds lamb meat, cubed
- 4 cloves
- 2 bay leaves
- 2 tablespoons vegetable oil
- 2 yellow onions, chopped
- 1 teaspoon cardamom, ground
- 1 tablespoon ginger, grated
- 1 teaspoon cinnamon powder
- 1 tablespoon garlic, minced
- ½ teaspoon turmeric powder
- 2 teaspoons garam masala
- 2 teaspoons coriander, ground
- ½ cup tomato puree
- ½ cup yogurt
- 2 cups water

Directions:
Set your instant pot on Sauté mode, add the oil, heat it up, add the meat, cloves, bay leaves, onions, garlic, ginger, cardamom and the cinnamon, stir and brown for 5 minutes. Add the rest of the ingredients, toss, put the lid on and cook on High for 25 minutes. Release the pressure naturally for 10 minutes, divide the mix into bowls and serve.

Nutrition: calories 323, fat 17, fiber 1, carbs 7, protein 33

Spiced Lamb Bowls

Preparation time: 10 minutes | Cooking time: 35 minutes | Servings: 4

Ingredients:
- 1 pound lamb meat, cubed
- 1 teaspoon cumin, ground
- 1 teaspoon sweet paprika
- ½ teaspoon turmeric powder
- 1 tablespoon cocoa powder
- ½ teaspoon garam masala
- 2 tablespoons canola oil
- A pinch of salt and black pepper
- 3 garlic cloves, minced
- 1 cup beef stock
- 1 tablespoon coriander, chopped

Directions:
Set your instant pot on Sauté mode, add the oil, heat it up, add the meat, cumin, paprika, turmeric, cocoa and garam masala, stir and brown for 5 minutes. Add the rest of the ingredients, put the lid on and cook on High for 30 minutes. Release the pressure naturally for 10 minutes, divide the lamb mix into bowls and serve.

Nutrition: calories 343, fat 12, fiber 3, carbs 16.7, protein 10

Creamy Lamb with Carrots Curry

Preparation time: 10 minutes | Cooking time: 30 minutes | Servings: 4

Ingredients:

- 2 pounds lamb meat, cubed
- 2 carrots, sliced
- 2 tablespoons vegetable oil
- ½ cup coconut cream
- 1 cup heavy cream
- 3 tablespoons curry powder
- ½ teaspoon garam masala
- ½ teaspoon turmeric powder
- 1 red onion, chopped
- A pinch of salt and black pepper
- 1 tablespoon cilantro, chopped

Directions:

Set your instant pot on Sauté mode, add the oil, heat it up, add the meat, curry powder, garam masala, turmeric and the onion, stir and brown for 5 minutes. Add the rest of the ingredients, put the lid on and cook on High for 25 minutes. Release the pressure naturally for 10 minutes, divide the mix into bowls and serve.

Nutrition: calories 333, fat 14.7, fiber 2, carbs 22.6, protein 12

Lamb with Coconut Green Beans

Preparation time: 10 minutes | Cooking time: 35 minutes | Servings: 4

Ingredients:

- 1 pound lamb meat, cubed
- 2 tablespoons ghee, melted
- 1 cup green beans, trimmed and halved
- ½ cup coconut, shredded
- A pinch of salt and black pepper
- 1 yellow onion, chopped
- ½ cup heavy cream
- 1 teaspoon cumin, ground
- ½ teaspoon turmeric powder
- ½ teaspoon garam masala
- 2 garlic cloves, minced
- 2 tablespoons parsley, chopped

Directions:

Set your instant pot on Sauté mode, add the ghee, heat it up, add the meat, coconut, the onion, and the garlic, stir and brown for 5 minutes. Add the rest of the ingredients, put the lid on and cook on High for 30 minutes. Release the pressure naturally for 10 minutes, divide the mix between plates and serve.

Nutrition: calories 435, fat 12, fiber 5, carbs 16.7, protein 10

Spiced Lamb with Corn

Preparation time: 10 minutes | Cooking time: 30 minutes | Servings: 4

Ingredients:
- 2 pounds lamb shoulder, cubed
- 2 tablespoons ghee, melted
- 1 cup corn
- ½ cup beef stock
- 1 yellow onion, chopped
- Salt and black pepper to the taste
- 2 garlic cloves, minced
- 1 teaspoon cumin powder
- 1 teaspoon ginger powder
- ½ teaspoon turmeric powder
- ½ teaspoon garam masala
- ½ teaspoon allspice, ground
- 1 teaspoon cinnamon powder

Directions:
Set the instant pot on Sauté mode, add the ghee, heat it up, add the meat, onion, garlic, cumin, ginger and turmeric, stir and brown for 5 minutes. Add the rest of the ingredients, toss, put the lid on and cook on High for 25 minutes. Release the pressure naturally for 10 minutes, divide mix into bowls and serve.

Nutrition: calories 291, fat 9, fiber 2, carbs 13.6, protein 12

Lamb with Spiced Sprouts

Preparation time: 10 minutes | Cooking time: 30 minutes | Servings: 4

Ingredients:
- 1 pound lamb shoulder, cubed
- 1 cup Brussels sprouts, trimmed and halved
- 1 yellow onion, chopped
- 2 tomatoes, cubed
- 2 garlic cloves, minced
- 2 tablespoons tomato paste
- 1 tablespoon vegetable oil
- ½ cup beef stock
- 1 teaspoon garam masala
- ½ teaspoon turmeric powder
- ½ teaspoon cinnamon powder
- ½ teaspoon allspice, ground
- A pinch of salt and black pepper
- A handful parsley, chopped

Directions:
Set your instant pot on Sauté mode, add the oil, heat it up, add the meat, onion, garlic, garam masala, turmeric, cinnamon and the allspice, stir and brown for 5 minutes. Add the rest of the ingredients except the parsley, put the lid on and cook on High for 25 minutes Release the pressure naturally for 10 minutes, divide everything between plates, sprinkle the parsley on top and serve.

Nutrition: calories 254, fat 12, fiber 3, carbs 8.6, protein 15.6

Beef with Chili Quinoa

Preparation time: 10 minutes | *Cooking time:* 30 minutes | *Servings:* 4

Ingredients:
- 1 cup quinoa
- 1 pound beef stew meat, cubed
- 1 yellow onions, chopped
- 2 cups beef stock
- 1 tablespoon chili powder
- ½ teaspoon smoked paprika
- ½ teaspoon turmeric powder
- ½ teaspoon allspice, ground
- ½ teaspoon dried fenugreek powder
- 1 tablespoon coriander, chopped
- A pinch of salt and black pepper

Directions:
In your instant pot, combine the meat with the quinoa and the rest of the ingredients, toss, put the lid on and cook on High for 30 minutes. Release the pressure naturally for 10 minutes, divide the mix between plates and serve.

Nutrition: calories 342, fat 10, fiber 11.5, carbs 16.7, protein 11

Indian Lamb Chops

Preparation time: 10 minutes | *Cooking time:* 30 minutes | *Servings:* 4

Ingredients:
- 4 lamb chops
- ¼ cup green chutney
- Juice of 1 lime
- 2 teaspoons chili powder
- 2 tablespoons ginger and garlic paste
- 2 tablespoons vegetable oil
- 1 teaspoon turmeric powder
- 1 teaspoon garam masala
- ½ cup beef stock

Directions:
Set the instant pot on Sauté mode, add the oil, heat it up, add the lamb chops, chili powder, ginger paste, turmeric and garam masala, stir and brown for 5 minutes. Add the remaining ingredients, toss, put the lid on and cook on High for 25 minutes. Release the pressure naturally for 10 minutes, divide the mix between plates and serve.

Nutrition: calories 343, fat 15, fiber 4, carbs 23.6, protein 10

Minty Lamb Mix

Preparation time: 10 minutes | Cooking time: 35 minutes | Servings: 4

Ingredients:
- 4 lamb chops
- 2 tablespoons ghee, melted
- 1 tablespoon mint, chopped
- ½ cup beef stock
- 1 teaspoon garam masala
- ½ teaspoon allspice, ground
- ½ teaspoon coriander, ground
- ½ teaspoon dried mango powder
- 3 garlic cloves, minced
- 1 red onion, chopped
- A pinch of salt and black pepper
- ½ bunch cilantro, chopped

Directions:
Set your instant pot on Sauté mode, add the ghee, heat it up, add the lamb chops, garam masala, allspice, coriander, mango powder, garlic and the onion and brown for 5 minutes. Add the rest of the ingredients, put the lid on and cook on High for 30 minutes. Release the pressure naturally for 10 minutes, divide the mix between plates and serve.

Nutrition: calories 332, fat 12.5, fiber 4, carbs 5.66, protein 9

Spiced Lamb and Cucumber

Preparation time: 10 minutes | Cooking time: 30 minutes | Servings: 4

Ingredients:
- 2 pounds lamb shoulder, cubed
- 1 cucumber, sliced
- 1 yellow onion, chopped
- 3 garlic cloves, minced
- 2 tablespoons ghee, melted
- ½ teaspoon garam masala
- ½ teaspoon turmeric powder
- ½ teaspoon dry fenugreek leaves
- 10 curry leaves, chopped
- ½ teaspoon cinnamon powder
- A pinch of salt and black pepper
- 1 cup beef stock
- 2 tablespoons coriander, chopped

Directions:
Set your instant pot on Sauté mode, add the ghee, heat it up, add the meat, onion, garlic, garam masala, turmeric and fenugreek leaves, stir and brown for 5 minutes. Add the rest of the ingredients, put the lid on and cook on High for 25 minutes. Release the pressure naturally for 10 minutes, divide the mix between plates and serve.

Nutrition: calories 274, fat 13.9, fiber 5, carbs 15.6, protein 12

Turmeric Lamb with Beets

Preparation time: 10 minutes | Cooking time: 30 minutes | Servings: 4

Ingredients:
- 1 pound lamb shoulder, cubed
- 2 tablespoons ghee, melted
- 2 beets, peeled and cubed
- A pinch of salt and black pepper
- 1 teaspoon turmeric powder
- 1 teaspoon cinnamon powder
- 1 tablespoon ginger, grated
- 2 garlic cloves, minced
- ½ cup beef stock
- 1 teaspoon coriander, chopped

Directions:
Set your instant pot on Sauté mode, add the ghee, heat it up, add the meat, turmeric, cinnamon, ginger and the garlic and brown for 5 minutes. Add the rest of the ingredients, put the lid on and cook on High for 25 minutes. Release the pressure naturally for 10 minutes, divide everything between plates and serve.

Nutrition: calories 332, fat 11.9, fiber 3, carbs 22.6, protein 10

Indian Pork Chops

Preparation time: 10 minutes | Cooking time: 25 minutes | Servings: 4

Ingredients:
- 4 pork chops
- 1 tablespoon canola oil
- 1 tablespoon cumin, ground
- 1 tablespoon brown sugar
- 2 green chilies, minced
- 1 teaspoon cloves, ground
- 1 teaspoon coriander seeds
- ½ teaspoon curry powder
- ½ teaspoon cardamom powder
- ½ teaspoon onion powder
- ½ teaspoon black peppercorns
- ½ teaspoon mustard seeds
- ¼ teaspoon garlic powder
- Salt and black pepper to the taste
- ½ cup beef stock

Directions:
Set your instant pot on Sauté mode, add the oil, heat it up, add pork chops and brown them for 5 minutes. Add the rest of the ingredients, put the lid on and cook on High for 20 minutes. Release the pressure naturally for 10 minutes, divide everything between plates and serve.

Nutrition: calories 320, fat 11, fiber 3, carbs 22.6, protein 15

Pork Chops with Allspice Spinach

Preparation time: 10 minutes | Cooking time: 25 minutes | Servings: 4

Ingredients:
- 4 pork chops
- 2 tablespoons ghee, melted
- 2 garlic cloves, minced
- 2 tablespoons lime juice
- ½ teaspoon sweet paprika
- ½ teaspoon chili powder
- ½ teaspoon turmeric powder
- 1 teaspoon allspice, ground
- 1 cup baby spinach
- 1 yellow onion, chopped
- ½ cup beef stock
- Salt and black pepper to the taste
- 1 tablespoon parsley, chopped

Directions:
Set your instant pot on Sauté mode, add the ghee, heat it up, add the pork chops, garlic, onion, paprika, chili powder and turmeric, stir and brown for 5 minutes. Add the rest of the ingredients except the parsley, put the lid on and cook on High for 20 minutes Release the pressure naturally for 10 minutes, divide everything between plates and serve with the parsley sprinkled on top.

Nutrition: calories 310, fat 14.5, fiber 3, carbs 22.8, protein 12

Pork and Tomato Chutney

Preparation time: 10 minutes | Cooking time: 30 minutes | Servings: 4

Ingredients:
- 1 pound pork stew meat, cubed
- 2 tablespoons sunflower oil
- ½ teaspoon coriander, ground
- ½ teaspoon garam masala
- 2 teaspoons chili powder
- 1 cup tomato chutney
- 2 garlic cloves, minced
- Salt and black pepper to the taste
- 1 bunch coriander, chopped

Directions:
Set the instant pot on Sauté mode, add the oil, heat it up, add the meat and brown for 5 minutes. Add the coriander, garam masala and the other ingredients, toss, put the lid on and cook on High for 25 minutes. Release the pressure naturally for 10 minutes, divide the mix into bowls and serve.

Nutrition: calories 248, fat 11, fiber 3, carbs 12.6, protein 15

Cocoa Pork Chops and Green Beans

Preparation time: 10 minutes | Cooking time: 25 minutes | Servings: 4

Ingredients:
- 4 pork chops
- 1 tablespoon cocoa powder
- 2 tablespoons coconut oil, melted
- 1 cup green beans, trimmed and halved
- 1 cup beef stock
- 2 teaspoons sweet paprika
- 1 teaspoon turmeric powder
- ½ teaspoon garam masala
- ½ teaspoon fenugreek leaves, dried
- 5 curry leaves, chopped
- A pinch of salt and black pepper

Directions:
Set the instant pot on Sauté mode, add the oil, heat it up, add the pork chops and the cocoa powder, toss and brown for 5 minutes. Add the rest of the ingredients, toss, put the lid on and cook on High for 20 minutes. Release the pressure naturally for 10 minutes, divide everything between plates and serve.

Nutrition: calories 333, fat 11.9, fiber 3, carbs 6.7, protein 14

Pork with Cinnamon Carrots Mix

Preparation time: 10 minutes | Cooking time: 25 minutes | Servings: 4

Ingredients:
- 4 pork chops
- 2 tablespoons canola oil
- 2 carrots, sliced
- 1 tablespoon cinnamon powder
- ½ teaspoon turmeric powder
- ½ teaspoon garam masala
- A pinch of salt and black pepper
- 2 garlic cloves, minced
- 1 yellow onion, chopped
- 1 cup beef stock
- ¼ cup tomato sauce
- 1 tablespoon parsley, chopped

Directions:
Set your instant pot on Sauté mode, add the oil, heat it up, add the pork chops, cinnamon, turmeric, garam masala, onion and the garlic and brown for 5 minutes Add the rest of the ingredients, put the lid on and cook on High for 20 minutes. Release the pressure naturally for 10 minutes, divide the mix between plates and serve.

Nutrition: calories 327, fat 14, fiber 4, carbs 13.6, protein 16

Sweet Pork Chops

Preparation time: 10 minutes | Cooking time: 25 minutes | Servings: 4

Ingredients:
- 4 pork chops
- 2 tablespoons ghee, melted
- 2 cups red onions, chopped
- 1 tablespoon ginger, grated
- 6 garlic cloves, minced
- 2 tablespoons coriander, ground
- 1 teaspoon chili powder
- ½ teaspoon meat masala
- 15 ounces tomato sauce
- 2 tablespoons honey
- Salt and black pepper to the taste

Directions:
Set your instant pot on Sauté mode, add the ghee, heat it up, add the pork chops, onions, ginger, garlic and the meat masala, toss and brown for 5 minutes. Add the rest of the ingredients except the sesame seeds, put the lid on and cook on High for 20 minutes. Release the pressure naturally for 10 minutes, divide mix between plates and serve.

Nutrition: calories 436, fat 12, fiber 2, carbs 22.7, protein 15

Pork with Broccoli

Preparation time: 10 minutes | Cooking time: 30 minutes | Servings: 4

Ingredients:
- 2 pounds pork loin, cubed
- 1 cup beef stock
- 2 cups broccoli florets
- 1 yellow onion, chopped
- 2 tablespoons ghee, melted
- ¼ teaspoon red pepper, crushed
- ½ cup green onions, chopped
- 1 tablespoon sugar
- 1 tablespoon ginger, grated
- 4 garlic cloves, minced
- 2 tablespoons soy sauce
- ½ cup cashews, chopped

Directions:
Set the instant pot on Sauté mode, add the ghee, heat it up, add the meat, the onion, red pepper, green onions, ginger and garlic and brown for 5 minutes. Add the rest of the ingredients, put the lid on and cook on High for 25 minutes. Release the pressure naturally for 10 minutes, divide the mix between plates and serve.

Nutrition: calories 473, fat 12, fiber 4, carbs 15.7, protein 17

Pork Chops and Turmeric Cauliflower

Preparation time: 10 minutes | Cooking time: 25 minutes | Servings: 4

Ingredients:
- 1 cup beef stock
- 1 tablespoon peppercorns, crushed
- 1 cup cauliflower florets
- 1 teaspoon turmeric powder
- 4 pork chops
- 4 garlic cloves, minced
- 1 yellow onion, chopped
- 2 tablespoons canola oil
- ½ teaspoon garam masala
- A pinch of salt and black pepper

Directions:
Set your instant pot on sauté mode, add the oil, heat it up, add the garlic, onion, the meat and the garam masala, stir and brown for 5 minutes. Add the rest of the ingredients, put the lid on and cook on High for 20 minutes. Release the pressure naturally for 10 minutes, divide the mix between plates and serve.

Nutrition: calories 244, fat 12, fiber 2, carbs 15.5, protein 16

Coriander Pork with Almonds

Preparation time: 10 minutes | Cooking time: 25 minutes | Servings: 4

Ingredients:
- 4 pork chops
- 2 tablespoons almonds, chopped
- ½ cup beef stock
- 3 garlic cloves, minced
- 1 yellow onion, chopped
- 1 bunch coriander, chopped
- ½ teaspoon turmeric powder
- ½ teaspoon meat masala
- A pinch of salt and black pepper

Directions:
In your instant pot, combine the pork chops with the almonds, the stock and the other ingredients, toss, put the lid on and cook on High for 25 minutes. Release the pressure naturally for 10 minutes, divide the mix between plates and serve.

Nutrition: calories 354, fat 14, fiber 3, carbs 17.6, protein 17

Mustard and Cumin Pork Chops

Preparation time: 10 minutes | Cooking time: 30 minutes | Servings: 6

Ingredients:
- 6 pork chops
- 2 tablespoons ghee, melted
- 1 teaspoon mustard seeds
- 1 teaspoon coriander seeds
- ½ teaspoon cumin, ground
- ½ teaspoon nutmeg, ground
- ½ teaspoon turmeric powder
- A pinch of salt and black pepper
- 1 tablespoon smoked paprika
- 2 tablespoons Dijon mustard
- 1 cup beef stock
- 1 tablespoon cilantro, chopped

Directions:
Set your instant pot on Sauté mode, add the ghee, heat it up, add the pork chops, mustard seeds, coriander seeds, cumin and turmeric, toss and brown for 5 minutes Add the remaining ingredients, toss, put the lid on and cook on High for 25 minutes. Release the pressure naturally for 10 minutes, divide the mix between plates and serve.

Nutrition: calories 263, fat 14, fiber 6.6, carbs 22.6, protein 20

Paprika Pork with Nutmeg Potatoes

Preparation time: 10 minutes | Cooking time: 25 minutes | Servings: 4

Ingredients:
- 4 pork chops
- 2 tablespoons vegetable oil
- ½ pound gold potatoes, peeled and cubed
- 1 teaspoon sweet paprika
- ½ teaspoon chili powder
- ½ teaspoon nutmeg, ground
- ½ teaspoon chana masala
- ½ teaspoon coriander, ground
- A pinch of salt and black pepper
- 1 teaspoon onion powder
- 1 yellow onion, chopped
- 1 cup beef stock
- ½ teaspoon cayenne pepper

Directions:
Set the instant pot on Sauté mode, add the oil, heat it up, add the meat, paprika, chili powder and the masala, stir and brown for 5 minutes. Add the potatoes, nutmeg and the other ingredients, toss, put the lid on and cook on High for 20 minutes. Release the pressure naturally for 10 minutes, divide the pork chops and potatoes mix between plates and serve.

Nutrition: calories 283, fat 13, fiber 4, carbs 15.6, protein 16

Pandi Masala

Preparation time: 10 minutes | *Cooking time:* 35 minutes | *Servings:* 4

Ingredients:

- 3 teaspoons cumin seeds
- 2 teaspoons red pepper, crushed
- 1 teaspoon mustard seeds
- 1 teaspoon fenugreek seeds
- ½ teaspoon held powder
- 2 cloves
- 2 tablespoons vegetable oil
- 2 curry leaves, chopped
- 1 tablespoon coriander seeds
- 2 pounds pork stew meat, cubed
- 1 teaspoon chili powder
- 4 garlic cloves, minced
- 2 yellow onions, chopped
- 1 tablespoon ginger, grated
- 2 green chilies, chopped
- 1 tablespoon coriander leaves, chopped
- 1 cup beef stock

Directions:

Set your instant pot on Sauté mode, add the oil, heat it up, add cumin, red pepper, mustard seeds, fenugreek seeds, cloves, curry leaves, haldi powder, coriander and the pork stew meat, toss and brown for 5 minutes. Add the rest of the ingredients, put the lid on and cook on High for 30 minutes. Release the pressure naturally for 10 minutes, divide the mix between plates and serve.

Nutrition: calories 353, fat 14, fiber 6.7, carbs 16.6, protein 18

Pork Indaad

Preparation time: 10 minutes | *Cooking time:* 30 minutes | *Servings:* 4

Ingredients:

- 1 pound pork loin, cubed
- 1 tablespoon vegetable oil
- 1 teaspoon white vinegar
- 4 cloves
- 1 tablespoon mint, chopped
- 2 teaspoons sugar
- Salt and black pepper to the taste
- 1 cinnamon stick
- ½ tablespoon cumin, ground
- 2 red chilies, chopped
- 10 peppercorns
- 1 teaspoon turmeric powder
- 1 tablespoon tamarind paste
- 2 yellow onions, chopped
- ½ cup beef stock

Directions:

Set your instant pot on Sauté mode, add the oil, heat it up, add the meat, cloves, cumin, chilies, peppercorns and the turmeric and brown for 5 minutes. Add the rest of the ingredients, put the lid on and cook on High for 25 minutes. Release the pressure naturally for 10 minutes, divide everything into bowls and serve.

Nutrition: calories 364, fat 14, fiber 3, carbs 17.6, protein 17

Hot Pork Mix

Preparation time: *10 minutes* | **Cooking time:** *35 minutes* | **Servings:** *4*

Ingredients:

- 2 tablespoons canola oil
- 1 pound pork stew meat, cubed
- 3 red chilies, chopped
- 1 teaspoon smoked paprika
- ½ teaspoon chili powder
- ½ teaspoon cumin, ground
- ½ teaspoon garam masala
- A pinch of salt and black pepper
- 1 red bell pepper, roughly chopped
- 1 green bell pepper, roughly chopped
- 3 garlic cloves, minced
- 1 cup beef stock
- 1 tablespoon coriander, chopped

Directions:

Set your instant pot on Sauté mode, add the oil, heat it up, add the meat, chilies, paprika, chili powder and garam masala, stir and brown for 5 minutes. Add all the other ingredients except the parsley, put the lid on and cook on High for 30 minutes. Release the pressure naturally for 10 minutes, divide the mix into bowls and serve.

Nutrition: calories 373, fat 13, fiber 2, carbs 156, protein 15

Orange Pork Mix

Preparation time: *10 minutes* | **Cooking time:** *35 minutes* | **Servings:** *4*

Ingredients:

- 1 pound pork shoulder, cubed
- 3 garlic cloves, minced
- ½ cup orange juice
- ½ teaspoon garam masala
- ½ teaspoon turmeric powder
- ½ teaspoon cumin, ground
- ½ teaspoon fenugreek leaves, dried
- 1 bay leaf
- A pinch of salt and black pepper
- 1 tablespoon ginger, grated
- ½ cup beef stock

Directions:

In your instant pot, combine the pork with the garlic, orange juice and all the other ingredients, put the lid on and cook on High for 35 minutes. Release the pressure naturally for 10 minutes, divide the mix between plates and serve.

Nutrition: calories 314, fat 14, fiber 6.2, carbs 13.6, protein 16

Ginger Pork Mix

Preparation time: 10 minutes | Cooking time: 35 minutes | Servings: 4

Ingredients:

- 1 cup basmati rice
- 2 pounds pork stew meat, cubed
- 3 cups water
- 2 carrots, sliced
- 1 yellow onion, chopped
- ½ teaspoon turmeric powder
- 1 tablespoon ginger paste
- 4 bay leaves
- 2 tablespoons sweet paprika
- 2 tablespoons ghee, melted
- Salt and black pepper to the taste
- ¼ cup mint, chopped

Directions:

Set the instant pot on Sauté mode, add the ghee, heat it up, add the meat, the onion, turmeric, ginger and the paprika, toss, and brown for 5 minutes. Add the rest of the ingredients, put the lid on and cook on High for 30 minutes. Release the pressure naturally for 10 minutes, divide the mix between plates and serve.

Nutrition: calories 264, fat 14, fiber 5.6, carbs 15.8, protein 12

Cocoa Pork and Tomatoes

Preparation time: 10 minutes | Cooking time: 30 minutes | Servings: 4

Ingredients:

- 4 pork chops
- 1 cup cherry tomatoes, halved
- A pinch of salt and black pepper
- 2 tablespoons cocoa powder
- 1 teaspoon chili powder
- ½ teaspoon cumin, ground
- ½ teaspoon allspice, ground
- ½ teaspoon coriander, ground
- ½ teaspoon garam masala
- 1 cup beef stock
- 1 tablespoon parsley, chopped

Directions:

In your instant pot, combine the pork chops with the tomatoes and with the rest of the ingredients, put the lid on and cook on High for 30 minutes. Release the pressure naturally for 10 minutes, divide the mix between plates and serve.

Nutrition: calories 300, fat 9, fiber 2, carbs 15.6, protein 12

Ema Datshi

Preparation time: 10 minutes | Cooking time: 35 minutes | Servings: 4

Ingredients:

- 2 pounds pork shoulder, cubed
- 4 gold potatoes, peeled and cut into wedges
- 10 dried chilies, minced
- A pinch of salt and black pepper
- 3 tomatoes, cubed
- 10 green onions, chopped
- 2 tablespoons ghee, melted
- ½ teaspoon turmeric powder
- 2 cups beef stock

Directions:

Set your instant pot on Sauté mode, add the ghee, heat it up, add the meat, chilies and the turmeric and brown for 5 minutes. Add the rest of the ingredients, put the lid on and cook on High for 30 minutes. Release the pressure naturally for 10 minutes, divide everything into bowls and serve.

Nutrition: calories 334, fat 11, fiber 3, carbs 11.7, protein 15

Pork with Bamboo Mix

Preparation time: 10 minutes | Cooking time: 30 minutes | Servings: 4

Ingredients:

- 2 pounds pork shoulder, cubed
- 2 tablespoons vegetable oil
- 1 cup bamboo shoots
- Salt and black pepper to the taste
- 2 yellow onions, chopped
- 1 tablespoon ginger, grated
- 1 tablespoon chili powder
- A bunch coriander, chopped
- 1 cup beef stock

Directions:

Set your instant pot on Sauté mode, add the oil, heat it up, add the pork, onions, ginger and chili powder, stir and brown for 5 minutes. Add the rest of the ingredients, put the lid on and cook on High for 25 minutes. Release the pressure naturally for 10 minutes, divide the mix into bowls and serve.

Nutrition: calories 273, fat 14, fiber 2, carbs 14.5, protein 15

Kaleez Ankiti

Preparation time: 10 minutes | *Cooking time:* 30 minutes | *Servings:* 4

Ingredients:
- 2 pounds pork stew meat, cubed
- 1 teaspoon garam masala
- 2 yellow onions, roughly chopped
- 6 garlic cloves, minced
- 1-inch ginger, grated
- 2 green chilies, chopped
- Juice of 1 lime
- 10 bay leaves
- 1 teaspoon vinegar
- 1 cup beef stock
- Salt and black pepper to the taste

Directions:
In your instant pot, mix the pork with the garam masala, onion, garlic ad the other ingredients, put the lid on and cook on High for 30 minutes. Release the pressure naturally for 10 minutes, divide everything into bowls and serve.

Nutrition: calories 292, fat 12, fiber 3, carbs 7, protein 16

Pork Chili Mix

Preparation time: 10 minutes | *Cooking time:* 30 minutes | *Servings:* 4

Ingredients:
- 2 pounds pork stew meat, cubed
- 2 tablespoons vegetable oil
- 2 yellow onions, chopped
- 3 red chilies, chopped
- 2 green chilies, chopped
- 1 teaspoon garlic, minced
- 2 potatoes, peeled and cut into wedges
- Salt and black pepper to the taste
- ½ teaspoon ginger, grated
- ¼ teaspoon turmeric powder
- 2 tomatoes, cubed
- 1 tablespoon white vinegar

Directions:
Set the instant pot on Sauté mode, add the oil, heat it up, add the onions, all the chilies, garlic, ginger and the meat and brown for 5 minutes. Add the rest of the ingredients, put the lid on and cook on High for 25 minutes. Release the pressure naturally for 10 minutes, divide everything between plates and serve.

Nutrition: calories 357, fat 14, fiber 6.5, carbs 14.7, protein 17

Pork Meatballs Mix

Preparation time: 10 minutes | Cooking time: 30 minutes | Servings: 4

Ingredients:
- ½ cup coconut cream
- 1 tablespoon ghee, melted
- 2 tablespoons coconut flour
- 2 eggs, whisked
- 2 pounds pork meat, ground
- ½ teaspoon sweet paprika
- ½ teaspoon turmeric powder
- 1 yellow onion, minced
- Salt and black pepper to the taste
- 2 pounds pork meat, ground
- ½ cup beef stock
- 1 tablespoon parsley, chopped

Directions:
In a bowl, mix the pork with the flour and the other ingredients except the oil, stock and the cream, stir well and shape medium meatballs out of this mix. Set the instant pot on Sauté mode, add the ghee, heat it up, add the meatballs and brown for 5 minutes. Add the cream and the stock, toss, put the lid on and cook on High for 25 minutes. Release the pressure naturally for 10 minutes, divide the mix between plates and serve.

Nutrition: calories 374, fat 12, fiber 4, carbs 15.7, protein 16

Tamarind Pork

Preparation time: 10 minutes | Cooking time: 30 minutes | Servings: 4

Ingredients:
- 2 pounds pork stew meat, cubed
- 2 tablespoons vegetable oil
- 2 garlic cloves, minced
- 1 cup beef stock
- 2 tablespoons brown sugar
- 2 tablespoons tamarind paste
- 3 shallots, chopped
- 1 teaspoon fish sauce
- 1 tablespoon soy sauce
- 1 red chili, chopped
- ½ teaspoon turmeric powder
- 1 tablespoon cilantro, chopped

Directions:
Set the instant pot on Sauté mode, add the oil, heat it up, add the meat, garlic, shallots, red chili and the turmeric, stir and brown for 5 minutes. Add the rest of the ingredients, toss, put the lid on and cook on High for 25 minutes. Release the pressure naturally for 10 minutes, divide the mix between plates and serve.

Nutrition: calories 269, fat 12, fiber 3, carbs 5, protein 16

Hot BBQ Ribs
Preparation time: 10 minutes | Cooking time: 30 minutes | Servings: 4

Ingredients:
- 2 tablespoons fennel seeds
- 2 tablespoon cumin seeds
- 1 teaspoon black peppercorns
- 2 tablespoons sunflower oil
- 1 tablespoon smoked paprika
- Salt and black pepper to the taste
- 2 tablespoons tomato Sauce
- 1 tablespoon hot chili sauce
- 1 teaspoon chili powder
- 2 tablespoons honey
- 1 tablespoon soy sauce
- 2 racks of ribs
- 1 cup beef stock

Directions:
Set the instant pot on Sauté mode, add the oil, heat it up, add the fennel, cumin, black peppercorns, paprika and chili sauce, stir and cook for 2 minutes. Add the rack of ribs, toss and brown for 3 minutes more. Add the rest of the ingredients, put the lid on and cook on High for 25 minutes. Release the pressure naturally for 10 minutes, divide everything between plates and serve.

Nutrition: calories 293, fat 14, fiber 4, carbs 12.6, protein 18

Spicy Pork and Artichokes
Preparation time: 10 minutes | Cooking time: 30 minutes | Servings: 4

Ingredients:
- 1 red onion, chopped
- 1 tablespoon ghee, melted
- ½ teaspoon turmeric powder
- ½ teaspoon garam masala
- ½ teaspoon chili powder
- ½ teaspoon hot paprika
- 2 artichokes, trimmed and quartered
- 2 tablespoons lemon juice
- A pinch of salt and black pepper
- 2 pounds pork stew meat, cubed
- 1 cup beef stock

Directions:
Set the instant pot on Sauté mode, add the ghee, heat it up, add the onion, turmeric, garam masala, chili powder, paprika and the meat and brown for 5 minutes. Add the rest of the ingredients, put the lid on and cook on High for 25 minutes. Release the pressure naturally for 10 minutes, divide the mix between plates and serve.

Nutrition: calories 263, fat 12, fiber 3, carbs 12.4, protein 13

Beef and Creamy Turmeric Potatoes

Preparation time: 10 minutes | Cooking time: 30 minutes | Servings: 4

Ingredients:

- 1 pound beef stew meat, cubed
- 2 gold potatoes, peeled and cubed
- 1 cup beef stock
- ½ cup heavy cream
- 1 yellow onion, chopped
- 2 tablespoons ghee, melted
- 1 teaspoon chili powder
- ½ teaspoon turmeric powder
- ½ teaspoon cumin, ground
- ½ teaspoon coriander seeds
- 1 tablespoon parsley, chopped
- A pinch of salt and black pepper

Directions:

Set your instant pot on Sauté mode, add the ghee, heat it up, add the meat, the onion, chili powder, turmeric, cumin and coriander, toss and brown for 5 minutes. Add the rest of the ingredients except the parsley, put the lid on and cook on High for 25 minutes. Release the pressure naturally for 10 minutes, divide the mix between plates, sprinkle the parsley on top and serve.

Nutrition: calories 263, fat 14, fiber 3, carbs 11.57, protein 19

Indian Instant Pot Vegetable Recipes

Masala Artichokes
Preparation time: 10 minutes | Cooking time: 20 minutes | Servings: 4

Ingredients:
- 5 garlic cloves, minced
- 1 tablespoon ginger, grated
- 2 tablespoons vegetable oil
- 1 yellow onion, chopped
- 3 tomatoes, cubed
- 1 teaspoon cumin seeds, ground
- 1 teaspoon coriander, ground
- ½ teaspoon garam masala
- ½ teaspoon turmeric powder
- 3 tablespoons yogurt
- 1 tablespoon lime juice
- 4 artichokes, trimmed and halved
- 1 cup water

Directions:
Set the instant pot on Sauté mode, add the oil, heat it up, add the garlic, ginger and the onion and sauté for 5 minutes. Add the rest of the ingredients, put the lid on and cook on High for 15 minutes. Release the pressure naturally for 10 minutes, divide everything between plates and serve.

Nutrition: calories 188, fat 7.7, fiber 10.9, carbs 27.5, protein 7.6

Turmeric Artichokes
Preparation time: 5 minutes | Cooking time: 15 minutes | Servings: 4

Ingredients:
- 10 ounces canned artichoke hearts, drained and halved
- A pinch of salt and black pepper
- ¼ cup chicken stock
- 2 tablespoons ghee, melted
- 1 teaspoon turmeric powder
- ½ teaspoon cumin, ground
- ½ teaspoon fenugreek leaves, dried

Directions:
Set the instant pot on Sauté mode, add the ghee, heat it up, add the artichokes and sauté for 2 minutes. Add the rest of the ingredients, put the lid on and cook on High for 13 minutes. Release the pressure fast for 5 minutes, divide the artichokes mix between plates and serve.

Nutrition: calories 94, fat 6.7, fiber 4.1, carbs 8.3, protein 2.6

Creamy Artichokes and Coconut

Preparation time: 5 minutes | Cooking time: 20 minutes | Servings: 4

Ingredients:
- 4 artichokes, trimmed and halved
- 1 cup coconut cream
- ½ teaspoon turmeric powder
- ½ teaspoon cumin, ground
- ½ teaspoon sweet paprika
- 1 teaspoon onion powder

Directions:

In your instant pot, combine the artichokes with the cream, turmeric and the other ingredients, put the lid on and cook on High for 20 minutes. Release the pressure fast for 5 minutes, divide the mix between plates and serve.

Nutrition: calories 219, fat 14.7, fiber 10.3, carbs 21.3, protein 6.8

Spiced Asparagus

Preparation time: 5 minutes | Cooking time: 12 minutes | Servings: 4

Ingredients:
- 1 bunch asparagus, trimmed and halved
- ½ teaspoon garam masala
- ½ teaspoon nutmeg, ground
- ½ teaspoon turmeric powder
- 1 bay leaf
- 1 cup chicken stock
- 1 tablespoon chili powder
- 2 garlic cloves, chopped

Directions:

In your instant pot, combine the asparagus with the rest of the ingredients, put the lid on and cook on High for 12 minutes. Release the pressure fast for 5 minutes, divide the mix between plates and serve.

Nutrition: calories 17, fat 0.6, fiber 1.2, carbs 2.8, protein 1

Cinnamon Artichokes and Rice

Preparation time: 5 minutes | Cooking time: 20 minutes | Servings: 4

Ingredients:
- 1 cup canned artichoke hearts, drained and quartered
- 2 tablespoons ghee, melted
- 1 yellow onion, chopped
- ½ cup basmati rice
- 1 cup chicken stock
- ½ teaspoon turmeric powder
- ½ teaspoon garam masala
- A pinch of salt and black pepper
- 1 tablespoon smoked paprika
- 1 tablespoon cilantro, chopped

Directions:

Set the instant pot on Sauté mode, add the ghee, heat it up, add the onion, turmeric, garam masala and the paprika, stir and sauté for 5 minutes. Add the rest of the ingredients, toss, put the lid on and cook on High for 15 minutes. Release the pressure fast for 5 minutes, divide the mix between plates and serve.

Nutrition: calories 217, fat 7.1, fiber 8.2, carbs 35.2, protein 6.4

Almond Asparagus Mix

Preparation time: 5 minutes | Cooking time: 10 minutes | Servings: 4

Ingredients:

- 1 tablespoon vegetable oil
- ½ teaspoon pepper flakes, crushed
- 1 bunch asparagus, trimmed and halved
- 2 tablespoons almonds, chopped
- ½ tablespoon chili powder
- ½ teaspoon garam masala
- ½ teaspoon coriander, ground
- A pinch of salt and black pepper
- 1 cup chicken stock

Directions:

Set the instant pot on Sauté mode, add the oil, heat it up, add the pepper flakes, almonds, chili powder, garam masala and the coriander, stir and cook for 2 minutes. Add the remaining ingredients, toss, put the lid on and cook on High for 8 minutes. Release the pressure fast for 5 minutes, divide the asparagus between plates and serve.

Nutrition: calories 56, fat 5.2, fiber 1, carbs 2, protein 1.3

Ginger Asparagus

Preparation time: 5 minutes | Cooking time: 10 minutes | Servings: 4

Ingredients:

- 1 bunch asparagus, trimmed and halved
- 2 tablespoons vegetable oil
- 1 tablespoon ginger, grated
- ½ teaspoon chili powder
- 1 teaspoon coriander, ground
- A pinch of salt and black pepper
- 1 cup chicken stock

Directions:

In your instant pot, mix the asparagus with the oil, ginger and the rest of the ingredients, put the lid on and cook on High for 10 minutes. Release the pressure fast for 5 minutes, divide everything between plates and serve.

Nutrition: calories 72, fat 7.1, fiber 0.6, carbs 2, protein 0.7

Spiced Green Beans

Preparation time: 10 minutes | Cooking time: 15 minutes | Servings: 4

Ingredients:
- 1 pound green beans, trimmed and halved
- 1 tablespoon vegetable oil
- A pinch of salt and black pepper
- 1 teaspoon sweet paprika
- 1 teaspoon turmeric powder
- 1 teaspoon cinnamon powder
- ½ teaspoon garam masala
- 1 cup chicken stock

Directions:
In your instant pot, combine the green beans with the oil, salt, pepper and the other ingredients, toss, put the lid on and cook on High for 15 minutes. Release the pressure naturally for 10 minutes, divide the mix between plates and serve.

Nutrition: calories 71, fat 3.8, fiber 4.2, carbs 9, protein 2.4

Green Beans and Orange Sauce

Preparation time: 5 minutes | Cooking time: 15 minutes | Servings: 4

Ingredients:
- 1 pound green beans, trimmed and halved
- 2 teaspoons orange zest, grated
- 1 cup orange juice
- 1 teaspoon chili powder
- ½ teaspoon garam masala
- ½ teaspoon turmeric powder
- ½ teaspoon dried fenugreek leaves
- A pinch of salt and black pepper

Directions:
In your instant pot, combine the green beans with the orange zest and the other ingredients, put the lid on and cook on High for 15 minutes. Release the pressure fast for 5 minutes, divide the mix between plates and serve.

Nutrition: calories 69, fat 0.4, fiber 4.5, carbs 15.6, protein 2.7

Coconut Beets

Preparation time: 10 minutes | Cooking time: 20 minutes | Servings: 4

Ingredients:
- 1 cup chicken stock
- 4 beets, peeled and roughly cubed
- 2 shallots, chopped
- ½ cup coconut cream
- 1 teaspoon chili powder
- 1 teaspoon turmeric powder
- A pinch of salt and black pepper
- 1 tablespoon dill, chopped

Directions:
In your instant pot, combine the beets with the stock, shallots and the rest of the ingredients, put the lid on and cook on High for 20 minutes. Release the pressure naturally for 10 minutes, divide everything between plates and serve.

Nutrition: calories 125, fat 7.7, fiber 3.1, carbs 13.8, protein 3

Hot Brussels Sprouts

Preparation time: 10 minutes | Cooking time: 20 minutes | Servings: 4

Ingredients:
- 1 pound Brussels sprouts, trimmed and halved
- 1 cup heavy cream
- 4 garlic cloves, minced
- 1 tablespoon chili powder
- 1 tablespoon sweet paprika
- 5 curry leaves, chopped
- ½ teaspoon garam masala
- A pinch of salt and black pepper
- 1 tablespoon cilantro, chopped

Directions:
In your instant pot, mix the Brussels sprouts with the cream, garlic and the rest of the ingredients, put the lid on and cook on High for 20 minutes. Release the pressure naturally for 10 minutes, divide the mix between plates and serve.

Nutrition: calories 176, fat 12.4, fiber 6.5, carbs 15.6, protein 5.5

Walnuts Bell Peppers Mix

Preparation time: 10 minutes | Cooking time: 20 minutes | Servings: 4

Ingredients:
- 1 pound red bell peppers, cut into wedges
- ½ cup coconut cream
- ½ teaspoon dry mango powder
- ½ teaspoon allspice, ground
- ½ teaspoon turmeric powder
- 1 bay leaf
- 1 tablespoon walnuts, chopped

Directions:
In your instant pot, mix the bell peppers with the cream, mango powder and the rest of the ingredients, put the lid on and cook on High for 20 minutes. Release the pressure naturally for 10 minutes, divide the mix into bowls and serve.

Nutrition: calories 93, fat 8.4, fiber 1.3, carbs 4.6, protein 1.5

Minty Peppers

Preparation time: 10 minutes | Cooking time: 20 minutes | Servings: 4

Ingredients:
- 1 red bell peppers, cut into wedges
- 1 tablespoon chili powder
- ½ teaspoon garam masala
- ½ teaspoon nutmeg, ground
- ¼ cup veggie stock
- 3 garlic cloves, minced
- 1 tablespoon mint, chopped
- 1 tablespoon cilantro, chopped

Directions:
In your instant pot, combine the bell peppers with the chili powder, garam masala and the rest of the ingredients, put the lid on and cook on High for 20 minutes. Release the pressure naturally for 10 minutes, divide the mix between plates and serve.

Nutrition: calories 22, fat 0.6, fiber 1.3, carbs 4.4, protein 0.8

Bell Peppers and Potatoes Mix

Preparation time: 10 minutes | Cooking time: 20 minutes | Servings: 4

Ingredients:
- 1 pound mixed bell peppers, cut into wedges
- 2 sweet potatoes, peeled and cut into wedges
- ½ cup chicken stock
- 1 teaspoon chili powder
- ½ teaspoon garam masala
- ½ teaspoon coriander, ground
- ½ teaspoon cumin, ground
- 1 tablespoon olive oil

Directions:
In your instant pot, combine the bell peppers with the potatoes, the stock and the rest of the ingredients, put the lid on and cook on High for 20 minutes. Release the pressure naturally for 10 minutes, divide the mix between plates and serve.

Nutrition: calories 132, fat 4, fiber 3.7, carbs 23.7, protein 1.7

Coriander Peppers Mix

Preparation time: 5 minutes | Cooking time: 20 minutes | Servings: 4

Ingredients:
- 1 pound mixed bell peppers, cut into wedges
- 1 teaspoon coriander, ground
- ½ teaspoon sweet paprika
- ½ teaspoon chana masala
- ½ teaspoon fenugreek leaves, dried
- 1 teaspoon mustard seeds
- 1 teaspoon chili powder
- ½ teaspoon cumin, ground
- Salt and black pepper to the taste
- 1 cup heavy cream

Directions:
In your instant pot, combine the bell peppers with the coriander, mustard seeds and the rest of the ingredients, put the lid on and cook on High for 20 minutes. Release the pressure naturally for 5 minutes, divide the mix between plates and serve.

Nutrition: calories 122, fat 11.7, fiber 1, carbs 4.3, protein 1.4

Beets with Yogurt

Preparation time: 10 minutes | Cooking time: 25 minutes | Servings: 4

Ingredients:
- 1 pound beets, peeled and cubed
- Juice of 1 lime
- 1 cup yogurt
- ½ teaspoon turmeric powder
- ½ teaspoon dried mango powder
- ½ teaspoon fenugreek leaves, dried
- A pinch of salt and black pepper

Directions:
In your instant pot, combine the beets with the lime juice and the rest of the ingredients, put the lid on and cook on High for 25 minutes. Release the pressure naturally for 10 minutes, divide the mix between plates and serve.

Nutrition: calories 99, fat 1, fiber 2.5, carbs 17, protein 5.6

Dill Potatoes

Preparation time: 10 minutes | Cooking time: 20 minutes | Servings: 4

Ingredients:
- 2 pounds sweet potatoes, peeled and cut into wedges
- 1 cup yogurt
- 1 tablespoon dill, chopped
- 1 teaspoon turmeric powder
- ½ teaspoon garam masala
- ½ teaspoon chili powder
- A pinch of salt and black pepper

Directions:
In your instant pot, mix the potatoes with the yogurt, dill and the rest of the ingredients, toss, put the lid on and cook on High for 20 minutes. Release the pressure naturally for 10 minutes, divide the mix between plates and serve.

Nutrition: calories 316, fat 1.3, fiber 9.7, carbs 68.5, protein 7.2

Creamy Potatoes

Preparation time: 10 minutes | Cooking time: 30 minutes | Servings: 4

Ingredients:
- 1 pound gold potatoes, peeled and roughly cubed
- 1 tablespoon coconut oil, melted
- 2 shallots, chopped
- ½ teaspoon cumin, ground
- ½ teaspoon coriander, ground
- ½ teaspoon chili powder
- ½ teaspoon turmeric powder
- 1 cup coconut cream
- A pinch of salt and black pepper
- 2 tablespoons cilantro, chopped

Directions:
Set the instant pot on Sauté mode, add the oil, heat it up, add the shallots, stir and sauté for 5 minutes. Add the potatoes and the rest of the ingredients, put the lid on and cook on High for 25 minutes. Release the pressure naturally for 10 minutes, divide the mix between plates and serve.

Nutrition: calories 250, fat 17.9, fiber 4.6, carbs 22.8, protein 3.1

Garlic Potato Masala

Preparation time: 10 minutes | Cooking time: 25 minutes | Servings: 4

Ingredients:
- 1 pound gold potatoes, peeled and roughly cubed
- 1 teaspoon garam masala
- ½ teaspoon turmeric powder
- ½ teaspoon coriander, ground
- 1 tablespoon ghee, melted
- 4 garlic cloves, minced
- 1 cup beef stock
- A pinch of salt and black pepper
- 1 tablespoon coriander, chopped

Directions:
Set your instant pot on Sauté mode, add the ghee, heat it up, add the garlic, garam masala, turmeric and the ground coriander, stir and cook for 5 minutes. Add the potatoes and the rest of the ingredients, put the lid on and cook on High for 20 minutes more. Release the pressure naturally for 10 minutes, divide the mix between plates and serve.

Nutrition: calories 113, fat 3.4, fiber 3.2, carbs 19.4, protein 2.4

Turmeric Zucchini

Preparation time: 10 minutes | *Cooking time:* 20 minutes | *Servings:* 4

Ingredients:
- 2 tablespoons ghee, melted
- 1 teaspoon turmeric powder
- ½ teaspoon garam masala
- ½ teaspoon dried fenugreek leaves
- 4 zucchinis, sliced
- 1 red onion, chopped
- 1 cup chicken stock
- A pinch of salt and black pepper
- 1 tablespoon dill, chopped

Directions:
Set the instant pot on Sauté mode, add the ghee, heat it up, add the onion, stir and sauté for 5 minutes. Add the zucchinis and the rest of the ingredients, put the lid on and cook on High for 15 minutes. Release the pressure naturally for 10 minutes, divide the mix between plates and serve.

Nutrition: calories 106, fat 7, fiber 3.1, carbs 10.4, protein 3.2

Cayenne Zucchinis Mix

Preparation time: 10 minutes | *Cooking time:* 15 minutes | *Servings:* 4

Ingredients:
- 4 zucchinis, sliced
- ½ teaspoon turmeric powder
- 1 teaspoon chili powder
- ¼ cup chicken stock
- 1 tablespoon chili powder
- ½ teaspoon cayenne pepper
- ½ teaspoon garam masala

Directions:
In your instant pot, mix the zucchinis with the turmeric, the stock and the rest of the ingredients, put the lid on and cook on High for 15 minutes. Release the pressure naturally for 10 minutes, divide the mix between plates and serve.

Nutrition: calories 42, fat 0.9, fiber 3.1, carbs 8.3, protein 2.8

Potato and Zucchini Masala

Preparation time: 10 minutes | Cooking time: 20 minutes | Servings: 4

Ingredients:
- 2 sweet potatoes, peeled and roughly cubed
- 2 zucchinis, roughly cubed
- 2 tablespoons ghee, melted
- 1 teaspoon garam masala
- ½ teaspoon turmeric powder
- ½ teaspoon cumin, ground
- ½ teaspoon nutmeg, ground
- A pinch of salt and black pepper
- ½ cup chicken stock
- 1 tablespoon parsley, chopped

Directions:
In your instant pot, mix the potatoes with the zucchinis, the melted ghee and the rest of the ingredients, put the lid on and cook on High for 20 minutes. Release the pressure naturally for 10 minutes, divide the mix between plates and serve.

Nutrition: calories 165, fat 7, fiber 4.4, carbs 24.8, protein 2.6

Spinach Mix

Preparation time: 5 minutes | Cooking time: 12 minutes | Servings: 4

Ingredients:
- 1 pound spinach leaves
- 1 tablespoon coconut oil, melted
- 2 shallots, chopped
- ½ teaspoon turmeric powder
- ½ teaspoon garam masala
- ½ teaspoon coriander, ground
- 1 tablespoon tomato sauce
- A pinch of salt and black pepper
- ¼ cup chicken stock
- 1 tablespoon parsley, chopped

Directions:
Set the instant pot on Sauté mode, add the oil, heat it up, add the shallots, stir and sauté for 2 minutes. Add the spinach, turmeric and the other ingredients, toss, put the lid on and cook on High for 10 minutes. Release the pressure naturally for 5 minutes, divide the mix between plates and serve.

Nutrition: calories 62, fat 3.9, fiber 2.7, carbs 5.5, protein 3.5

Spiced Okra

Preparation time: 10 minutes | Cooking time: 20 minutes | Servings: 4

Ingredients:
- 1 pound okra, trimmed
- ½ cup chicken stock
- 1 tablespoon ghee, melted
- 1 red onion, chopped
- ½ teaspoon nutmeg, ground
- ½ teaspoon garam masala
- ½ teaspoon chili powder
- ½ teaspoon coriander, ground
- A pinch of salt and black pepper
- 1 tablespoon sweet paprika
- 2 tablespoon cilantro, chopped

Directions:
Set the instant pot on Sauté mode, add the ghee, heat it up, add the onion and sauté for 4 minutes. Add the okra, the nutmeg and the rest of the ingredients, put the lid on and cook on High for 16 minutes. Release the pressure naturally for 10 minutes, divide the mix between plates and serve.

Nutrition: calories 93, fat 3.9, fiber 5.1, carbs 12.4, protein 2.9

Turmeric Broccoli and Onions

Preparation time: 10 minutes | Cooking time: 20 minutes | Servings: 4

Ingredients:
- 1 pound broccoli florets
- 1 tablespoon sunflower oil
- 1 yellow onion, chopped
- 2 spring onions, chopped
- 1 teaspoon turmeric powder
- ½ teaspoon chili powder
- ½ teaspoon garam masala
- 2 garlic cloves, minced
- 1 cup chicken stock
- A pinch of salt and black pepper
- 1 tablespoon coriander, chopped

Directions:
Set the instant pot on Sauté mode, add the oil, heat it up, add the onion and spring onions, stir and sauté for 5 minutes. Add the broccoli, turmeric and the rest of the ingredients except the dill, put the lid on and cook on High for 15 minutes. Release the pressure naturally for 10 minutes, divide the mix between plates and serve.

Nutrition: calories 91, fat 4.2, fiber 4, carbs 11.9, protein 4

Nutmeg Cauliflower Mix

Preparation time: 10 minutes | Cooking time: 20 minutes | Servings: 4

Ingredients:
- 1 pound cauliflower florets
- 1 teaspoon nutmeg, ground
- ½ teaspoon garam masala
- 1 cup coconut cream
- 1 tablespoon chili powder
- A pinch of salt and black pepper
- 1 tablespoon cilantro, chopped

Directions:
In your instant pot, combine the cauliflower with the nutmeg, garam masala and the other ingredients, toss, put the lid on and cook on High for 20 minutes. Release the pressure naturally for 10 minutes, divide the mix between plates and serve.

Nutrition: calories 122, fat 2.5, fiber4. 2, carbs 5, protein 3.56

Hot Spinach and Potato Mix

Preparation time: 10 minutes | Cooking time: 20 minutes | Servings: 4

Ingredients:
- 1 pound gold potatoes, peeled and roughly cubed
- 1 cup baby spinach
- ½ cup chicken stock
- 1 teaspoon turmeric powder
- 1 teaspoon cumin, ground
- ½ teaspoon hot paprika
- 1 teaspoon chili powder
- A pinch of salt and black pepper
- 1 tablespoon dill, chopped

Directions:
In your instant pot, mix the potatoes with the spinach, the stock and the rest of the ingredients, put the lid on and cook on High for 20 minutes. Release the pressure naturally for 10 minutes, divide the mix between plates and serve.

Nutrition: calories 130, fat 7.2, fiber 2, carbs 4, protein 4.6

Cinnamon Potato Mix

Preparation time: 10 minutes | Cooking time: 20 minutes | Servings: 4

Ingredients:
- 1 yellow onion, chopped
- 2 tablespoons vegetable oil
- 3 garlic cloves, minced
- 2 pounds gold potatoes, peeled and cubed
- 1 tablespoon cinnamon powder
- ½ teaspoon garam masala
- ½ teaspoon dried mango powder
- A pinch of salt and black pepper
- 1 cup chicken stock
- 1 tablespoon cilantro, chopped

Directions:
Set the instant pot on Sauté mode, add the oil, heat it up, add the onion, garlic, garam masala and mango powder, stir and sauté for 5 minutes. Add the potatoes and the rest of the ingredients, put the lid on and cook on High for 15 minutes. Release the pressure naturally for 10 minutes, divide the mix between plates and serve.

Nutrition: calories 210, fat 5.2, fiber 2, carbs 7.5, protein 4.7

Coconut Fennel Mix

Preparation time: 10 minutes | Cooking time: 20 minutes | Servings: 4

Ingredients:
- 2 fennel bulbs, trimmed and sliced
- 2 tablespoons ghee, melted
- ½ cup coconut, shredded
- 1 cup coconut cream
- A pinch of salt and black pepper
- 1 teaspoon garam masala
- ½ teaspoon turmeric powder
- 1 tablespoon dill, chopped

Directions:
Set the instant pot on Sauté mode, add the ghee, heat it up, add the fennel and the coconut and cook for 5 minutes. Add the rest of the ingredients, put the lid on and cook on High for 15 minutes. Release the pressure naturally for 10 minutes, divide the mix between plates and serve.

Nutrition: calories 114, fat 4.2, fiber 2, carbs 4.4, protein 4

Masala Endives

Preparation time: 10 minutes | Cooking time: 15 minutes | Servings: 4

Ingredients:
- 4 endives, trimmed and halved
- 1 tablespoon garam masala
- 1 cup chicken stock
- 1 teaspoon chili powder
- 4 curry leaves, chopped
- A pinch of salt and black pepper
- ½ teaspoon nutmeg, ground

Directions:
In your instant pot, combine the endives with the garam masala, the stock and the rest of the ingredients, put the lid on and cook on High for 15 minutes. Release the pressure naturally for 10 minutes, divide the mix between plates and serve.

Nutrition: calories 144, fat 3.2, fiber 1, carbs 5.3, protein 4

Spinach and Okra Mix

Preparation time: 5 minutes | Cooking time: 20 minutes | Servings: 4

Ingredients:
- 1 cup baby spinach
- 2 cups okra, trimmed
- 1 cup chicken stock
- 1 tablespoon sweet paprika
- 1 tablespoon lemon juice
- 1 tablespoon lime juice
- A pinch of salt and black pepper
- 1 teaspoon turmeric powder
- ½ teaspoon cumin, ground
- 2 tablespoons parsley, chopped

Directions:
In your instant pot, mix the okra with the spinach, the stock and the rest of the ingredients, put the lid on and cook on High for 20 minutes. Release the pressure fast for 5 minutes, divide the mix between plates and serve.

Nutrition: calories 171, fat 3.1, fiber 4.1, carbs 8.4, protein 3.5

Creamy Potato and Apples Mix

Preparation time: 10 minutes | Cooking time: 20 minutes | Servings: 4

Ingredients:
- 2 sweet potatoes, peeled and cut into wedges
- 2 green apples, peeled, cored and cut into wedges
- 1 tablespoon chili powder
- 1 teaspoon coriander, ground
- 1 teaspoon mustard seeds
- 1 teaspoon cumin, ground
- 2 cups coconut cream
- A pinch of salt and black pepper
- 1 tablespoon cilantro, chopped

Directions:
In your instant pot, combine the potatoes with the apples, chili powder and the rest of the ingredients, toss, put the lid on and cook on High for 20 minutes. Release the pressure naturally for 10 minutes, divide the mix between plates and serve.

Nutrition: calories 200, fat 7, fiber 3.2, carbs 11.4, protein 6.6

Eggplant Masala

Preparation time: 5 minutes | Cooking time: 20 minutes | Servings: 4

Ingredients:
- 1 pound eggplant, roughly cubed
- 1 yellow onion, chopped
- 2 garlic cloves, minced
- 1 tablespoon vegetable oil
- A pinch of salt and black pepper
- 1 tablespoon sweet paprika
- 1 teaspoon cumin, ground
- 1 teaspoon garam masala
- 2 black peppercorns, crushed
- 1 teaspoon mustard seeds
- 1 teaspoon turmeric powder
- 1 cup tomato sauce

Directions:
Set the instant pot on Sauté mode, add the oil, heat it up, add the onion, garlic, cumin, garam masala, peppercorns and the mustard seeds, stir and cook for 5 minutes. Add the eggplant and the rest of the ingredients, put the lid on and cook on High for 15 minutes. Release the pressure fast for 5 minutes, divide the mix between plates and serve.

Nutrition: calories 99, fat 4.4, fiber 6.5, carbs 14.9, protein 2.9

Spiced Eggplant Mix
Preparation time: 10 minutes | Cooking time: 12 minutes | Servings: 4

Ingredients:
- 1 pound eggplant, cubed
- 1 teaspoon cumin, ground
- 1 teaspoon dried fenugreek leaves
- 4 curry leaves, chopped
- 1 teaspoon turmeric powder
- 1 teaspoon dried mango powder
- 1 teaspoon nutmeg, ground
- 1 tablespoon canola oil
- 1 red onion, chopped
- 1 cup chicken stock
- 1 teaspoon chili powder
- A pinch of salt and black pepper

Directions:
Set the instant pot on Sauté mode, add the oil, heat it up, add the onion, cumin, fenugreek, curry leaves, turmeric, mango powder and the nutmeg, stir and cook for 2 minutes. Add the eggplant and the rest of the ingredients, put the lid on and cook on High for 10 minutes. Release the pressure naturally for 10 minutes, divide the mix between plates and serve.

Nutrition: calories 105, fat 3.5, fiber 3.2, carbs 8.3, protein 2.4

Lime Zucchinis and Eggplant Mix
Preparation time: 10 minutes | Cooking time: 20 minutes | Servings: 4

Ingredients:
- 1 pound eggplant, roughly cubed
- 2 zucchinis, sliced
- 2 tablespoons sweet paprika
- 1 teaspoon mustard seeds
- 2 black peppercorns, crushed
- 1 teaspoon turmeric powder
- 1 teaspoon coriander, ground
- A pinch of salt and black pepper
- ½ cup chicken stock
- ¼ cup lime juice
- 1 tablespoon lime zest, grated
- 1 tablespoon cilantro, chopped

Directions:
In your instant pot, mix the eggplants with the zucchinis and the rest of the ingredients except the cilantro, put the lid on and cook on High for 20 minutes. Release the pressure naturally for 10 minutes, divide the mix between plates, sprinkle the cilantro on top and serve.

Nutrition: calories 128, fat 3.3, fiber 1.2, carbs 9.4, protein 2.5

Coconut Eggplants

Preparation time: 10 minutes | Cooking time: 15 minutes | Servings: 4

Ingredients:
- 2 eggplants, roughly cubed
- 1 cup coconut, shredded
- 1 cup coconut cream
- 2 tablespoons lime juice
- 1 bunch coriander, chopped
- ½ cup chicken stock
- 1 tablespoon ginger, grated

Directions:
In your instant pot, combine the eggplants with the coconut, the cream and the rest of the ingredients, put the lid on and cook on High for 15 minutes. Release the pressure naturally for 10 minutes, divide the mix between plates and serve.

Nutrition: calories 126, fat 5.4, fiber 2, carbs 11.4, protein 2.6

Coconut Tomatoes

Preparation time: 10 minutes | Cooking time: 15 minutes | Servings: 4

Ingredients:
- 1 pound cherry tomatoes, halved
- 2 garlic cloves, chopped
- 2 spring onions, chopped
- 1 tablespoon vegetable oil
- 1 teaspoon turmeric powder
- 1 teaspoon garam masala
- ½ cup coconut, shredded
- 1 red chili pepper, chopped
- ¾ cup veggie stock
- 1 tablespoon cilantro, chopped

Directions:
Set your instant pot on Sauté mode, add the oil, heat it up, add the garlic, spring onions, the chili and the coconut, stir and cook for 3 minutes. Add the tomatoes and the rest of the ingredients, put the lid on and cook on High for 12 minutes. Release the pressure naturally for 10 minutes, divide the mix between plates and serve.

Nutrition: calories 136, fat 3.4, fiber 2, carbs 9.4, protein 2.7

Zucchini and Cauliflower Mix

Preparation time: 10 minutes | Cooking time: 15 minutes | Servings: 4

Ingredients:

- cup cauliflower florets
- 1 zucchini, roughly cubed
- 1 red onion, chopped
- 1 cup chicken stock
- 1 tablespoon vegetable oil
- 1 teaspoon chili powder
- ½ teaspoon turmeric powder
- ½ teaspoon garam masala
- 1 teaspoon hot paprika
- A pinch of salt and black pepper
- ½ teaspoon coriander, ground

Directions:

Set your instant pot on Sauté mode, add the oil, heat it up, add the onion, chili powder, turmeric, garam masala and the paprika, stir and cook for 2 minutes. Add the cauliflower and the rest of the ingredients, put the lid on and cook on High for 13 minutes. Release the pressure naturally for 10 minutes, divide the mix into bowls and serve.

Nutrition: calories 61, fat 3.8, fiber 2.1, carbs 6.3, protein 1.7

Turmeric Kale

Preparation time: 5 minutes | Cooking time: 15 minutes | Servings: 4

Ingredients:

- 3 garlic cloves, chopped
- 1 tablespoon coconut oil, melted
- 1 teaspoon turmeric powder
- ½ teaspoon cumin, ground
- ½ teaspoon dried mango powder
- 1 pound kale, trimmed
- 1 tablespoon lime zest, grated
- 1 tablespoon lime juice
- ½ cup chicken stock

Directions:

Set the instant pot on Sauté mode, add the oil, heat it up, add the garlic, turmeric, cumin and mango powder, stir and sauté for 2 minutes. Add the rest of the ingredients, put the lid on and cook on High for 13 minutes. Release the pressure fast for 5 minutes, divide the mix between plates and serve.

Nutrition: calories 109, fat 4.4, fiber 2, carbs 5.3, protein 1.2

Cocoa Zucchinis and Peppers

Preparation time: 10 minutes | Cooking time: 20 minutes | Servings: 6

Ingredients:
- 1 pound zucchinis, sliced
- 1 pound red bell peppers, cut into strips
- 1 yellow onion, chopped
- 1 tablespoon vegetable oil
- 1 tablespoon cocoa powder
- ½ teaspoon turmeric powder
- ½ teaspoon garam masala
- ½ teaspoon chili powder
- 1 cup chicken stock
- 4 garlic cloves, chopped
- A pinch of salt and black pepper
- ¼ teaspoon red pepper flakes, crushed

Directions:
Set the instant pot on Sauté mode, add the oil, heat it up, add the onion, cocoa powder, turmeric, garam masala and chili powder, stir and cook for 5 minutes. Add the rest of the ingredients, toss, put the lid on and cook on High for 15 minutes. Release the pressure naturally for 10 minutes, divide the mix into bowls and serve.

Nutrition: calories 119, fat 4.2, fiber 2, carbs 6.4, protein 1.5

Orange Zucchinis

Preparation time: 10 minutes | Cooking time: 20 minutes | Servings: 4

Ingredients:
- A pinch of salt and black pepper
- ½ teaspoon cayenne pepper
- 2 zucchinis, sliced
- 1 cup orange juice
- 1 red onion, chopped
- 1 tablespoon vegetable oil
- 1 teaspoon turmeric powder
- ½ teaspoon garam masala
- ½ teaspoon cumin, ground
- 1 teaspoon chili powder

Directions:
Set the instant pot on Sauté mode, add the oil, heat it up, add the onion, the turmeric, garam masala, cumin and chili powder and sauté for 5 minutes. Add the rest of the ingredients, put the lid on and cook on High for 15 minutes. Release the pressure naturally for 10 minutes, stir the mix, divide it between plates and serve.

Nutrition: calories 91, fat 4, fiber 2.2, carbs 13.3, protein 2.1

Tomatoes and Citrus Rice

Preparation time: 10 minutes | Cooking time: 20 minutes | Servings: 4

Ingredients:
- 1 cup basmati rice
- 2 cups chicken stock
- 2 garlic cloves, minced
- 2 cups cherry tomatoes, halved
- 1 tablespoon orange juice
- 1 tablespoon orange zest, grated
- 2 tablespoon vegetable oil
- 1 yellow onion, chopped
- 1 teaspoon cumin, ground
- ½ teaspoon turmeric powder
- ½ teaspoon garam masala
- 2 tablespoons cilantro, chopped

Directions:
Set your instant pot on Sauté mode, add the oil, heat it up, add the onion, garlic and the tomatoes and cook for 5 minutes. Add rest of the ingredients, put the lid on and cook on High for 15 minutes. Release the pressure naturally for 10 minutes, divide the mix between plates and serve.

Nutrition: calories 200, fat 8.1, fiber 4, carbs 11.6, protein 3.7

Allspice Zucchini Mix

Preparation time: 5 minutes | Cooking time: 20 minutes | Servings: 4

Ingredients:
- 2 tablespoons ghee, melted
- 1 pound zucchinis, roughly cubed
- 1 yellow onion, chopped
- 2 garlic cloves, minced
- 1 teaspoon turmeric powder
- ½ teaspoon garam masala
- ½ teaspoon nutmeg, ground
- ½ teaspoon ginger, grated
- ½ teaspoon allspice, ground

Directions:
Set your instant pot on Sauté mode, add the ghee, heat it up, add onion and garlic, stir and sauté for 5 minutes. Add the zucchinis and the rest of the ingredients, toss, put the lid on and cook on High for 15 minutes. Release the pressure fast for 5 minutes, divide the mix between plates and serve.

Nutrition: calories 110, fat 4.7, fiber 2.3, carbs 7.8, protein 1.6

Spiced Zucchinis and Carrots

Preparation time: 5 minutes | Cooking time: 20 minutes | Servings: 4

Ingredients:
- 1 pound carrots, sliced
- 2 zucchinis, sliced
- 1 cup chicken stock
- ½ teaspoon dried mango powder
- 1 teaspoon chili powder
- 1 teaspoon sweet paprika
- ½ teaspoon ginger, grated
- 3 garlic cloves, minced
- 2 tablespoons ghee, melted
- 1 yellow onion, chopped
- 1 teaspoon cardamom, ground
- A pinch of salt and black pepper

Directions:
Set the instant pot on sauté mode, add the ghee, heat it up, add the onion, garlic, mango powder, chili powder and the paprika, and sauté for 5 minutes. Add the remaining ingredients, put the lid on and cook on High for 15 minutes. Release the pressure fast for 5 minutes, stir the mix, divide between plates and serve.

Nutrition: calories 100, fat 5.8, fiber 2.4, carbs 8.6, protein 1.8

Cumin Potato and Carrots Mix

Preparation time: 10 minutes | Cooking time: 20 minutes | Servings: 4

Ingredients:
- 2 spring onions, chopped
- 2 carrots, grated
- 1 pound gold potatoes, peeled and cubed
- A pinch of salt and black pepper
- 1 teaspoon chili powder
- ½ teaspoon garam masala
- 1 teaspoon cumin, ground
- ¼ cup coconut cream

Directions:
In your instant pot, combine the potatoes with the carrots and the other ingredients, toss, put the lid on and cook on High for 20 minutes. Release the pressure naturally for 10 minutes, divide the mix between plates and serve.

Nutrition: calories 129, fat 3.8, fiber 4.6, carbs 23.1, protein 2.4

Cardamom Beets
Preparation time: 10 minutes | Cooking time: 20 minutes | Servings: 4

Ingredients:
- 2 tablespoons sunflower oil
- 1 teaspoon cardamom, crushed
- 1 pound beets, peeled and roughly cubed
- ½ teaspoon chili powder
- 1 cup chicken stock
- 1 teaspoon turmeric powder
- ½ teaspoon garam masala
- A pinch of salt and black pepper
- ½ cup currants, chopped

Directions:
Set your instant pot on Sauté mode, add the oil, heat it up, add the currants, cardamom, chili powder, turmeric powder and garam masala, stir and cook for 5 minutes. Add the rest of the ingredients, stir, put the lid on and cook on High for 15 minutes. Release the pressure naturally for 10 minutes, divide the mix between plates and serve.

Nutrition: calories 127, fat 7.5, fiber 3.3, carbs 14.3, protein 2.4

Minty Tomatoes Mix
Preparation time: 10 minutes | Cooking time: 20 minutes | Servings: 4

Ingredients:
- 1 tablespoon sunflower oil
- 1 pound cherry tomatoes, halved
- 2 shallots, chopped
- 1 tablespoon lime zest, grated
- 1 teaspoon lime juice
- 1 teaspoon garam masala
- 1 teaspoon cumin, ground
- 1 teaspoon coriander, ground
- A pinch of salt and black pepper
- 1 cup chicken stock
- 2 tablespoons mint leaves, chopped

Directions:
Set the instant pot on Sauté mode, add the shallots, garam masala, cumin and coriander, stir and sauté for 5 minutes. Add the tomatoes and the rest of the ingredients, toss, put the lid on and cook on High for 15 minutes. Release the pressure naturally for 10 minutes, divide between plates and serve.

Nutrition: calories 110, fat 3.8, fiber 3.3, carbs 7.7, protein 1.8

Spinach with Broccoli

Preparation time: *10 minutes* | ***Cooking time:*** *20 minutes* | ***Servings:*** *4*

Ingredients:
- 2 garlic cloves, minced
- 2 tablespoons vegetable oil
- 1 cup baby spinach
- 1 yellow onion, chopped
- 1 cup broccoli florets
- 1 teaspoon red pepper flakes, crushed
- 1 teaspoon cumin, ground
- 1 teaspoon garam masala
- 1 teaspoon coriander, ground
- A pinch of salt and black pepper
- 2 tablespoons lemon juice

Directions:
Set your instant pot on sauté mode, add the oil, heat it up, add the onion, garlic, pepper flakes, cumin and garam masala, stir and sauté for 5 minutes. Add the rest of the ingredients, toss, put the lid on and cook on High for 15 minutes. Release the pressure naturally for 10 minutes, divide the mix between plates and serve.

Nutrition: calories 88, fat 7.2, fiber 1.6, carbs 5.5, protein 1.5

Beets and Onions Mix

Preparation time: *10 minutes* | ***Cooking time:*** *20 minutes* | ***Servings:*** *4*

Ingredients:
- 1 tablespoon sunflower oil
- 2 beets, peeled and roughly cubed
- 2 yellow onions, chopped
- 1 cup chicken stock
- 1 teaspoon garam masala
- 1 teaspoon chili powder
- ½ teaspoon fenugreek seeds
- 1 teaspoon mustard seeds
- 2 garlic cloves, minced
- 1 and ½ tablespoons thyme, chopped
- A pinch of salt and black pepper

Directions:
Set your instant pot on Sauté mode, add the oil, heat up, add the onions, garlic, garam masala, chili powder, fenugreek seeds and mustard seeds, stir and cook for 5 minutes. Add the rest of the ingredients, toss, put the lid on and cook on High for 15 minutes. Release the pressure naturally for 10 minutes, divide the mix between plates and serve.

Nutrition: calories 105, fat 4.6, fiber 3.4, carbs 7.6, protein 2.4

Basil Potato and Cream

Preparation time: 10 minutes | Cooking time: 20 minutes | Servings: 4

Ingredients:
- 1 cup heavy cream
- ½ cup yellow onion, chopped
- 2 tablespoons ghee, melted
- 4 potatoes, peeled and cut into wedges
- A pinch of salt and black pepper
- 1 teaspoon cumin, ground
- 4 curry leaves, chopped
- 1 teaspoon garam masala
- 1 teaspoon turmeric powder
- 1 tablespoon basil, chopped

Directions:
Set your instant pot on Sauté mode, add the ghee, heat it up, add the onion, cumin, curry leaves, garam masala and the turmeric, stir and sauté for 5 minutes. Add the potatoes, and the rest of the ingredients, toss, put the lid on and cook on High for 15 minutes. Release the pressure naturally for 10 minutes, divide the mix between plates and serve.

Nutrition: calories 323, fat 18.1, fiber 6.3, carbs 37.4, protein 4.8

Indian Instant Pot Dessert Recipes

Gajar Ka Halwa

Preparation time: 10 minutes | **Cooking time:** 15 minutes | **Servings:** 8

Ingredients:
- 2 pounds carrots, grated
- 2 cinnamon sticks
- 1 cup sugar
- 1 cup ghee, melted
- 1 cup condensed milk
- 1 tablespoon almonds, chopped
- 1 tablespoon pistachios, chopped

Directions:
In your instant pot, combine the carrots with the cinnamon and the other ingredients, toss, put the lid on and cook on High for 15 minutes. Release the pressure naturally for 10 minutes, divide the mix into bowls and serve.

Nutrition: calories 496, fat 29.4, fiber 3.2, carbs 57.7, protein 4.3

Aam Shrikhand

Preparation time: 10 minutes | *Cooking time:* 20 minutes | *Servings:* 4

Ingredients:
- 1 cup yogurt
- 1 teaspoon cardamom powder
- 1 mango, peeled and chopped
- ½ teaspoon saffron powder
- ¾ cup sugar
- ½ cup mango puree
- Juice of 1 lemon
- 1 tablespoon mint
- 2 teaspoons chaat masala

Directions:
In your instant pot, combine the yogurt with the cardamom, the mango and the other ingredients, toss, put the lid on and cook on High for 20 minutes. Release the pressure naturally for 10 minutes, blend the mix using an immersion blender, divide into bowls and serve.

Nutrition: calories 252, fat 1.3, fiber 2, carbs 58.3, protein 4.6

Payasam

Preparation time: 10 minutes | Cooking time: 30 minutes | Servings: 4

Ingredients:
- 1 cup white rice
- 2 cups milk
- 1 teaspoon cardamom powder
- 3 tablespoons sugar
- 1 tablespoon ghee, melted
- 1 tablespoon cashews, chopped
- 1 tablespoon raisins, chopped

Directions:
In your instant pot, combine the rice with the milk, cardamom and the other ingredients, toss, put the lid on and cook on Low for 30 minutes. Release the pressure naturally for 10 minutes, divide the mix into bowls and serve.

Nutrition: calories 312, fat 7, fiber 0.9, carbs 54.8, protein 7.8

Pistachio Phirni

Preparation time: 10 minutes | Cooking time: 20 minutes | Servings: 4

Ingredients:
- 2 cups milk
- 1 tablespoon pistachios, chopped
- 1 tablespoon gram rice flour
- 1 teaspoon cardamom powder
- 1 tablespoon sugar

Directions:
In your instant pot, combine the milk with the pistachios and the other ingredients, toss, put the lid on and cook on High for 20 minutes. Release the pressure naturally for 10 minutes, divide the mix into bowls, cool down completely and serve.

Nutrition: calories 88, fat 3, fiber 0.3, carbs 11.6, protein 4.4

Indian Kulfi

Preparation time: 10 minutes | Cooking time: 20 minutes | Servings: 4

Ingredients:
- 1 quart milk
- ½ teaspoon saffron powder
- ½ cup sugar
- 12 almonds, blanched and chopped
- 4 green cardamoms
- 2 tablespoons pistachios, chopped

Directions:
In your instant pot, combine the milk with the saffron and the other ingredients, toss, put the lid on and cook on High for 20 minutes. Release the pressure naturally for 10 minutes, divide the mix into moulds and freeze before serving.

Nutrition: calories 250, fat 7.8, fiber 0.9, carbs 39, protein 9.3

Rice Kheer

Preparation time: 10 minutes | Cooking time: 25 minutes | Servings: 4

Ingredients:
- ½ cup red rice vermicelli
- 1 tablespoon butter
- 2 and ½ cups milk
- 1 tablespoon almonds, chopped
- ¼ teaspoon cardamom powder
- ½ teaspoon saffron powder
- 3 tablespoons sugar

Directions:

In your instant pot, combine the rice vermicelli with the butter and the other ingredients, toss, put the lid on and cook on High for 25 minutes. Release the pressure naturally for 10 minutes, divide everything into bowls and serve.

Nutrition: calories 156, fat 6.3, fiber 0.5, carbs 20.7, protein 5.2

Mixed Fruits

Preparation time: 5 minutes | Cooking time: 10 minutes | Servings: 4

Ingredients:
- 1 quart milk
- 1 teaspoon saffron powder
- 1 teaspoon cardamom powder
- 1 tablespoon almonds, chopped
- ½ cup kiwi, peeled and cubed
- ½ cup grapes, halved
- ½ cup apples, peeled, cored and cubed
- ½ cup orange, peeled and cut into segments
- 2 tablespoons sugar

Directions:

In your instant pot, combine the milk with the saffron and the other ingredients, toss, put the lid on and cook on High for 10 minutes. Release the pressure fast for 5 minutes, divide the mix into bowls and serve cold.

Nutrition: calories 201, fat 6, fiber 2.3, carbs 30.5, protein 9

Gehun Ki Kheer

Preparation time: 10 minutes | Cooking time: 20 minutes | Servings: 4

Ingredients:
- 1 cup broken wheat
- 1 tablespoon ghee, melted
- 1 tablespoon raisins
- 2 cardamom pods
- 1 tablespoon sugar
- ½ cup gram cashew nut
- ½ quart milk

Directions:
In your instant pot, combine the wheat with the ghee and the other ingredients, stir, put the lid on and cook on High for 20 minutes. Release the pressure naturally for 10 minutes, divide the mix into bowls and serve.

Nutrition: calories 227, fat 15.2, fiber 0.6, carbs 16.3, protein 7.6

Ada Pradhaman

Preparation time: 10 minutes | Cooking time: 20 minutes | Servings: 4

Ingredients:
- 1 cup rice flat pasta
- 1 cup palm jaggery
- 2 cups coconut milk
- 1 teaspoon cardamom powder
- 1 tablespoon coconut, shredded
- 1 tablespoon cashews, chopped
- 1 tablespoon raisins
- 1 tablespoon ghee, melted

Directions:
In your instant pot, combine the rice with the jaggery and the other ingredients, toss, put the lid on and cook on High for 20 minutes. Release the pressure naturally for 10 minutes, divide the mix into bowls and serve.

Nutrition: calories 400, fat 34.7, fiber 4.3, carbs 22.9, protein 4.5

Pistachio Parfait

Preparation time: 10 minutes | Cooking time: 20 minutes | Servings: 4

Ingredients:
- 1 tablespoon pistachios, chopped
- 2 eggs, whisked
- 1 tablespoon sugar
- 2 cups double cream
- 1 cup raspberries
- 1 tablespoon lemon juice

Directions:
In your instant pot, combine the pistachios with the eggs, sugar and the other ingredients, toss, put the lid on and cook on High for 20 minutes. Release the pressure naturally for 10 minutes, divide the mix into bowls and serve cold.

Nutrition: calories 272, fat 25.1, fiber 2.1, carbs 8.8, protein 4.6

Saffron Zucchini Pudding

Preparation time: 10 minutes | Cooking time: 20 minutes | Servings: 4

Ingredients:
- 3 cups zucchinis, grated
- 1 cup caster sugar
- 2 eggs, whisked
- 2 tablespoons ghee, melted
- 1 cup milk
- ½ teaspoon saffron powder

Directions:
In your instant pot, combine the zucchinis with the sugar and the other ingredients, toss, put the lid on and cook on High for 20 minutes Release the pressure naturally for 10 minutes, divide the pudding into bowls and serve cold.

Nutrition: calories 252, fat 5.5, fiber 2, carb 11.6, protein 3.6

Turmeric Pear Bowls

Preparation time: 10 minutes | Cooking time: 20 minutes | Servings: 4

Ingredients:
- 2 tablespoons almonds, chopped
- 1 tablespoon raisins
- 1 teaspoon turmeric powder
- 1 teaspoon vanilla extract
- 2 cups pears, cored and cubed
- 1 cup coconut cream

Directions:
In your instant pot, combine the almonds with the pears and the other ingredients, toss, put the lid on and cook on High for 20 minutes. Release the pressure naturally for 10 minutes, divide the dessert into bowls and serve.

Nutrition: calories 220, fat 11.4, fiber 4.2, carbs 9.4, protein 2.4

Banana and Rice Pudding

Preparation time: 10 minutes | Cooking time: 30 minutes | Servings: 4

Ingredients:
- 2 egg, whisked
- 3 tablespoons sugar
- 2 tablespoons ghee, melted
- 1 cup white rice
- 2 and ½ cups milk
- 2 bananas, peeled and mashed
- 1 teaspoon saffron powder

Directions:
In your instant pot, mix the rice with the milk, the eggs and the other ingredients, whisk, put the lid on and cook on High for 30 minutes. Release the pressure naturally for 10 minutes, divide the pudding into bowls and serve.

Nutrition: calories 262, fat 11.7, fiber 5.2, carbs 14.5, protein 2.8

Turmeric Apples

Preparation time: 10 minutes | Cooking time: 15 minutes | Servings: 4

Ingredients:
- 2 teaspoons turmeric powder
- ½ teaspoon cinnamon powder
- 4 apples, cored and cut into chunks
- 2 tablespoons sugar
- ½ cup milk

Directions:
In your instant pot, mix the apples with the cinnamon, turmeric and the rest of the ingredients, put the lid on and cook on High for 15 minutes. Release the pressure naturally for 10 minutes, divide the mix into bowls and serve.

Nutrition: calories 220, fat 9.2, fiber 4.2, carbs 14.4, protein 3.6

Grapes Rice

Preparation time: 10 minutes | Cooking time: 25 minutes | Servings: 4

Ingredients:
- 1 cup grapes, halved
- ½ cup white rice
- 2 cups milk
- ¼ cup raisins
- 2 tablespoons sugar
- ½ teaspoon lime juice
- 1 teaspoon vanilla extract

Directions:
In your instant pot, combine grapes with the rice, milk and the other ingredients, toss, put the lid on and cook on High for 25 minutes. Release the pressure naturally for 10 minutes, divide the mix into bowls and serve.

Nutrition: calories 262, fat 12.2, fiber 4.2, carbs 11.4, protein 3.5

Cocoa Grapes Mix

Preparation time: 5 minutes | Cooking time: 15 minutes | Servings: 4

Ingredients:
- 1 cup grapes, halved
- 1 tablespoon cocoa powder
- 1 cup milk
- 1 tablespoon sugar
- ½ teaspoon cardamom, ground

Directions:
In your instant pot, combine the grapes with the cocoa and the other ingredients, toss, put the lid on and cook on High for 15 minutes. Release the pressure fast for 5 minutes, divide the mix into bowls and serve.

Nutrition: calories 272, fat 11.2, fiber 4.3, carbs 13.4, protein 2.5

Cranberries with Pistachios Cream

Preparation time: 10 minutes | Cooking time: 20 minutes | Servings: 4

Ingredients:
- 4 ounces cranberries, chopped
- 2 cups milk
- 2 tablespoons pistachios, chopped
- 4 tablespoons sugar
- 1 teaspoon ginger powder
- 1 teaspoon cinnamon powder
- ½ teaspoon turmeric powder
- 2 cups water

Directions:
In a bowl, combine the cranberries with the milk, pistachios and the other ingredients, whisk well and divide into 4 ramekins. Add the water to the instant pot, add the steamer basket inside, add the ramekins inside, put the lid on and cook on High for 20 minutes. Release the pressure naturally for 10 minutes, and serve the dessert cold.

Nutrition: calories 134, fat 3.4, fiber 1.3, carbs 21.6, protein 4.4

Carrots Pudding

Preparation time: 10 minutes | Cooking time: 20 minutes | Serving: 4

Ingredients:
- 1 pound carrots, grated
- 2 eggs, whisked
- 2 cups milk
- ¾ cup sugar
- 1 teaspoon cinnamon powder
- 1 teaspoon turmeric powder
- ½ teaspoon saffron powder
- 1 cup water

Directions:
In a bowl, mix the carrots with the eggs and the other ingredients except the water, whisk well and transfer to a pudding mould. Add the water to the instant pot, add the steamer basket, put the pudding pan inside, put the lid on and cook on High for 20 minutes. Release the pressure naturally for 10 minutes, cool the pudding down and serve.

Nutrition: calories 200, fat 8.5, fiber 3.2, carbs 11.5, protein 4.6

Apples Quinoa Pudding

Preparation time: 10 minutes | Cooking time: 20 minutes | Servings: 4

Ingredients:
- 2 cups milk
- ½ cup quinoa
- 2 apples, cored, peeled and cubed
- ½ cup sugar
- 1 teaspoon turmeric powder
- ½ teaspoon cardamom powder
- 1 teaspoon cinnamon powder

Directions:
In your instant pot, mix the quinoa with the milk and the other ingredients, toss, put the lid on and cook on High for 20 minutes. Release the pressure naturally for 10 minutes, divide the pudding into bowls and serve.

Nutrition: calories 272, fat 7.6, fiber 2, carbs 11.4, protein 2.5

Almond Pudding

Preparation time: 10 minutes | Cooking time: 20 minutes | Servings: 4

Ingredients:
- ¼ cup almonds, chopped
- 1 cup rice
- 2 eggs, whisked
- 2 cups milk
- 3 tablespoons sugar
- 1 teaspoon turmeric powder
- 1 teaspoon cinnamon powder
- 1 teaspoon vanilla extract

Directions:
In your instant pot, mix the rice with the almonds, the eggs and the other ingredients, whisk, put the lid on and cook on High for 20 minutes. Release the pressure naturally for 10 minutes, divide the pudding into bowls and serve.

Nutrition: calories 334, fat 8, fiber 1.5, carbs 53.9, protein 11.4

Coconut and Rice

Preparation time: 10 minutes | Cooking time: 20 minutes | Servings: 4

Ingredients:
- 1 cup white rice
- 1 cup coconut cream
- 1 cup milk
- 1 tablespoon cinnamon powder
- ½ cup sugar
- 1 teaspoon saffron powder

Directions:
In your instant pot, combine the rice with the cream and the other ingredients, whisk, put the lid on and cook on High for 20 minutes. Release the pressure naturally for 10 minutes, divide everything into bowls and serve.

Nutrition: calories 431, fat 15.9, fiber 1.9, carbs 68.3, protein 6.7

Saffron Lime Cream

Preparation time: 10 minutes | Cooking time: 15 minutes | Servings: 4

Ingredients:
- 1 cup heavy cream
- 1 cup coconut cream
- ½ teaspoon saffron powder
- 1 teaspoon vanilla extract
- 4 tablespoons sugar
- Zest of 1 lime, grated
- 1 tablespoon lime juice
- 1 cup water

Directions:
In a bowl, mix the cream with the coconut cream and the other ingredients except the water, whisk well and divide into 4 ramekins. Add the water to the instant pot, add the steamer basket, put the ramekins inside, put the lid on and cook on High for 15 minutes. Release the pressure naturally for 10 minutes and serve the mix cold.

Nutrition: calories 292, fat 25.4, fiber 1.4, carbs 17.2, protein 2

Raisins Pudding

Preparation time: 10 minutes | Cooking time: 20 minutes | Servings: 4

Ingredients:
- 1 cup white rice
- 2 cups milk
- ½ cup raisins
- 4 tablespoons sugar
- ½ teaspoon vanilla extract
- ½ teaspoon turmeric powder

Directions:
In your instant pot, combine the rice with the milk, raisins and the other ingredients, whisk, put the lid on and cook on High for 20 minutes. Release the pressure naturally for 10 minutes, and serve the pudding cold.

Nutrition: calories 270, fat 6.4, fiber 2.4, carbs 11.5, protein 4.2

Banana and Avocado Mix

Preparation time: 5 minutes | Cooking time: 10 minutes | Servings: 4

Ingredients:
- 2 bananas, peeled and sliced
- 1 avocado, peeled, pitted and cut into wedges
- 1 teaspoon vanilla extract
- ½ teaspoon cardamom, ground
- ½ teaspoon turmeric powder
- 1 tablespoon cinnamon powder
- 1 cup milk
- 2 tablespoons sugar

Directions:
In your instant pot, mix the bananas with the avocado and the other ingredients, toss, put the lid on and cook on High for 10 minutes. Release the pressure fast for 5 minutes, divide the mix into bowls and serve cold.

Nutrition: calories 282, fat 5.4, fiber 2.3, carbs 11.4, protein 4.6

Lemon Grapes and Bananas

Preparation time: 5 minutes | Cooking time: 10 minutes | Servings: 4

Ingredients:

- 1 cup grapes, halved
- 2 bananas, peeled and sliced
- Juice of ½ lemon
- 1 tablespoon lemon zest, grated
- 1 cup coconut cream
- ½ teaspoon turmeric powder
- ½ teaspoon chana masala
- ½ teaspoon vanilla extract

Directions:

In your instant pot, mix grapes with the bananas and the other ingredients, toss, put the lid on and cook on High for 10 minutes. Release the pressure fast for 5 minutes, divide the mix into bowls and serve.

Nutrition: calories 162, fat 4.2, fiber 2.1, carbs 7.4, protein 1.6

Saffron Cauliflower Rice Pudding

Preparation time: 10 minutes | Cooking time: 15 minutes | Servings: 4

Ingredients:

- 1 cup cauliflower rice
- 1 tablespoon raisins
- 1 tablespoon pistachios, chopped
- 2 cups milk
- ½ teaspoon saffron powder
- 3 tablespoon sugar
- 1 teaspoon vanilla extract
- 1 tablespoon cinnamon powder

Directions:

In your instant pot, mix the cauliflower rice with the raisins, the pistachios and the rest of the ingredients, put the lid on and cook on High for 15 minutes. Release the pressure naturally for 10 minutes, divide the mix into bowls and serve.

Nutrition: calories 124, fat 3.4, fiber 0.2, carbs 18.9, protein 5.3

Sweet Wheat Bowls

Preparation time: 10 minutes | Cooking time: 20 minutes | Servings: 4

Ingredients:

- 1 cup broken wheat
- 2 cups milk
- 3 tablespoons sugar
- 1 tablespoon lemon juice
- ½ teaspoon turmeric powder
- 1 teaspoon lemon zest, grated

Directions:

In your instant pot, combine the wheat with the milk and the other ingredients, whisk, put the lid on and cook on High for 20 minutes. Release the pressure naturally for 10 minutes, divide the mix into bowls and serve.

Nutrition: calories 195, fat 2.6, fiber 0.1, carbs 15.4, protein 4.1

Sweet Potatoes Pudding

Preparation time: 10 minutes | *Cooking time:* 20 minutes | *Servings:* 4

Ingredients:

- 1 cup sweet potatoes, peeled and grated
- 1 eggs, whisked
- 2 cups milk
- 3 tablespoons sugar
- 1 cup coconut cream
- 1 teaspoon vanilla extract
- 1 teaspoon saffron powder
- ½ teaspoon cardamom, ground

Directions:

In your instant pot, combine the potatoes with the egg and the other ingredients, whisk, put the lid on and cook on High for 20 minutes. Release the pressure naturally for 10 minutes, divide the pudding into bowls and serve.

Nutrition: calories 297, fat 18, fiber 2.9, carbs 29.2, protein 7.4

Lime Apples Bowls

Preparation time: 10 minutes | *Cooking time:* 15 minutes | *Servings:* 4

Ingredients:

- 1 cup cashew milk
- 1 tablespoon lime zest, grated
- 1 tablespoon lime juice
- 2 apples, cored and cubed
- 1 teaspoon vanilla extract
- 1 cup water

Directions:

In your instant pot, combine the apples with the milk and the other ingredients, toss, put the lid on and cook on High for 15 minutes. Release the pressure naturally for 10 minutes, divide into bowls and serve.

Nutrition: calories 92, fat 1.5, fiber 2.9, carbs 18.4, protein 2.3

Orange Cream

Preparation time: 10 minutes | *Cooking time:* 20 minutes | *Servings:* 4

Ingredients:

- Juice of 1 orange
- 1 pound orange, peeled and cut into segments
- 1 tablespoon lime zest, grated
- 4 tablespoons sugar
- 1 cup heavy cream

Directions:

In your instant pot, mix the oranges with the orange juice and the rest of the ingredients, put the lid on and cook on High for 20 minutes. Release the pressure naturally for 10 minutes, blend the mix using an immersion blender, divide into bowls and serve cold.

Nutrition: calories 162, fat 9.1, fiber 3.2, carbs 11.3, protein 2.6

Raspberries and Rice

Preparation time: 10 minutes | Cooking time: 20 minutes | Servings: 4

Ingredients:
- 1 cup raspberries, chopped
- Zest of 1 lemon
- 1 cup white rice
- 2 cups milk
- 3 tablespoons sugar
- 1 teaspoon saffron powder
- 1 teaspoon vanilla extract

Directions:

In your instant pot, combine the raspberries with the rice and the other ingredients, whisk, put the lid on and cook on High for 20 minutes. Release the pressure naturally for 10 minutes and serve cold.

Nutrition: calories 240, fat 7.1, fiber 4.2, carbs 11.4, protein 3.3

Turmeric Carrot Cream

Preparation time: 10 minutes | Cooking time: 20 minutes | Servings: 4

Ingredients:
- 1 pound carrots, peeled and grated
- 2 tablespoons lime juice
- 1 cup sugar
- 2 cups heavy cream
- 1 teaspoon turmeric powder
- ½ teaspoon cardamom powder
- 1 teaspoon cinnamon powder

Directions:

In your instant pot, combine the carrots with the lime juice and the other ingredients, whisk, put the lid on and cook on High for 20 minutes. Release the pressure naturally for 10 minutes, blend the mix using an immersion blender, divide into bowls and serve cold.

Nutrition: calories 224, fat 9.2, fiber 2.2, carbs 8.4, protein 3.5

Cardamom Pears Cream

Preparation time: 10 minutes | Cooking time: 15 minutes | Servings: 4

Ingredients:
- 4 pears, cored, peeled and chopped
- 1 cup heavy cream
- 1 cup milk
- 1 teaspoon cardamom, ground
- ½ teaspoon turmeric powder
- 1 teaspoon vanilla extract

Directions:

In your instant pot, mix the pears with the cream and the rest of the ingredients, put the lid on and cook on High for 15 minutes. Release the pressure naturally for 10 minutes, blend using an immersion blender, divide into bowls and serve.

Nutrition: calories 229, fat 5.2, fiber 3.2, carbs 11.4, protein 5.7

Ginger Cauliflower Rice

Preparation time: 10 minutes | Cooking time: 15 minutes | Servings: 4

Ingredients:
- 2 cups cauliflower rice
- ½ teaspoon saffron powder
- 2 tablespoons caster sugar
- 1 tablespoon ginger, grated
- 2 cups milk
- 1 teaspoon vanilla extract

Directions:
In your instant pot, mix the rice with the saffron powder and the rest of the ingredients, whisk, put the lid on and cook on High for 15 minutes. Release the pressure naturally for 10 minutes, divide the rice mix in to bowls and serve.

Nutrition: calories 91, fat 10.9, fiber 4.3, carbs 40.1, protein 8.3

Turmeric Blackberries Bowls

Preparation time: 10 minutes | Cooking time: 15 minutes | Servings: 4

Ingredients:
- 3 cups blackberries
- 1 teaspoon turmeric powder
- 2 tablespoons zest, grated
- 2 tablespoons sugar
- 1 and ½ cups milk
- 1 teaspoon vanilla extract

Directions:
In your instant pot, mix the berries with the turmeric, lime zest and the other ingredients, toss, put the lid on and cook on High for 15 minutes. Release the pressure naturally for 10 minutes, divide the mix into bowls and serve cold.

Nutrition: calories 120, fat 1.3, fiber 6.4, carbs 25.1, protein 3.3

Apple Quinoa Mix

Preparation time: 10 minutes | Cooking time: 15 minutes | Servings: 4

Ingredients:
- 2 cups apples, cored and cubed
- 2 tablespoons lemon juice
- 1 cup quinoa
- 2 cups milk
- ½ teaspoon cardamom powder
- ¾ cup sugar
- 1 teaspoon vanilla extract

Directions:
In your instant pot, mix the quinoa with the apples and the rest of the ingredients, put the lid on and cook on High for 15 minutes. Release the pressure naturally for 10 minutes, divide the mix into bowls and serve.

Nutrition: calories 252, fat 4.1, fiber 3.2, carbs 7.4, protein 2.5

Avocado Cream

Preparation time: 5 minutes | Cooking time: 10 minutes | Servings: 4

Ingredients:
- 2 avocados, peeled, pitted and cut into wedges
- 1 teaspoon saffron powder
- 1 cup heavy cream
- 2 tablespoons lime juice
- 3 tablespoons sugar

Directions:
In your instant pot, mix the avocados with the saffron and the other ingredients, whisk, put the lid on and cook on High for 10 minutes. Release the pressure fast for 5 minutes, blend the mix using an immersion blender, divide into bowls and serve.

Nutrition: calories 210, fat 11.2, fiber 2.2, carbs 8.5, protein 2.5

Apricots Rice

Preparation time: 10 minutes | Cooking time: 25 minutes | Servings: 4

Ingredients:
- 2 cups apricots, cubed
- 1 cup white rice
- 2 cups milk
- 4 tablespoons sugar
- 1 tablespoon almonds, chopped
- 2 tablespoons ghee, melted
- 1 teaspoon turmeric powder

Directions:
In your instant pot, mix the apricots with the rice and the rest of the ingredients, put the lid on and cook on High for 25 minutes. Release the pressure naturally for 10 minutes, divide everything into bowls and serve cold.

Nutrition: calories 258, fat 5.4, fiber 1, carbs 7.5, protein 2

Zucchinis Rice

Preparation time: 10 minutes | Cooking time: 15 minutes | Servings: 4

Ingredients:
- 2 cups zucchinis, grated
- 1 cup heavy cream
- 1 cup milk
- ½ teaspoon saffron powder
- ½ teaspoon cardamom powder
- 4 tablespoons sugar
- 1 teaspoon vanilla extract

Directions:
In your instant pot, mix the zucchinis with the cream, the milk and with the rest of the ingredients, put the lid on and cook on High for 15 minutes. Release the pressure naturally for 10 minutes, divide the mix into bowls and serve.

Nutrition: calories 252, fat 7.2, fiber 2, carbs 8.4, protein 1.4

Dates Quinoa

Preparation time: *10 minutes* | ***Cooking time:*** *20 minutes* | ***Servings:*** *4*

Ingredients:
- 1 cup quinoa
- 2 cups milk
- ½ cup dates, pitted
- ½ teaspoon turmeric powder
- ½ teaspoon saffron powder
- 1 teaspoon cinnamon powder
- 1 teaspoon vanilla extract

Directions:
In your instant pot, mix the quinoa with the milk and the other ingredients, whisk, put the lid on and cook on High for 20 minutes. Release the pressure naturally for 10 minutes, divide the mix into bowls and serve cold.

Nutrition: calories 210, fat 6.1, fiber 2, carbs 8.4, protein 3.6

Coconut Banana Mix

Preparation time: *10 minutes* | ***Cooking time:*** *15 minutes* | ***Servings:*** *4*

Ingredients:
- 2 bananas, peeled and sliced
- ½ teaspoon cinnamon powder
- 1 cup yogurt
- 2 tablespoons sugar
- 2 tablespoons coconut flakes

Directions:
In your instant pot, combine the bananas with the cinnamon and the rest of the ingredients, put the lid on and cook on High for 15 minutes. Release the pressure naturally for 10 minutes, divide the mix into bowls and serve.

Nutrition: calories 127, fat 1.8, fiber 1.8, carbs 24.2, protein 4.2

Walnuts Cream

Preparation time: *10 minutes* | ***Cooking time:*** *20 minutes* | ***Servings:*** *4*

Ingredients:
- 1 cup milk
- 1 cup heavy cream
- 3 eggs, whisked
- 1 teaspoon vanilla extract
- 3 tablespoons sugar
- 2 cups walnuts, chopped
- 1 teaspoon cardamom powder
- 1 teaspoon turmeric powder
- 1 teaspoon cinnamon powder

Directions:
In your instant pot, combine the milk with the cream and the other ingredients, stir, put the lid on and cook on High for 20 minutes. Release the pressure naturally for 10 minutes, blend using an immersion blender, divide into bowls and serve cold.

Nutrition: calories 608, fat 52.6, fiber 4.5, carbs 20.1, protein 21.

Coconut Strawberry Mix

Preparation time: 10 minutes | Cooking time: 20 minutes | Servings: 4

Ingredients:
- 1 cup coconut cream
- 1 cup strawberries, chopped
- 3 tablespoons sugar
- 1 cup milk
- 1 teaspoon vanilla extract
- 2 eggs, whisked
- 2 cups water

Directions:

In a bowl, mix the cream with the strawberries and the other ingredients except the water, blend using an immersion blender, and divide into 4 ramekins. Add the water to the instant pot, add the steamer basket, put the ramekins inside, put the lid on and cook on High for 20 minutes. Release the pressure naturally for 10 minutes, and serve the dessert cold.

Nutrition: calories 248, fat 17.9, fiber 2, carbs 18.4, protein 6.4

Pineapple Pudding

Preparation time: 10 minutes | Cooking time: 20 minutes | Servings: 4

Ingredients:
- 2 cups milk
- 1 cup white rice
- ½ cup pineapple, peeled and cubed
- 1 teaspoon saffron powder
- ½ teaspoon cardamom powder
- ½ cup sugar
- ½ teaspoon vanilla extract

Directions:

In your instant pot, mix the rice with the pineapple and the other ingredients, put the lid on and cook on High for 20 minutes. Release the pressure naturally for 10 minutes, divide the pudding into bowls and serve cold.

Nutrition: calories 262, fat 6.3, fiber 2, carbs 11.5, protein 4.6

Coconut Parfait

Preparation time: 10 minutes | Cooking time: 15 minutes | Servings: 4

Ingredients:
- 3 eggs, whisked
- 2 cups heavy cream
- 1/3 cup sugar
- 1 tablespoon ghee, melted
- ½ cup coconut cream
- 1 teaspoon turmeric powder
- ½ cup coconut flakes
- 1 teaspoon vanilla extract

Directions:

In your instant pot, mix the eggs with the cream and the rest of the ingredients, whisk, put the lid on and cook on High for 15 minutes. Release the pressure naturally for 10 minutes, blend the mix using an immersion blender, divide the mix in bowls and serve.

Nutrition: calories 228, fat 7.5, fiber 3.1, carbs 12.2, protein 1.6

Cardamom Pudding

Preparation time: 10 minutes | Cooking time: 20 minutes | Servings: 4

Ingredients:
- 1 cup quinoa
- 2 cups milk
- 2 eggs, whisked
- 3 tablespoon sugar
- 2 teaspoons vanilla extract
- ½ teaspoon saffron powder
- ¼ teaspoon cardamom, ground

Directions:

In your instant pot, combine the quinoa with the milk and the other ingredients, whisk, put the lid on and cook on High for 20 minutes. Release the pressure naturally for 10 minutes, divide the mix into bowls and serve cold.

Nutrition: calories 289, fat 7.3, fiber 3, carbs 42.8, protein 12.8

Saffron Chocolate Cream

Preparation time: 10 minutes | Cooking time: 20 minutes | Servings: 4

Ingredients:
- 2 cups milk
- 1 cup heavy cream
- ¼ cup sugar
- 1/3 cup ghee, melted
- ½ teaspoon saffron powder
- 1 teaspoon vanilla extract
- ¼ cup dark chocolate, chopped
- 2 cups water

Directions:

In a bowl, combine the milk with the cream and the other ingredients except the water, whisk well and divide into 4 ramekins. Put the water in the instant pot, add the steamer basket, add the ramekins, put the lid on and cook on High for 20 minutes. Release the pressure naturally for 10 minutes, and serve the cream cold.

Nutrition: calories 420, fat 33.7, fiber 0.4, carbs 25.7, protein 5.5

Rhubarb Quinoa

Preparation time: 10 minutes | Cooking time: 15 minutes | Servings: 4

Ingredients:
- 1 cup milk
- ½ cup quinoa
- ½ teaspoon saffron powder
- 2 tablespoons sugar
- ½ teaspoon cardamom powder
- 2 cups rhubarb, chopped
- 1 teaspoon vanilla extract

Directions:

In your instant pot, combine the milk with the quinoa and the other ingredients, whisk, put the lid on and cook on High for 15 minutes. Release the pressure naturally for 10 minutes, divide into bows and serve cold.

Nutrition: calories 148, fat 2.7, fiber 2.7, carbs 25.7, protein 5.6

Mango and Banana Mix

Preparation time: 10 minutes | Cooking time: 10 minutes | Servings: 4

Ingredients:
- 1 cup mango, peeled and cubed
- 2 bananas, peeled and sliced
- 1 tablespoon lime juice
- ½ teaspoon cardamom powder
- ½ teaspoon dry mango powder
- ½ teaspoon cinnamon powder
- 1 cup milk
- 2 tablespoons sugar

Directions:
In your instant pot, combine the mango with the bananas, lime juice and the other ingredients, toss gently, put the lid on and cook on High for 10 minutes. Release the pressure naturally for 10 minutes, divide the mix into bowls and serve cold.

Nutrition: calories 134, fat 1.6, fiber 2.3, carbs 29.8, protein 3.1

Nutmeg Pumpkin Mix

Preparation time: 10 minutes | Cooking time: 15 minutes | Servings: 4

Ingredients:
- 1 cup milk
- ½ cup sugar
- 1 cup heavy cream
- ½ teaspoon saffron powder
- 1 teaspoon nutmeg, ground
- 2 tablespoons ghee, melted
- 2 cups pumpkin flesh

Directions:
In your instant pot, combine the milk with the pumpkin and the other ingredients, toss gently, put the lid on and cook on High for 15 minutes. Release the pressure naturally for 10 minutes, cool the mix down, divide into bowls and serve.

Nutrition: calories 311, fat 19, fiber 1.5, carbs 35.1, protein 3.6

Conclusion

This Indian instant pot recipes collection will really surprise you. The rich, flavored and textured dishes you've discovered here will make your taste buds dance. The Indian meals you learned how to make will transform you into a real start in the kitchen.

All you need to do is to get an instant pot (if you don't already have one) and to get your hands on a copy of this useful and original Indian instant pot cooking guide.

You will have so much fun playing with Indian spices, ingredients, tastes and flavors. You will obtain such great dishes and you will learn to love Indian cuisine.
So, what are you still waiting for? Discover Indian cuisine and make the most delicious Indian dishes using only one useful kitchen tool: the instant pot!
Have fun!

Ingredients Index

AJOWAN SEEDS
Fruit Masala, 39

ALLSPICE
Spicy Beef, 187
Beef with Cinnamon Zucchini Mix, 190
Beef and Beets Mix, 191
Spiced Lamb with Corn, 194
Lamb with Spiced Sprouts, 194
Beef with Chili Quinoa, 195
Minty Lamb Mix, 196
Pork Chops with Allspice Spinach, 198
Cocoa Pork and Tomatoes, 205
Walnuts Bell Peppers Mix, 216
Allspice Zucchini Mix, 231

ALMOND MILK
Ghee Carrot Pudding, 64
Cheese Dip, 112

ALMONDS
Sweet Dalia, 21
Healthy Kheer, 35
Ragi Malt Java, 43
Garlic Rice Mix, 91
Beets and Almonds, 95
Peppers Dip, 104
Quinoa, Almonds and Avocado Salad, 120
Cardamom Shrimp and Zucchinis, 140
Coriander Pork with Almonds, 201
Almond Asparagus Mix, 213
Gajar Ka Halwa, 236
Indian Kulfi, 237
Rice Kheer, 238
Mixed Fruits, 238
Turmeric Pear Bowls, 240
Almond Pudding, 243
Apricots Rice, 249

APPLES
Chicken Masala, 56
Ghee Carrot Pudding, 64
Narangi Pulao, 90
Ginger Beef Curry, 182
Apple Ragi Halwa, 43
Mulligatawny Soup, 58
Mixed Fruits, 238
Turmeric Apples, 241
Apples Quinoa Pudding, 243
Lime Apples Bowls, 246
Apple Quinoa Mix, 248

APRICOTS
Apricots Rice, 249

ARTICHOKES
Cumin Chicken and Artichokes, 154
Spicy Pork and Artichokes, 209
Masala Artichokes, 211
Creamy Artichokes and Coconut, 212

ARUGULA
Chicken Chutney Salad, 110

ASAFETIDA
Beet Poriyal, 77

ASPARAGUS
Asparagus Rice Mix, 91
Indian Cumin Asparagus, 98
Charred Salmon, 127
Indian Salmon and Asparagus, 131
Spiced Asparagus, 212
Almond Asparagus Mix, 213
Ginger Asparagus, 213
Curry Turkey, Asparagus and Tomatoes, 158
Turkey and Chili Asparagus, 174

AVOCADO
Spinach and Avocado Dip, 107

255

Quinoa, Almonds and Avocado Salad, 120
Tuna and Avocado Mix, 139
Chicken, Avocado and Turmeric Rice, 159
Chicken with Avocado and Cucumber Mix, 171
Banana and Avocado Mix, 244
Avocado Raita, 102
Avocado Cream, 249

BAMBOO SHOOTS
Pork with Bamboo Mix, 206

BANANAS
Banana Moong Dal, 27
Fruit Masala, 39
Banana Salad, 39
Banana and Rice Pudding, 240
Banana and Avocado Mix, 244
Lemon Grapes and Bananas, 245
Coconut Banana Mix, 250
Mango and Banana Mix, 253

BARLEY
Barley and Turmeric Salad, 118
Barley and Olives Salad, 119
Barley and Chickpea Bowls, 120

BASMATI RICE
Tomato Rice, 29
Veggie Masala, 31
Green Peas Masala Rice, 31
Spinach and Lentils Rice, 32
Rose Rice Bowls, 39
Veggie Pulao, 46
Chicken Biryani, 47
Shrimp Biryani, 53
Indian Fish Soup, 59
Aromatic Rice Mix, 73
Spicy Rice, 74
Beet Rice, 77
Peas Pulao, 80
Orange Pulao, 90

Narangi Pulao, 90
Rice and Kale, 91
Asparagus Rice Mix, 91
Cabbage Rice, 93
Creamy Beans and Rice, 94
Spicy Artichokes and Rice, 95
Turmeric Fennel and Rice, 98
Chicken Chutney Salad, 110
Lemon Cod and Rice, 128
Chicken, Avocado and Turmeric Rice, 159
Turkey, Cauliflower and Rice Mix, 163
Chicken and Zucchini Rice Mix, 165
Chicken and Endives Rice Mix, 176
Turkey with Brussels Sprouts Rice, 177
Chicken, Rice and Mango Mix, 179
Coconut Turkey and Carrots Rice, 180
Cheesy Beef and Rice, 190
Ginger Pork Mix, 205
Cinnamon Artichokes and Rice, 212
Tomatoes and Citrus Rice, 231
Rice Salad, 40

BEANS
Turkey with Chili Black Beans, 173

BEEF
Kheema Masala, 185
Saag Gosht, 187
Beef and Veggies Curry, 188
Keema Matar, 51
Beef Curry, 180
Ribs Curry, 181
Coconut Pork Mix, 181
Madras Beef Mix, 182
Ginger Beef Curry, 182
Beef with Veggies Mix, 183
Aromatic Beef, 183
Lemony Beef Mix, 184
Beef and Lentils Curry, 184
Kheema Masala, 185

Beef and Peas, 186
Coconut Beef and Cilantro Mix, 186
Spicy Beef, 187
Beef with Squash Curry, 188
Beef with Squash Curry, 188
Indian Beef and Pumpkin Mix, 189
Beef with Lemony Scallions, 189
Cheesy Beef and Rice, 190
Beef with Cinnamon Zucchini Mix, 190
Cumin Beef, 191
Beef and Beets Mix, 191
Spiced Lamb Bowls, 192
Lamb with Spiced Sprouts, 194
Beef with Chili Quinoa, 195
Indian Lamb Chops, 195
Minty Lamb Mix, 196
Spiced Lamb and Cucumber, 196
Turmeric Lamb with Beets, 197
Indian Pork Chops, 197
Pork Chops with Allspice Spinach, 198
Cocoa Pork Chops and Green Beans, 199
Pork with Cinnamon Carrots Mix, 199
Pork with Broccoli, 200
Pork Chops and Turmeric Cauliflower, 201
Coriander Pork with Almonds, 201
Mustard and Cumin Pork Chops, 202
Paprika Pork with Nutmeg Potatoes, 202
Pandi Masala, 203
Pork Indaad, 203
Hot Pork Mix, 204
Orange Pork Mix, 204
Cocoa Pork and Tomatoes, 205
Ema Datshi, 206
Pork with Bamboo Mix, 206
Kaleez Ankiti, 207
Pork Meatballs Mix, 208
Tamarind Pork, 208
Hot BBQ Ribs, 209

Spicy Pork and Artichokes, 209
Beef and Creamy Turmeric Potatoes, 210
Garlic Potato Masala, 219

BEET
Chicken with Turmeric Beets and Broccoli, 170
Beet Sabzi, 76
Beet Rice, 77
Beet Poriyal, 77
Beet Thoran, 78
Beet and Carrot Poriyal, 78
Beets and Almonds, 95
Turmeric Lamb with Beets, 197
Coconut Beets, 215
Beets with Yogurt, 218
Cardamom Beets, 233
Beets and Onions Mix, 234

BHINDI
Bhindi Masala, 24

BIRYANI MASALA
Spinach and Lentils Rice, 32

BLACKBERRIES
Turmeric Blackberries Bowls, 248

BROCCOLI
Egg and Broccoli Bhurji, 43
Cream of Broccoli, 57
Curry Cauliflower and Broccoli Soup, 58
Broccoli Junka, 66
Turmeric Broccoli Mix, 89
Ginger Broccoli and Orange Mix, 92
Spiced Broccoli Spread, 116
Broccoli Bites, 119
Mushroom and Broccoli Dip, 122
Salmon and Broccoli, 127
Citrus Turkey and Spiced Broccoli, 151
Chives Chicken and Broccoli, 170

257

Chicken with Turmeric Beets and Broccoli, 170
Chicken with Coriander Broccoli Sauté, 175
Pork with Broccoli, 200
Turmeric Broccoli and Onions, 222
Spinach with Broccoli, 234

BROWN RICE
Millet Pongal, 42
Rice with Lamb, 52
Cheesy Turkey and Rice, 166

BRUSSELS SPROUTS
Brussels Sprouts Subzi, 86
Spiced Brussels Sprouts, 86
Curried Brussels Sprouts, 87
Turkey with Brussels Sprouts Rice, 177
Lamb with Spiced Sprouts, 194
Hot Brussels Sprouts, 215

BUTTER
Paneer Butter Masala, 22
Bread Upma, 34
Masala Omelet, 41
Paneer Butter Masala, 44
Buttery Chicken, 47
Tomato Soup, 61
Curry Turkey Soup, 62
Mutton Stew, 65
Garlic Rice Mix, 91
Khara Biscuits, 100
Mushroom and Broccoli Dip, 122
Creamy Mushroom Spread, 122
Cod and Butter Sauce, 132
Tuna and Turmeric Green Beans Mix, 139
Rice Kheer, 238

BUTTERMILK
Onion Rava Dosa, 16

BUTTERNUT
Squash and Lentils Stew, 67
Beef with Squash Curry, 188

CANNED ARTICHOKE
Spicy Artichokes and Rice, 95
Turmeric Artichokes, 211
Cinnamon Artichokes and Rice, 212

CANNED BEANS
Balkan Bean Stew, 68

CANNED CHICKPEAS
Quinoa and Chickpeas Mix, 76
Garam Masala Hummus, 102
Chickpea Dip, 114
Barley and Chickpea Bowls, 120
Chicken and Chickpeas Mix, 167
Turkey, Chickpeas and Zucchinis, 168

CANNED LENTILS
Thyme Lentils and Tomatoes Bowls, 121
Turkey and Curried Lentils, 168

CANNED NAVY BEANS
Beans Dip, 108

CANNED RED KIDNEY BEANS
Cocoa Turkey and Beans, 163

CANNED TOMATOES
Buttery Chicken, 47
Keema Matar, 51
Mulligatawny Soup, 58
Chickpeas and Tomatoes Masala, 65
Veggie Sabjee, 73
Quinoa and Chickpeas Mix, 76
Trout and Sauce, 130
Curry Chicken Thighs, 152
Beef and Lentils Curry, 184
Beef and Veggies Curry, 188
Indian Beef and Pumpkin Mix, 189

CANNED TUNA
Spicy Tuna, 134

CANNED WHITE BEANS
White Beans Spread, 108

CANOLA OIL
Curry Chicken Thighs, 152
Ginger Chicken and Sweet Potatoes, 156
Coconut Chicken and Tomatoes, 157
Chicken and Turmeric Zucchini Mix, 162
Chicken Meatballs Curry, 164
Chicken and Lime Turmeric Carrots, 165
Chives Chicken and Broccoli, 170
Chicken Wings and Turmeric Sauce, 174
Turkey with Brussels Sprouts Rice, 177
Chicken with Chili Onions, 178
Coconut Turkey and Carrots Rice, 180
Madras Beef Mix, 182
Beef and Peas, 186
Coconut Beef and Cilantro Mix, 186
Spicy Beef, 187
Beef and Veggies Curry, 188
Cheesy Beef and Rice, 190
Cumin Beef, 191
Spiced Lamb Bowls, 192
Indian Pork Chops, 197
Pork Chops and Turmeric Cauliflower, 201
Hot Pork Mix, 204
Spiced Eggplant Mix, 227

CAPSICUMS
Aloo Capsicum, 25

CARROT
Green Dosa, 30
Broken Wheat Upma, 32
Millet Upma, 33
Veggie Khichdi, 46
Mulligatawny Soup, 58
Curry Turkey Soup, 62
Beef Stew, 63
Veggie Stew, 64
Veggie Sabjee, 73
Quinoa Pilaf, 75
Chicken Chutney Salad, 110
Warm Cucumber Salad, 118
Sea Bass and Lentils, 143
Oats Upma, 19
Oats Khichdi, 23
Gajar Matar, 24
Carrot Rasam and Moong Dal, 29
Veggie Masala, 31
Masala Pasta, 55
Avial, 56
Chicken Soup, 57
Beans and Rutabaga Soup, 60
Turkey and Coriander Soup, 62
Ghee Carrot Pudding, 64
Mutton Stew, 65
Beet and Carrot Poriyal, 78
Gajar Matar, 81
Parsnips Mix, 83
Orange Pulao, 90
Barley and Turmeric Salad, 118
Curry Chicken Thighs, 152
Chicken and Lime Turmeric Carrots, 165
Coconut Turkey and Carrots Rice, 180
Beef and Veggies Curry, 188
Creamy Lamb with Carrots Curry, 193
Pork with Cinnamon Carrots Mix, 199
Ginger Pork Mix, 205
Spiced Zucchinis and Carrots, 232
Cumin Potato and Carrots Mix, 232
Gajar Ka Halwa, 236
Carrots Pudding, 242
Turmeric Carrot Cream, 247

Veggie Pulao, 46

CASHEW MILK
Lime Apples Bowls, 246

CASHEW NUT
Gehun Ki Kheer, 239

CASHEWS
Rave Upma, 14
Poori Masala, 18
Chura Matar, 20
Sweet Pongal, 21
Sweet Dalia, 21
Paneer Butter Masala, 22
Millet Pongal, 42
Paneer Butter Masala, 44
Aloo Baingan Masala, 44
Dum Aloo, 45
Shrimp Biryani, 53
Ghee Carrot Pudding, 64
Spiced Quinoa, 74
Hara Bhara Kabab, 81
Creamy Cauliflower Mix, 85
Cashew Dip, 103
Cilantro Turkey and Lemon Mix, 150
Pork with Broccoli, 200
Payasam, 237
Ada Pradhaman, 239

CAULIFLOWER
Indian Farro Masala, 34
Spiced Quinoa, 74
Spiced Gobi, 84
Turkey, Cauliflower and Rice Mix, 163
Green Dosa, 30
Veggie Masala, 31
Broken Wheat Upma, 32
Millet Upma, 33
Curry Cauliflower and Broccoli Soup, 58
Cauliflower Mix, 84
Spicy Gobi Mix, 85

Creamy Cauliflower Mix, 85
Citrus Cauliflower Mix, 89
Hot Cauliflower Dip, 116
Cod and Cauliflower, 130
Cinnamon Turkey and Cauliflower, 152
Chicken with Cauliflower and Pomegranate Mix, 171
Garlic Turkey, Tomatoes and Rice, 172
Ribs Curry, 181
Beef and Veggies Curry, 188
Pork Chops and Turmeric Cauliflower, 201
Nutmeg Cauliflower Mix, 223
Zucchini and Cauliflower Mix, 229
Saffron Cauliflower Rice Pudding, 245
Ginger Cauliflower Rice, 248

CELERY
Beans and Rutabaga Soup, 60
Curry Turkey Soup, 62
Tuna and Avocado Mix, 139
Chicken with Turmeric Beets and Broccoli, 170

CHAAT MASALA
Kurkuri Bhindi, 27
Indian Farro Masala, 34
Poha Bowls with Sprouts, 37
Hara Bhara Kabab, 81
Aam Shrikhand, 236

CHANA DAL
Garlic Dip, 101
Potato Masala, 14
Rave Upma, 14
Poori Masala, 18
Oats Upma, 19
Tomato Upma, 19
Spinach and Lentils Rice, 32
Langar Dal, 54
Creamy Cauliflower Mix, 85

Broccoli Bites, 119

CHANA MASALA
Quinoa, Almonds and Avocado Salad, 120
Cod and Cauliflower, 130
Indian Salmon and Asparagus, 131
Fenugreek Tuna and Mushroom Curry, 141
Citrus Turkey and Spiced Broccoli, 151
Coconut Chicken and Tomatoes, 157
Chicken and Zucchini Rice Mix, 165
Turkey with Chili Black Beans, 173
Turkey Bowls, 177
Coriander Peppers Mix, 217
Lemon Grapes and Bananas, 245

CHERRY TOMATOES
Figs and Tomatoes Salad, 42
Warm Cucumber Salad, 118
Barley and Turmeric Salad, 118
Barley and Olives Salad, 119
Thyme Lentils and Tomatoes Bowls, 121
Cod and Tomato Bowls, 126
Tilapia, Tomatoes and Radish Saad, 136
Coriander Cod Mix, 149
Cinnamon Chicken and Rice Mix, 155
Curry Turkey, Asparagus and Tomatoes, 158
Chicken, Tomatoes and Mushrooms, 166
Garlic Turkey, Tomatoes and Rice, 172
Coconut Tomatoes, 228
Tomatoes and Citrus Rice, 231
Minty Tomatoes Mix, 233

CHICKEN
Chicken Masala, 48
Chicken Masala, 56
Chicken Soup, 57
Curry Cauliflower and Broccoli Soup, 58
Mango and Kale Mix, 88
Turmeric Broccoli Mix, 89
Rice and Kale, 91
Endives and Walnuts Mix, 97
Chicken Chutney Salad, 110
Chives Tuna Curry, 135
Salmon, Spinach and Coconut Mix, 136
Spicy Tamarind Clams, 145
Chicken and Lime Turmeric Carrots, 165
Buttery Chicken, 47
Chicken Biryani, 47
Mulligatawny Soup, 58
Indian Fish Soup, 59
Curry Turkey Soup, 62
Beet Sabzi, 76
Beet Thoran, 78
Beet and Carrot Poriyal, 78
Parsnips Mix, 83
Spicy Gobi Mix, 85
Citrus Cauliflower Mix, 89
Garlic Rice Mix, 91
Asparagus Rice Mix, 91
Spicy Eggplant Mix, 92
Beets and Almonds, 95
Spicy Artichokes and Rice, 95
Endives with Orange Mix, 97
Indian Cumin Asparagus, 98
Turmeric Fennel and Rice, 98
Curd Chicken Salad, 109
Broccoli Bites, 119
Lemon Cod and Rice, 128
Shrimp and Lime Rice, 128
Spiced Cod, 129
Seafood Salad, 129
Turmeric Salmon and Lime Sauce, 132
Indian Halibut, 133
Tilapia, Tomatoes and Radish Saad, 136

Shrimp and Okra, 138
Shrimp and Spiced Potatoes, 138
Tuna and Turmeric Green Beans Mix, 139
Tilapia Masala, 141
Crab Curry, 146
Spicy Crab and Eggplant Mix, 146
Mustard Seed Mahi Mahi, 147
Turkey Meatballs and Sauce, 151
Cinnamon Turkey and Cauliflower, 152
Curry Chicken Thighs, 152
Curry Chicken Thighs, 152
Ginger Chicken Mix, 153
Masala Chicken and Peppers, 153
Cumin Chicken and Artichokes, 154
Curry Chicken and Eggplants, 154
Cardamom Turkey Mix, 155
Cinnamon Chicken and Rice Mix, 155
Ginger Chicken and Sweet Potatoes, 156
Turkey with Spiced Potatoes, 156
Coconut Chicken and Tomatoes, 157
Coconut Chicken and Tomatoes, 157
Sage Chicken and Mango, 157
Curry Turkey, Asparagus and Tomatoes, 158
Creamy Chicken Mix, 158
Chicken, Avocado and Turmeric Rice, 159
Cinnamon Turkey and Green Beans, 159
Chicken and Masala Fennel, 160
Chicken and Masala Fennel, 160
Turkey and Lime Sauce, 160
Cumin Chicken with Tomato Chutney, 161
Hot Chicken and Pineapple Mix, 161
Chicken and Turmeric Zucchini Mix, 162
Fenugreek Chicken Mix, 162
Turkey, Cauliflower and Rice Mix, 163

Cocoa Turkey and Beans, 163
Chicken Meatballs Curry, 164
Paprika Turkey Mix, 164
Chicken and Zucchini Rice Mix, 165
Cheesy Turkey and Rice, 166
Chicken, Tomatoes and Mushrooms, 166
Turkey and Masala Corn, 167
Chicken and Chickpeas Mix, 167
Turkey and Curried Lentils, 168
Turkey, Chickpeas and Zucchinis, 168
Chicken with Turmeric Cabbage, 169
Coriander Chicken Masala, 169
Chives Chicken and Broccoli, 170
Chicken with Turmeric Beets and Broccoli, 170
Chicken with Avocado and Cucumber Mix, 171
Chicken with Cauliflower and Pomegranate Mix, 171
Chicken with Cauliflower and Pomegranate Mix, 171
Garlic Turkey, Tomatoes and Rice, 172
Hot Cayenne Chicken Mix, 172
Turkey with Chili Black Beans, 173
Chicken Wings and Turmeric Sauce, 174
Chicken with Coriander Broccoli Sauté, 175
Chicken, Zucchini and Mushrooms Curry, 175
Chicken and Endives Rice Mix, 176
Lime Turmeric Chicken Wings, 176
Turkey Bowls, 177
Turkey with Brussels Sprouts Rice, 177
Creamy Turkey and Peas Mix, 178
Chicken with Chili Onions, 178
Masala Turkey with Nutmeg Potatoes, 179
Chicken, Rice and Mango Mix, 179
Turmeric Artichokes, 211

Spiced Asparagus, 212
Cinnamon Artichokes and Rice, 212
Almond Asparagus Mix, 213
Ginger Asparagus, 213
Spiced Green Beans, 214
Coconut Beets, 215
Bell Peppers and Potatoes Mix, 217
Turmeric Zucchini, 220
Cayenne Zucchinis Mix, 220
Potato and Zucchini Masala, 221
Spinach Mix, 221
Spiced Okra, 222
Turmeric Broccoli and Onions, 222
Hot Spinach and Potato Mix, 223
Cinnamon Potato Mix, 224
Masala Endives, 225
Spinach and Okra Mix, 225
Spiced Eggplant Mix, 227
Lime Zucchinis and Eggplant Mix, 227
Coconut Eggplants, 228
Zucchini and Cauliflower Mix, 229
Turmeric Kale, 229
Cocoa Zucchinis and Peppers, 230
Tomatoes and Citrus Rice, 231
Spiced Zucchinis and Carrots, 232
Cardamom Beets, 233
Minty Tomatoes Mix, 233
Beets and Onions Mix, 234

CHICKEN BREASTS
Chicken and Lime Turmeric Carrots, 165

CHICKEN STOCK
Turkey Bowls, 111

CHICKPEAS
Kadala Curry, 22
Chana Masala, 50
Sookha Kana Chana, 54
Chickpeas and Tomatoes Masala, 65
Barley and Turmeric Salad, 118

CHILI FLAKES
Okra Mix, 70
Aromatic Rice Mix, 73

CHILI PASTE
Turmeric Tuna, 134
Beef with Cinnamon Zucchini Mix, 190

CHILI PEPPER
Baingan Ka Bharta, 83
Cumin Eggplant and Tomato Bowls, 106
Lentils Dip, 114
Lemongrass Shrimp and Corn, 140
Beef and Peas, 186
Gajar Matar, 24
Spiced Quinoa, 74
Tilapia, Tomatoes and Radish Saad, 136

CHIVES
Curry Cauliflower and Broccoli Soup, 58
Chives Tuna Curry, 135
Sea Bass with Fennel, 137
Chives Chicken and Broccoli, 170
Chicken and Endives Rice Mix, 176

CHOCOLATE
Saffron Chocolate Cream, 252

CHUTNEY
Tamarind Dip, 103

CLAMS
Curry Clams, 145
Spicy Tamarind Clams, 145

COCONUT
Potato Poha, 17
Kadala Curry, 22
Beans Masala, 38
Avial, 56

Squash and Lentils Stew, 67
Cabbage Thoran, 72
Beet Sabzi, 76
Beet Poriyal, 77
Beet Thoran, 78
Beet and Carrot Poriyal, 78
Creamy Cauliflower Mix, 85
Curried Brussels Sprouts, 87
Salmon, Spinach and Coconut Mix, 136
Shrimp and Radish Curry, 137
Tilapia Curry, 142
Spicy Tamarind Clams, 145
Crab Curry, 146
Spicy Crab and Eggplant Mix, 146
Coconut Chicken and Tomatoes, 157
Creamy Chicken Mix, 158
Turkey with Chili Black Beans, 173
Coconut Turkey and Carrots Rice, 180
Coconut Pork Mix, 181
Beef with Veggies Mix, 183
Lamb with Coconut Green Beans, 193
Coconut Fennel Mix, 224
Coconut Eggplants, 228
Coconut Tomatoes, 228
Ada Pradhaman, 239
Banana Moong Dal, 27

COCONUT CREAM
Paneer Butter Masala, 44
Buttery Chicken, 47
Curry Cauliflower and Broccoli Soup, 58
Coconut Veggies, 71
Cauliflower Mix, 84
Creamy Beans and Rice, 94
Turmeric Fennel and Rice, 98
Peas and Fennel Mix, 98
Spinach and Avocado Dip, 107
Mango Salad, 110
Potato Dip, 112
Endives Dip, 113
Saffron Shrimp, 113
Turmeric Onion Dip, 115
Spiced Broccoli Spread, 116
Hot Cauliflower Dip, 116
Quinoa, Almonds and Avocado Salad, 120
Barley and Chickpea Bowls, 120
Thyme Lentils and Tomatoes Bowls, 121
Creamy Mushroom Spread, 122
Shrimp and Green Beans Bowls, 123
Chili Fish Mix, 125
Cod and Cauliflower, 130
Salmon and Chili Sauce, 131
Indian Salmon and Asparagus, 131
Simple Masala, 133
Turmeric Tuna, 134
Sea Bass with Fennel, 137
Spicy Tilapia, 142
Cilantro Turkey and Lemon Mix, 150
Creamy Chicken Mix, 158
Chicken Meatballs Curry, 164
Chicken, Tomatoes and Mushrooms, 166
Turkey with Turmeric Yogurt Mix, 173
Chicken Wings and Turmeric Sauce, 174
Chicken with Coriander Broccoli Sauté, 175
Lime Turmeric Chicken Wings, 176
Chicken with Chili Onions, 178
Ribs Curry, 181
Beef with Squash Curry, 188
Creamy Lamb with Carrots Curry, 193
Pork Meatballs Mix, 208
Creamy Artichokes and Coconut, 212
Coconut Beets, 215
Walnuts Bell Peppers Mix, 216
Creamy Potatoes, 219
Nutmeg Cauliflower Mix, 223
Coconut Fennel Mix, 224

Creamy Potato and Apples Mix, 226
Coconut Eggplants, 228
Cumin Potato and Carrots Mix, 232
Turmeric Pear Bowls, 240
Coconut and Rice, 243
Saffron Lime Cream, 244
Lemon Grapes and Bananas, 245
Sweet Potatoes Pudding, 246
Coconut Strawberry Mix, 251
Coconut Parfait, 251

COCONUT FLAKES
Coconut Banana Mix, 250
Coconut Parfait, 251

COCONUT MILK
Shrimp Curry, 50
Mulligatawny Soup, 58
Indian Fish Soup, 59
Turkey and Coriander Soup, 62
Coconut Shrimp Stew, 63
Ghee Carrot Pudding, 64
Zucchini and Peas Curry, 67
Quinoa Curry, 75
Cod Curry, 126
Lemongrass Shrimp and Corn, 140
Cardamom Shrimp and Zucchinis, 140
Tilapia Curry, 142
Spiced Mussels, 144
Curry Clams, 145
Coconut Turkey and Carrots Rice, 180
Pork with Red Lentils Mix, 185
Coconut Beef and Cilantro Mix, 186
Ada Pradhaman, 239

COCONUT OIL
Kadala Curry, 22
Avial, 56
Beef Stew, 63
Veggie Stew, 64
Zucchini Curry, 66
Zucchini and Peas Curry, 67

Turnips Soup, 68
Cabbage Thoran, 72
Beet Poriyal, 77
Beet Thoran, 78
Beet and Carrot Poriyal, 78
Hara Bhara Kabab, 81
Parsnips Mix, 83
Creamy Cauliflower Mix, 85
Brussels Sprouts Subzi, 86
Citrus Cauliflower Mix, 89
Spicy Eggplant Mix, 92
Saffron Red Cabbage, 93
Cabbage Rice, 93
Beets and Almonds, 95
Spicy Artichokes and Rice, 95
Spicy Tomatoes, 96
Endives and Tomatoes Mix, 96
Endives and Walnuts Mix, 97
Endives with Orange Mix, 97
Tamarind Dip, 103
Hot Shrimp and Peppers Salad, 106
Turmeric Shrimp Salad, 109
Turkey Bowls, 111
Endives Dip, 113
Lentils Dip, 114
Turmeric Onion Dip, 115
Spiced Broccoli Spread, 116
Zucchini Dip, 117
Shrimp and Green Beans Bowls, 123
Cod and Tomato Bowls, 126
Cod and Cauliflower, 130
Chives Tuna Curry, 135
Salmon, Spinach and Coconut Mix, 136
Tilapia, Tomatoes and Radish Saad, 136
Sea Bass with Fennel, 137
Shrimp and Radish Curry, 137
Shrimp and Okra, 138
Fish and Onions Paste, 148
Cinnamon Chicken and Rice Mix, 155
Fenugreek Chicken Mix, 162

Chicken with Avocado and Cucumber Mix, 171
Turkey with Chili Black Beans, 173
Turkey and Chili Asparagus, 174
Chicken, Zucchini and Mushrooms Curry, 175
Coconut Pork Mix, 181
Cocoa Pork Chops and Green Beans, 199
Creamy Potatoes, 219
Spinach Mix, 221
Turmeric Kale, 229

COD
Fish Tikka, 124
Cod and Tomato Bowls, 126
Cod Curry, 126
Lemon Cod and Rice, 128
Spiced Cod, 129
Cod and Cauliflower, 130
Cod and Butter Sauce, 132
Simple Masala, 133
Fish and Onions Paste, 148
Cod and Cilantro Chutney, 148
Coriander Cod Mix, 149

CORIANDER
Spicy Tamarind Clams, 145

CORN
Indian Farro Masala, 34
Avial, 56
Chicken Soup, 57
Quinoa Pilaf, 75
Corn and Leeks Bowls, 117
Lemongrass Shrimp and Corn, 140
Cardamom Shrimp and Zucchinis, 140
Turkey and Masala Corn, 167
Spiced Lamb with Corn, 194

COTTAGE CHEESE
Paneer Butter Masala, 22

CRAB
Seafood Salad, 129
Crab Curry, 146
Spicy Crab and Eggplant Mix, 146

CRANBERRIES
Cranberries with Pistachios Cream, 242

CREAM
Chicken Masala, 48
Cream of Broccoli, 57
Tomato Soup, 61
Curry Turkey Soup, 62
Spiced Peas, 79
Spiced Gobi, 84
Lemongrass Shrimp and Corn, 140
Tandoori Sea Bass, 144
Curry Chicken Thighs, 152
Fenugreek Chicken Mix, 162
Chicken, Zucchini and Mushrooms Curry, 175
Creamy Turkey and Peas Mix, 178
Coconut Pork Mix, 181
Creamy Lamb with Carrots Curry, 193
Lamb with Coconut Green Beans, 193
Beef and Creamy Turmeric Potatoes, 210
Hot Brussels Sprouts, 215
Coriander Peppers Mix, 217
Basil Potato and Cream, 235
Saffron Lime Cream, 244
Orange Cream, 246
Turmeric Carrot Cream, 247
Cardamom Pears Cream, 247
Avocado Cream, 249
Zucchinis Rice, 249
Walnuts Cream, 250
Coconut Parfait, 251
Saffron Chocolate Cream, 252
Nutmeg Pumpkin Mix, 253
Tomato Upma, 19

CREAM CHEESE
Cheese Dip, 112
Cheesy Turkey and Rice, 166
Cheesy Beef and Rice, 190
Cheesy Beef and Rice, 190

CUCUMBERS
Rice Salad, 40
Figs and Tomatoes Salad, 42
Minty Dip, 101
Sea Bass with Fennel, 137
Spiced Lamb and Cucumber, 196
Cucumber and Mango Salad, 111
Warm Cucumber Salad, 118
Chicken with Avocado and Cucumber Mix, 171

CURD
Banana Salad, 39
Green Peas Mix, 79
Spiced Gobi, 84
Tomato Salad, 94
Marinated Shrimp Bowls, 105
Turmeric Shrimp Salad, 109
Curd Chicken Salad, 109
Zucchini Dip, 117
Barley and Turmeric Salad, 118
Barley and Olives Salad, 119
Mushroom Dip, 121

CURRANTS
Cardamom Beets, 233

CURRY
Onion Rava Dosa, 16
Potato Poha, 17

CURRY LEAVES
Kanda Poha, 17
Poori Masala, 18
Tomato Upma, 19
Semiya Upma, 20
Kadala Curry, 22
Broken Wheat Upma, 32

Millet Upma, 33
Quinoa Poha, 36
Poha Bowls with Sprouts, 37
Shrimp Biryani, 53
Avial, 56
Indian Fish Soup, 59
Beef Stew, 63
Veggie Stew, 64
Turmeric Aloo, 71
Cabbage Thoran, 72
Beet Sabzi, 76
Beet Rice, 77
Beet Poriyal, 77
Beet Thoran, 78
Beet and Carrot Poriyal, 78
Brussels Sprouts Subzi, 86
Spiced Brussels Sprouts, 86
Orange Pulao, 90
Cabbage Rice, 93
Khara Biscuits, 100
Salmon Curry, 125
Lemongrass Shrimp and Corn, 140
Spicy Crab and Eggplant Mix, 146
Cumin Chicken with Tomato Chutney, 161
Chicken and Zucchini Rice Mix, 165
Chicken, Tomatoes and Mushrooms, 166
Chives Chicken and Broccoli, 170
Garlic Turkey, Tomatoes and Rice, 172
Ginger Beef Curry, 182
Beef with Veggies Mix, 183
Beef with Squash Curry, 188
Spiced Lamb and Cucumber, 196
Cocoa Pork Chops and Green Beans, 199
Pandi Masala, 203
Hot Brussels Sprouts, 215
Masala Endives, 225
Spiced Eggplant Mix, 227
Oats Upma, 19
Turkey and Curried Lentils, 168
Pork with Red Lentils Mix, 185

Bread Upma, 34

DATES
Kale Salad, 87
Dates Quinoa, 250

DIJON MUSTARD
Turkey Meatballs and Sauce, 151
Mustard and Cumin Pork Chops, 202

DOUBLE CREAM
Pistachio Parfait, 239

EGGPLANT
Spicy Crab and Eggplant Mix, 146
Turkey Bowls, 177
Beef with Squash Curry, 188
Eggplant Masala, 226
Spiced Eggplant Mix, 227
Lime Zucchinis and Eggplant Mix, 227
Aloo Baingan Masala, 44
Eggplant Bhurtha, 82
Baingan Ka Bharta, 83
Spicy Eggplant Mix, 92
Cumin Eggplant and Tomato Bowls, 106
Curry Chicken and Eggplants, 154
Coconut Eggplants, 228

EGGS
Banana and Rice Pudding, 241
Aloo Egg Curry, 36
Bell Pepper Omelet, 41
Masala Omelet, 41
Egg and Broccoli Bhurji, 43
Chicken Meatballs Curry, 164
Pork Meatballs Mix, 208
Pistachio Parfait, 239
Saffron Zucchini Pudding, 240
Carrots Pudding, 242
Almond Pudding, 243
Sweet Potatoes Pudding, 246
Walnuts Cream, 250

Coconut Strawberry Mix, 251
Coconut Parfait, 251
Cardamom Pudding, 252

ENDIVES
Endives and Tomatoes Mix, 96
Endives and Walnuts Mix, 97
Endives with Orange Mix, 97
Endives Dip, 113
Chicken and Endives Rice Mix, 176
Masala Endives, 225

ERACHII MASALA
Veggie Stew, 64

FARRO
Indian Farro Masala, 34

FENNEL
Creamy Cauliflower Mix, 85
Indian Halibut, 133
Sea Bass with Fennel, 137
Kadala Curry, 22
Bhindi Masala, 24
Green Peas Masala Rice, 31
Rice with Lamb, 52
Curried Brussels Sprouts, 87
Turmeric Fennel and Rice, 98
Peas and Fennel Mix, 98
Capsicum Masala, 104
Seafood Salad, 129
Chicken and Masala Fennel, 160
Beef with Veggies Mix, 183
Hot BBQ Ribs, 209
Coconut Fennel Mix, 224

FENUGREEK
Fenugreek Chicken Mix, 162
Methi Paratha, 18
Spiced Gobi, 84
Fish Tikka, 124
Salmon Curry, 125
Lemon Cod and Rice, 128
Salmon and Chili Sauce, 131

Ginger Trout and Tomatoes, 135
Fenugreek Tuna and Mushroom Curry, 141
Citrus Turkey and Spiced Broccoli, 151
Cumin Chicken and Artichokes, 154
Turkey, Chickpeas and Zucchinis, 168
Lime Turmeric Chicken Wings, 176
Spiced Lamb and Cucumber, 196
Cocoa Pork Chops and Green Beans, 199
Pandi Masala, 203
Orange Pork Mix, 204
Turmeric Artichokes, 211
Green Beans and Orange Sauce, 214
Coriander Peppers Mix, 217
Beets with Yogurt, 218
Turmeric Zucchini, 220
Spiced Eggplant Mix, 227
Beets and Onions Mix, 234
Ribs Curry, 181
Tamarind Pork, 208

FRENCH BEANS
Oats Upma, 19
Millet Upma, 33
Beans Masala, 38

GARAM MASALA
Spinach and Lentils Rice, 32
Aloo Egg Curry, 36
Mushrooms Korma, 37
Aloo Baingan Masala, 44
Palak Paneer, 45
Dum Aloo, 45
Veggie Pulao, 46
Buttery Chicken, 47
Chicken Biryani, 47
Chicken Masala, 48
Lamb Rogan Josh, 49
Shrimp Curry, 50
Chana Masala, 50
Keema Matar, 51
Toor Dal, 51
Rice with Lamb, 52
Potato and Pea Curry, 52
Shrimp Biryani, 53
Sookha Kana Chana, 54
Langar Dal, 54
Masala Pasta, 55
Kidney Beans Curry, 55
Chicken Masala, 56
Cream of Broccoli, 57
Indian Fish Soup, 59
Aloo Ki Kadhi, 60
Beef Stew, 63
Chickpeas and Tomatoes Masala, 65
Zucchini Curry, 66
Okra Mix, 70
Turmeric Aloo, 71
Coconut Veggies, 71
Veggie Sabjee, 73
Quinoa and Chickpeas Mix, 76
Green Peas Mix, 79
Spiced Peas, 79
Peas and Mushrooms, 80
Gajar Matar, 81
Matar Ka Nimona, 82
Baingan Ka Bharta, 83
Parsnips Mix, 83
Cauliflower Mix, 84
Brussels Sprouts Subzi, 86
Spiced Brussels Sprouts, 86
Kale Salad, 87
Turmeric Broccoli Mix, 89
Citrus Cauliflower Mix, 89
Ginger Broccoli and Orange Mix, 92
Creamy Beans and Rice, 94
Tomato Salad, 94
Spicy Artichokes and Rice, 95
Endives with Orange Mix, 97
Indian Cumin Asparagus, 98
Turmeric Fennel and Rice, 98
Garam Masala Hummus, 102
Marinated Shrimp Bowls, 105
Cumin Eggplant and Tomato Bowls, 106

Spinach Spread, 107
White Beans Spread, 108
Curd Chicken Salad, 109
Turkey Bowls, 111
Endives Dip, 113
Lentils Dip, 114
Hot Cauliflower Dip, 116
Barley and Olives Salad, 119
Broccoli Bites, 119
Barley and Chickpea Bowls, 120
Fish Tikka, 124
Fish Pulusu, 124
Salmon and Broccoli, 127
Charred Salmon, 127
Spiced Cod, 129
Trout and Sauce, 130
Cod and Butter Sauce, 132
Turmeric Tuna, 134
Salmon, Spinach and Coconut Mix, 136
Shrimp and Okra, 138
Shrimp and Spiced Potatoes, 138
Tuna and Turmeric Green Beans Mix, 139
Cardamom Shrimp and Zucchinis, 140
Spicy Tilapia, 142
Fish and Onions Paste, 148
Coriander Cod Mix, 149
Spiced Yogurt Turkey, 150
Turkey Meatballs and Sauce, 151
Cinnamon Turkey and Cauliflower, 152
Masala Chicken and Peppers, 153
Curry Chicken and Eggplants, 154
Cinnamon Chicken and Rice Mix, 155
Ginger Chicken and Sweet Potatoes, 156
Turkey with Spiced Potatoes, 156
Curry Turkey, Asparagus and Tomatoes, 158
Chicken, Avocado and Turmeric Rice, 159

Cinnamon Turkey and Green Beans, 159
Chicken and Masala Fennel, 160
Turkey and Lime Sauce, 160
Cumin Chicken with Tomato Chutney, 161
Hot Chicken and Pineapple Mix, 161
Chicken and Turmeric Zucchini Mix, 162
Cocoa Turkey and Beans, 163
Chicken and Lime Turmeric Carrots, 165
Turkey and Masala Corn, 167
Turkey, Chickpeas and Zucchinis, 168
Chicken with Turmeric Cabbage, 169
Coriander Chicken Masala, 169
Chives Chicken and Broccoli, 170
Chicken with Turmeric Beets and Broccoli, 170
Chicken with Cauliflower and Pomegranate Mix, 171
Garlic Turkey, Tomatoes and Rice, 172
Hot Cayenne Chicken Mix, 172
Chicken Wings and Turmeric Sauce, 174
Turkey and Chili Asparagus, 174
Chicken with Coriander Broccoli Sauté, 175
Chicken, Zucchini and Mushrooms Curry, 175
Chicken and Endives Rice Mix, 176
Lime Turmeric Chicken Wings, 176
Chicken with Chili Onions, 178
Masala Turkey with Nutmeg Potatoes, 179
Beef Curry, 180
Ribs Curry, 181
Coconut Pork Mix, 181
Ginger Beef Curry, 182
Aromatic Beef, 183
Beef and Peas, 186
Coconut Beef and Cilantro Mix, 186

Saag Gosht, 187
Beef with Squash Curry, 188
Beef with Lemony Scallions, 189
Cheesy Beef and Rice, 190
Beef with Cinnamon Zucchini Mix, 190
Cumin Beef, 191
Lamb Curry, 192
Spiced Lamb Bowls, 192
Creamy Lamb with Carrots Curry, 193
Lamb with Coconut Green Beans, 193
Spiced Lamb with Corn, 194
Indian Lamb Chops, 195
Minty Lamb Mix, 196
Spiced Lamb and Cucumber, 196
Pork and Tomato Chutney, 198
Cocoa Pork Chops and Green Beans, 199
Pork with Cinnamon Carrots Mix, 199
Pork Chops and Turmeric Cauliflower, 201
Hot Pork Mix, 204
Orange Pork Mix, 204
Cocoa Pork and Tomatoes, 205
Kaleez Ankiti, 207
Spicy Pork and Artichokes, 209
Masala Artichokes, 211
Spiced Asparagus, 212
Cinnamon Artichokes and Rice, 212
Almond Asparagus Mix, 213
Spiced Green Beans, 214
Green Beans and Orange Sauce, 214
Hot Brussels Sprouts, 215
Minty Peppers, 216
Bell Peppers and Potatoes Mix, 217
Dill Potatoes, 218
Garlic Potato Masala, 219
Turmeric Zucchini, 220
Cayenne Zucchinis Mix, 220
Potato and Zucchini Masala, 221
Spinach Mix, 221
Spiced Okra, 222
Turmeric Broccoli and Onions, 222
Cinnamon Potato Mix, 224
Coconut Fennel Mix, 224
Masala Endives, 225
Eggplant Masala, 226
Coconut Tomatoes, 228
Zucchini and Cauliflower Mix, 229
Cocoa Zucchinis and Peppers, 230
Orange Zucchinis, 230
Tomatoes and Citrus Rice, 231
Allspice Zucchini Mix, 231
Cumin Potato and Carrots Mix, 232
Cardamom Beets, 233
Minty Tomatoes Mix, 233
Spinach with Broccoli, 234
Beets and Onions Mix, 234
Basil Potato and Cream, 235
Spiced Gobi, 84

GHEE
Rave Upma, 14
Aloo Paratha, 15
Onion Rava Dosa, 16
Methi Paratha, 18
Oats Upma, 19
Tomato Upma, 19
Sweet Pongal, 21
Sweet Dalia, 21
Oats Khichdi, 23
Mango Moong Dal, 28
Carrot Rasam and Moong Dal, 29
Paneer Spread, 30
Veggie Masala, 31
Broken Wheat Upma, 32
Millet Upma, 33
Aloo Egg Curry, 36
Poha Bowls with Sprouts, 37
Millet Pongal, 42
Apple Ragi Halwa, 43
Ragi Malt Java, 43
Palak Paneer, 45
Dum Aloo, 45
Veggie Khichdi, 46

Veggie Pulao, 46
Chicken Biryani, 47
Goat Curry, 48
Keema Matar, 51
Shrimp Biryani, 53
Sookha Kana Chana, 54
Langar Dal, 54
Masala Pasta, 55
Kidney Beans Curry, 55
Chicken Soup, 57
Cream of Broccoli, 57
Mulligatawny Soup, 58
Aloo Ki Kadhi, 60
Beans and Rutabaga Soup, 60
Ghee Carrot Pudding, 64
Chickpeas and Tomatoes Masala, 65
Quinoa and Chickpeas Mix, 76
Green Peas Mix, 79
Spiced Peas, 79
Peas Pulao, 80
Baingan Ka Bharta, 83
Spiced Gobi, 84
Narangi Pulao, 90
Rice and Kale, 91
Spinach Spread, 107
Curd Chicken Salad, 109
Chicken Chutney Salad, 110
Saffron Shrimp, 113
Hot Cauliflower Dip, 116
Corn and Leeks Bowls, 117
Barley and Olives Salad, 119
Barley and Chickpea Bowls, 120
Thyme Lentils and Tomatoes Bowls, 121
Mushroom Dip, 121
Salmon and Broccoli, 127
Lemon Cod and Rice, 128
Turmeric Salmon and Lime Sauce, 132
Simple Masala, 133
Spicy Tuna, 134
Ginger Trout and Tomatoes, 135
Shrimp and Spiced Potatoes, 138

Cardamom Shrimp and Zucchinis, 140
Fenugreek Tuna and Mushroom Curry, 141
Spicy Tilapia, 142
Mahi Mahi Tikka, 147
Coriander Cod Mix, 149
Cilantro Turkey and Lemon Mix, 150
Turkey Meatballs and Sauce, 151
Cinnamon Turkey and Cauliflower, 152
Masala Chicken and Peppers, 153
Cardamom Turkey Mix, 155
Turkey with Spiced Potatoes, 156
Sage Chicken and Mango, 157
Creamy Chicken Mix, 158
Turkey and Lime Sauce, 160
Paprika Turkey Mix, 164
Chicken, Tomatoes and Mushrooms, 166
Turkey, Chickpeas and Zucchinis, 168
Coriander Chicken Masala, 169
Hot Cayenne Chicken Mix, 172
Lime Turmeric Chicken Wings, 176
Turkey Bowls, 177
Creamy Turkey and Peas Mix, 178
Saag Gosht, 187
Beef with Squash Curry, 188
Indian Beef and Pumpkin Mix, 189
Beef with Lemony Scallions, 189
Beef with Cinnamon Zucchini Mix, 190
Lamb with Coconut Green Beans, 193
Spiced Lamb with Corn, 194
Minty Lamb Mix, 196
Spiced Lamb and Cucumber, 196
Turmeric Lamb with Beets, 197
Pork Chops with Allspice Spinach, 198
Sweet Pork Chops, 200
Pork with Broccoli, 200
Mustard and Cumin Pork Chops, 202

Ginger Pork Mix, 205
Ema Datshi, 206
Pork Meatballs Mix, 208
Spicy Pork and Artichokes, 209
Beef and Creamy Turmeric Potatoes, 210
Turmeric Artichokes, 211
Cinnamon Artichokes and Rice, 212
Garlic Potato Masala, 219
Turmeric Zucchini, 220
Potato and Zucchini Masala, 221
Spiced Okra, 222
Coconut Fennel Mix, 224
Allspice Zucchini Mix, 231
Spiced Zucchinis and Carrots, 232
Basil Potato and Cream, 235
Gajar Ka Halwa, 236
Payasam, 237
Gehun Ki Kheer, 239
Ada Pradhaman, 239
Saffron Zucchini Pudding, 240
Banana and Rice Pudding, 240
Apricots Rice, 249
Coconut Parfait, 251
Saffron Chocolate Cream, 252
Nutmeg Pumpkin Mix, 253
Tuna and Avocado Mix, 139

GINGER PASTE
Aloo Ki Kadhi, 60
Classic Indian Sea Bass Mix, 143
Crab Curry, 146
Ginger Pork Mix, 205

GRAPES
Mixed Fruits, 238
Grapes Rice, 241
Cocoa Grapes Mix, 241
Lemon Grapes and Bananas, 245

GREEN APPLES
Curry Turkey Soup, 62
Creamy Potato and Apples Mix, 226

GREEN BEANS
Veggie Masala, 31
Broken Wheat Upma, 32
Green Beans Curry, 69
Coconut Veggies, 71
Creamy Beans and Rice, 94
Shrimp and Green Beans Bowls, 123
Tuna and Turmeric Green Beans Mix, 139
Cinnamon Turkey and Green Beans, 159
Beef and Veggies Curry, 188
Lamb with Coconut Green Beans, 193
Cocoa Pork Chops and Green Beans, 199
Spiced Green Beans, 214
Green Beans and Orange Sauce, 214

GREEN BELL PEPPER
Bell Pepper Omelet, 41
Masala Omelet, 41
Coconut Veggies, 71
Chili Paneer, 99
Chili Fish Mix, 125
Creamy Chicken Mix, 158
Hot Pork Mix, 204
Capsicum Masala, 104

GREEN CABBAGE
Spicy Cabbage Soup, 61
Cabbage Thoran, 72
Cabbage Rice, 93
Chicken with Turmeric Cabbage, 169

GREEN CHILI
Rave Upma, 14
Onion Rava Dosa, 16
Kanda Poha, 17
Semiya Upma, 20
Oats Khichdi, 23
Mushrooms Korma, 37
Millet Pongal, 42
Keema Matar, 51

Shrimp Biryani, 53
Mushroom Mix, 70
Quinoa Pilaf, 75
Quinoa and Chickpeas Mix, 76
Beet Rice, 77
Beet Poriyal, 77
Beet Thoran, 78
Beet and Carrot Poriyal, 78
Peas and Mushrooms, 80
Hara Bhara Kabab, 81
Brussels Sprouts Subzi, 86
Curried Brussels Sprouts, 87
Avocado Raita, 102
Zucchini Salad, 115
Spicy Tilapia, 142
Tandoori Sea Bass, 144
Beef and Lentils Curry, 184

GREEN CHILI PASTE
Green Dosa, 30
Mushroom and Broccoli Dip, 122

GREEN CHILI PEPPER
Masala Omelet, 41
Palak Paneer, 45
Veggie Pulao, 46
Goat Curry, 48
Shrimp Curry, 50
Avial, 56
Spiced Yogurt Turkey, 150

GREEN CHILIES
Potato Masala, 14
Aloo Paratha, 15
Potato Poha, 17
Methi Paratha, 18
Poori Masala, 18
Oats Upma, 19
Chura Matar, 20
Kadala Curry, 22
Paneer Butter Masala, 22
Jeera Aloo, 25
Banana Moong Dal, 27
Tomato Rice, 29

Green Peas Masala Rice, 31
Broken Wheat Upma, 32
Millet Upma, 33
Sabudana Knichdi, 33
Bread Upma, 34
Quinoa Poha, 36
Poha Bowls with Sprouts, 37
Banana Salad, 39
Aloo Baingan Masala, 44
Beef Stew, 63
Veggie Stew, 64
Turmeric Aloo, 71
Coconut Veggies, 71
Cumin Potatoes, 72
Beet Sabzi, 76
Gajar Matar, 81
Matar Ka Nimona, 82
Creamy Cauliflower Mix, 85
Spiced Greens, 88
Saffron Red Cabbage, 93
Cabbage Rice, 93
Khara Biscuits, 100
Pyaaz Chutney, 100
Cucumber and Mango Salad, 111
Creamy Mushroom Spread, 122
Fish Pulusu, 124
Spicy Tuna, 134
Coriander Cod Mix, 149
Turkey and Lime Sauce, 160
Cumin Chicken with Tomato Chutney, 161
Cocoa Turkey and Beans, 163
Turkey with Chili Black Beans, 173
Turkey and Chili Asparagus, 174
Beef with Veggies Mix, 183
Kheema Masala, 185
Indian Pork Chops, 197
Pandi Masala, 203
Kaleez Ankiti, 207
Pork Chili Mix, 207

GREEN CHUTNEY
Indian Lamb Chops, 195

GREEN CURRY PASTE
Chicken Meatballs Curry, 164
Chicken, Zucchini and Mushrooms Curry, 175

GREEN LENTILS
Beef and Lentils Curry, 184

GREEN MOONG
Poha Bowls with Sprouts, 37

GREEN ONIONS
Cilantro Turkey and Lemon Mix, 150
Ginger Chicken and Sweet Potatoes, 156
Pork with Broccoli, 200
Ema Datshi, 206

GREEN PEAS
Oats Upma, 19
Chura Matar, 20
Oats Khichdi, 23
Gajar Matar, 24
Green Dosa, 30
Green Peas Masala Rice, 31
Veggie Khichdi, 46
Zucchini and Peas Curry, 67
Gajar Matar, 81
Hara Bhara Kabab, 81
Curried Brussels Sprouts, 87

HONEY
Paneer Butter Masala, 44
Ghee Carrot Pudding, 64
Squash and Lentils Stew, 67
Mango and Kale Mix, 88
Sweet Pork Chops, 200
Sweet Pork Chops, 200
Hot BBQ Ribs, 209

HOT CHILI SAUCE
Hot BBQ Ribs, 209

JAGGERY
Sweet Pongal, 21
Paneer Spread, 30
Apple Ragi Halwa, 43
Ada Pradhaman, 239

JEERA
Beans Masala, 38

KALE
Kale Salad, 87
Mango and Kale Mix, 88
Rice and Kale, 91
Turmeric Kale, 229
Ragi and Kale Idli, 38

KARELA
Bharwa Karela, 26

KIDNEY BEANS
Beans and Rutabaga Soup, 60

KIWI
Mixed Fruits, 238

LAMB
Lamb Rogan Josh, 49
Rice with Lamb, 52
Lamb Curry, 192
Spiced Lamb Bowls, 192
Creamy Lamb with Carrots Curry, 193
Lamb with Coconut Green Beans, 193
Spiced Lamb with Corn, 194
Lamb with Spiced Sprouts, 194
Indian Lamb Chops, 195
Minty Lamb Mix, 196
Spiced Lamb and Cucumber, 196
Turmeric Lamb with Beets, 197

LEEK
Corn and Leeks Bowls, 117
Coconut Pork Mix, 181

LEMON
Raspberries and Rice, 247
Salmon and Chili Sauce, 131
Tuna and Avocado Mix, 139
Beef Curry, 180
Beef with Lemony Scallions, 189
Lemon Grapes and Bananas, 245
Sweet Wheat Bowls, 245

LEMON JUICE
Spiced Mussels, 144
Cod and Cilantro Chutney, 148
Spiced Yogurt Turkey, 150
Aam Shrikhand, 236
Chura Matar, 20
Jeera Aloo, 25
Sabudana Knichdi, 33
Indian Farro Masala, 34
Poha Bowls with Sprouts, 37
Chicken Biryani, 47
Goat Curry, 48
Chicken Soup, 57
Spicy Cabbage Soup, 61
Turnips Soup, 68
Green Beans Curry, 69
Spiced Quinoa, 74
Spiced Brussels Sprouts, 86
Kale Salad, 87
Spiced Greens, 88
Mango and Kale Mix, 88
Cabbage Rice, 93
Tomato Salad, 94
Spicy Tomatoes, 96
Garam Masala Hummus, 102
Avocado Raita, 102
Capsicum Masala, 104
Hot Shrimp and Peppers Salad, 106
Spinach and Avocado Dip, 107
White Beans Spread, 108
Chickpea Dip, 114
Zucchini Dip, 117
Corn and Leeks Bowls, 117
Warm Cucumber Salad, 118
Mushroom Dip, 121

Fish Tikka, 124
Lemon Cod and Rice, 128
Spiced Cod, 129
Cod and Butter Sauce, 132
Shrimp and Spiced Potatoes, 138
Tuna and Avocado Mix, 139
Tuna and Turmeric Green Beans Mix, 139
Tilapia Masala, 141
Tandoori Sea Bass, 144
Cumin Chicken with Tomato Chutney, 161
Turkey Bowls, 177
Madras Beef Mix, 182
Aromatic Beef, 183
Lemony Beef Mix, 184
Beef with Lemony Scallions, 189
Spinach and Okra Mix, 225
Spinach with Broccoli, 234
Pistachio Parfait, 239
Apple Quinoa Mix, 248
Spicy Artichokes and Rice, 95
Indian Cumin Asparagus, 98
Endives Dip, 113
Lentils Dip, 114
Salmon and Chili Sauce, 131
Simple Masala, 133
Chives Tuna Curry, 135
Sea Bass with Fennel, 137
Cilantro Turkey and Lemon Mix, 150
Spicy Pork and Artichokes, 209
Lemon Grapes and Bananas, 245
Sweet Wheat Bowls, 245

LEMONGRASS
Spiced Yogurt Turkey, 150
Turmeric Tuna, 134
Lemongrass Shrimp and Corn, 140

LENTILS
Sweet Pongal, 21
Oats Khichdi, 23

LIME
Mushroom and Broccoli Dip, 122
Shrimp and Lime Rice, 128
Indian Lamb Chops, 195
Saffron Lime Cream, 244
Turmeric Salmon and Lime Sauce, 132
Lime Turmeric Chicken Wings, 176
Lime Zucchinis and Eggplant Mix, 227
Turmeric Kale, 229
Minty Tomatoes Mix, 233
Lime Apples Bowls, 246
Orange Cream, 246
Turmeric Blackberries Bowls, 248

LIME JUICE
Banana Moong Dal, 27
Carrot Rasam and Moong Dal, 29
Quinoa Poha, 36
Chicken Masala, 48
Shrimp Curry, 50
Indian Fish Soup, 59
Turkey and Coriander Soup, 62
Squash and Lentils Stew, 67
Quinoa Pilaf, 75
Endives and Tomatoes Mix, 96
Seafood Salad, 129
Turmeric Salmon and Lime Sauce, 132
Cardamom Shrimp and Zucchinis, 140
Curry Clams, 145
Mustard Seed Mahi Mahi, 147
Fish and Onions Paste, 148
Coriander Cod Mix, 149
Turkey Meatballs and Sauce, 151
Chicken and Masala Fennel, 160
Lime Turmeric Chicken Wings, 176
Cumin Beef, 191
Pork Chops with Allspice Spinach, 198
Kaleez Ankiti, 207
Masala Artichokes, 211
Beets with Yogurt, 218
Lime Zucchinis and Eggplant Mix, 227
Turmeric Kale, 229
Minty Tomatoes Mix, 233
Turmeric Carrot Cream, 247
Avocado Cream, 249
Mango and Banana Mix, 253
Fruit Masala, 39
Cashew Dip, 103
Marinated Shrimp Bowls, 105
Cumin Eggplant and Tomato Bowls, 106
Turmeric Shrimp Salad, 109
Chicken Chutney Salad, 110
Cucumber and Mango Salad, 111
Zucchini Salad, 115
Thyme Lentils and Tomatoes Bowls, 121
Mushroom and Broccoli Dip, 122
Cod Curry, 126
Shrimp and Lime Rice, 128
Turkey and Lime Sauce, 160
Chicken and Lime Turmeric Carrots, 165
Spinach and Okra Mix, 225
Coconut Eggplants, 228
Grapes Rice, 241
Saffron Lime Cream, 244
Lime Apples Bowls, 246
Fenugreek Tuna and Mushroom Curry, 141

MAHI MAHI
Mustard Seed Mahi Mahi, 147
Mahi Mahi Tikka, 147

MANGO
Mango Moong Dal, 28
Rice Salad, 40
Mango and Kale Mix, 88
Mango Salad, 110
Quinoa, Almonds and Avocado Salad, 120

Sage Chicken and Mango, 157
Chicken, Rice and Mango Mix, 179
Aam Shrikhand, 236
Mango and Banana Mix, 253
Indian Fish Soup, 59
Beans Dip, 108
Chicken Chutney Salad, 110
Fenugreek Tuna and Mushroom Curry, 141
Aam Shrikhand, 236

MANGOES
Peach and Mango Lassi, 35
Cucumber and Mango Salad, 111

MASALA PASTE
Veggie Masala, 31

MEAT MASALA
Lemony Beef Mix, 184
Sweet Pork Chops, 200
Coriander Pork with Almonds, 201

MILK
Sweet Dalia, 21
Oats Porridge, 23
Paneer Spread, 30
Healthy Kheer, 35
Peach and Mango Lassi, 35
Rose Rice Bowls, 39
Apricot Rava Pudding, 40
Masala Omelet, 41
Ragi Malt Java, 43
Dum Aloo, 45
Cream of Broccoli, 57
Veggie Stew, 64
Narangi Pulao, 90
Spinach Spread, 107
Cheese Dip, 112
Mushroom and Broccoli Dip, 122
Gajar Ka Halwa, 236
Payasam, 237
Pistachio Phirni, 237
Indian Kulfi, 237
Mixed Fruits, 238
Gehun Ki Kheer, 239
Saffron Zucchini Pudding, 240
Banana and Rice Pudding, 240
Grapes Rice, 241
Cocoa Grapes Mix, 241
Cranberries with Pistachios Cream, 242
Carrots Pudding, 242
Apples Quinoa Pudding, 243
Almond Pudding, 243
Coconut and Rice, 243
Raisins Pudding, 244
Banana and Avocado Mix, 244
Saffron Cauliflower Rice Pudding, 245
Sweet Wheat Bowls, 245
Sweet Potatoes Pudding, 246
Raspberries and Rice, 247
Cardamom Pears Cream, 247
Ginger Cauliflower Rice, 248
Apple Quinoa Mix, 248
Apricots Rice, 249
Zucchinis Rice, 249
Dates Quinoa, 250
Walnuts Cream, 250
Coconut Strawberry Mix, 251
Pineapple Pudding, 251
Cardamom Pudding, 252
Saffron Chocolate Cream, 252
Rhubarb Quinoa, 252
Mango and Banana Mix, 253
Nutmeg Pumpkin Mix, 253
Khara Biscuits, 100
Turmeric Apples, 241
Turmeric Blackberries Bowls, 248

MILLET
Millet Pongal, 42

MIXED BELL PEPPERS
Bell Peppers and Potatoes Mix, 217
Coriander Peppers Mix, 217

MIXED MILLET
Millet Upma, 33

MOONG DAL
Millet Pongal, 42

MOONG LENTILS
Veggie Khichdi, 46

MUNG DAL
Mango Moong Dal, 28

MUSHROOMS
Mushrooms Korma, 37
Balkan Bean Stew, 68
Mushroom Mix, 70
Coconut Veggies, 71
Mushroom Dip, 121
Mushroom and Broccoli Dip, 122
Creamy Mushroom Spread, 122
Fenugreek Tuna and Mushroom Curry, 141
Chicken, Tomatoes and Mushrooms, 166
Chicken, Zucchini and Mushrooms Curry, 175

MUTTON
Mutton Stew, 65

NUTMEG
Kadala Curry, 22
Healthy Kheer, 35
Mutton Stew, 65
Tilapia Masala, 141
Citrus Turkey and Spiced Broccoli, 151
Turkey with Spiced Potatoes, 156
Chicken and Lime Turmeric Carrots, 165
Turkey with Turmeric Yogurt Mix, 173
Masala Turkey with Nutmeg Potatoes, 179

Mustard and Cumin Pork Chops, 202
Paprika Pork with Nutmeg Potatoes, 202
Spiced Asparagus, 212
Minty Peppers, 216
Potato and Zucchini Masala, 221
Spiced Okra, 222
Nutmeg Cauliflower Mix, 223
Masala Endives, 225
Spiced Eggplant Mix, 227
Allspice Zucchini Mix, 231
Nutmeg Pumpkin Mix, 253

OATS
Oats Upma, 19
Oats Porridge, 23
Oats Khichdi, 23
Healthy Kheer, 35

OKRA
Avial, 56
Okra Mix, 70
Okra Bowls, 99
Shrimp and Okra, 138
Spiced Okra, 222
Spinach and Okra Mix, 225
Kurkuri Bhindi, 27

ONION
Masala Pasta, 55
Peas Pulao, 80
Paprika Pork with Nutmeg Potatoes, 202
Creamy Artichokes and Coconut, 212

ONION MASALA
Toor Dal, 51
Potato and Pea Curry, 52
Langar Dal, 54
Chicken Masala, 56

ONIONS
Oats Upma, 19

ORANGE JUICE
Citrus Cauliflower Mix, 89
Orange Pulao, 90
Narangi Pulao, 90
Barley and Chickpea Bowls, 120
Citrus Turkey and Spiced Broccoli, 151
Orange Pork Mix, 204
Orange Zucchinis, 230
Tomatoes and Citrus Rice, 231
Turmeric Onion Dip, 115
Green Beans and Orange Sauce, 214
Orange Cream, 246

ORANGES
Citrus Cauliflower Mix, 89
Ginger Broccoli and Orange Mix, 92
Mixed Fruits, 238
Orange Cream, 246
Asparagus Rice Mix, 91
Green Beans and Orange Sauce, 214
Tomatoes and Citrus Rice, 231
Endives with Orange Mix, 97

PANEER
Paneer Butter Masala, 44
Chili Paneer, 99
Cashew Dip, 103
Mushroom and Broccoli Dip, 122

PAPAYA
Fruit Masala, 39

PARSNIPS
Parsnips Mix, 83

PEACHES
Peach and Mango Lassi, 35

PEANUTS
Potato Poha, 17
Kanda Poha, 17
Oats Upma, 19
Sabudana Knichdi, 33

Poha Bowls with Sprouts, 37
Cabbage Rice, 93
Cucumber and Mango Salad, 111
Zucchini Salad, 115
Barley and Turmeric Salad, 118

PEARL ONIONS
Fish and Onions Paste, 148

PEARS
Turmeric Pear Bowls, 240
Cardamom Pears Cream, 247

PEAS
Quinoa Poha, 36
Keema Matar, 51
Toor Dal, 51
Potato and Pea Curry, 52
Avial, 56
Veggie Sabjee, 73
Spiced Quinoa, 74
Green Peas Mix, 79
Spiced Peas, 79
Peas Pulao, 80
Peas and Mushrooms, 80
Matar Ka Nimona, 82
Peas and Fennel Mix, 98
Creamy Turkey and Peas Mix, 178
Beef and Peas, 186

PECANS
Apricot Rava Pudding, 40

PEPITAS
Mango and Kale Mix, 88

PEPPER FLAKES
Spicy Eggplant Mix, 92
Almond Asparagus Mix, 213

PEPPERCORNS
Millet Pongal, 42

PIGEON PEAS
Squash and Lentils Stew, 67

PINE NUTS
Turmeric Broccoli Mix, 89

PINEAPPLE
Fruit Masala, 39
Hot Chicken and Pineapple Mix, 161
Pineapple Pudding, 251

PISTACHIOS
Paneer Spread, 30
Rose Rice Bowls, 39
Kale Salad, 87
Gajar Ka Halwa, 236
Pistachio Phirni, 237
Indian Kulfi, 237
Pistachio Parfait, 239
Cranberries with Pistachios Cream, 242
Saffron Cauliflower Rice Pudding, 245

PLANTAIN
Beef Stew, 63

POHA
Ragi and Kale Idli, 38

POMEGRANATE
Fruit Masala, 39
Chicken with Cauliflower and Pomegranate Mix, 171
Turkey Bowls, 177

PORK
Pork Vindaloo, 49
Coconut Pork Mix, 181
Pork with Red Lentils Mix, 185
Indian Pork Chops, 197
Pork Chops with Allspice Spinach, 198
Pork and Tomato Chutney, 198

Cocoa Pork Chops and Green Beans, 199
Pork with Cinnamon Carrots Mix, 199
Sweet Pork Chops, 200
Pork with Broccoli, 200
Pork Chops and Turmeric Cauliflower, 201
Coriander Pork with Almonds, 201
Mustard and Cumin Pork Chops, 202
Paprika Pork with Nutmeg Potatoes, 202
Pandi Masala, 203
Pork Indaad, 203
Hot Pork Mix, 204
Orange Pork Mix, 204
Cocoa Pork and Tomatoes, 205
Ema Datshi, 206
Pork with Bamboo Mix, 206
Kaleez Ankiti, 207
Pork Chili Mix, 207
Pork Meatballs Mix, 208
Tamarind Pork, 208
Spicy Pork and Artichokes, 209

POTATO
Potato Poha, 17
Tomato Rice, 29
Spinach and Lentils Rice, 32
Sabudana Knichdi, 33
Quinoa Poha, 36
Mushrooms Korma, 37
Poha Bowls with Sprouts, 37
Masala Omelet, 41
Veggie Khichdi, 46
Veggie Pulao, 46
Cream of Broccoli, 57
Veggie Stew, 64
Mutton Stew, 65
Veggie Sabjee, 73
Kheema Masala, 185
Potato Masala, 14
Aloo Paratha, 15
Poori Masala, 18

Oats Khichdi, 23
Aloo Capsicum, 25
Jeera Aloo, 25
Aloo Moongre Ki Sabzi, 26
Sweet Potato Dhal, 28
Green Dosa, 30
Veggie Masala, 31
Aloo Egg Curry, 36
Aloo Baingan Masala, 44
Dum Aloo, 45
Potato and Pea Curry, 52
Aloo Ki Kadhi, 60
Turkey and Coriander Soup, 62
Green Beans Curry, 69
Turmeric Aloo, 71
Cumin Potatoes, 72
Hara Bhara Kabab, 81
Shrimp and Spiced Potatoes, 138
Ginger Chicken and Sweet Potatoes, 156
Turkey with Spiced Potatoes, 156
Masala Turkey with Nutmeg Potatoes, 179
Paprika Pork with Nutmeg Potatoes, 202
Ema Datshi, 206
Pork Chili Mix, 207
Beef and Creamy Turmeric Potatoes, 210
Bell Peppers and Potatoes Mix, 217
Dill Potatoes, 218
Creamy Potatoes, 219
Garlic Potato Masala, 219
Potato and Zucchini Masala, 221
Hot Spinach and Potato Mix, 223
Cinnamon Potato Mix, 224
Creamy Potato and Apples Mix, 226
Cumin Potato and Carrots Mix, 232
Basil Potato and Cream, 235
Sweet Potatoes Pudding, 246

PUMPKIN
Indian Beef and Pumpkin Mix, 189
Nutmeg Pumpkin Mix, 253

PUNJABI
Aloo Paratha, 15

PUNJAM GARAM MASALA
Bharwa Karela, 26

QUINOA
Quinoa Poha, 36
Quinoa Pilaf, 75
Quinoa and Chickpeas Mix, 76
Beef with Chili Quinoa, 195
Apples Quinoa Pudding, 243
Apple Quinoa Mix, 248
Dates Quinoa, 250
Cardamom Pudding, 252
Rhubarb Quinoa, 252

RADISH
Aloo Moongre Ki Sabzi, 26
Warm Cucumber Salad, 118
Salmon, Spinach and Coconut Mix, 136
Tilapia, Tomatoes and Radish Saad, 136
Sea Bass with Fennel, 137
Shrimp and Radish Curry, 137
Shrimp Biryani, 53
Ghee Carrot Pudding, 64
Potato Dip, 112
Payasam, 237
Gehun Ki Kheer, 239
Ada Pradhaman, 239
Turmeric Pear Bowls, 240
Grapes Rice, 241
Raisins Pudding, 244

RASPBERRIES
Pistachio Parfait, 239
Raspberries and Rice, 247

RAVA
Rave Upma, 14
Broken Wheat Upma, 32

RED BEATEN RICE
Kanda Poha, 17

RED BELL PEPPER
Veggie Masala, 31
Coconut Veggies, 71
Quinoa and Chickpeas Mix, 76
Chili Paneer, 99
Chicken Chutney Salad, 110
Cheese Dip, 112
Zucchini Salad, 115
Chili Fish Mix, 125
Sea Bass and Lentils, 143
Masala Chicken and Peppers, 153
Creamy Chicken Mix, 158
Hot Pork Mix, 204
Aloo Baingan Masala, 44
Peppers Dip, 104
Hot Shrimp and Peppers Salad, 106
Walnuts Bell Peppers Mix, 216
Minty Peppers, 216
Cocoa Zucchinis and Peppers, 230

RED CABBAGE
Saffron Red Cabbage, 93
Barley and Turmeric Salad, 118

RED CHILI
Semiya Upma, 20
Sweet Potato Dhal, 28
Aloo Ki Kadhi, 60
Tomato Chutney, 101
Cardamom Shrimp and Zucchinis, 140
Tamarind Pork, 208

RED CHILI PEPPER
Mulligatawny Soup, 58
Citrus Cauliflower Mix, 89
Hot Cauliflower Dip, 116
Warm Cucumber Salad, 118
Charred Salmon, 127
Chili Fish Mix, 125
Tomato Upma, 19

Mango Moong Dal, 28
Beans Masala, 38
Pork Vindaloo, 49
Indian Fish Soup, 59
Cabbage Thoran, 72
Beet Sabzi, 76
Beet Thoran, 78
Spiced Brussels Sprouts, 86
Pyaaz Chutney, 100
Garlic Dip, 101
Crab Curry, 146
Masala Chicken and Peppers, 153
Turkey and Curried Lentils, 168
Chicken, Rice and Mango Mix, 179
Pork Indaad, 203
Hot Pork Mix, 204
Pork Chili Mix, 207

RED CURRY PASTE
Curry Cauliflower and Broccoli Soup, 58
Curry Chicken and Eggplants, 154
Curry Turkey, Asparagus and Tomatoes, 158
Ribs Curry, 181

RED KIDNEY BEANS
Kidney Beans Curry, 55

RED LENTILS
Sweet Potato Dhal, 28
Mulligatawny Soup, 58
Lentils Dip, 114
Sea Bass and Lentils, 143
Pork with Red Lentils Mix, 185

RED ONION
Sweet Potato Dhal, 28
Lamb Rogan Josh, 49
Masala Pasta, 55
Tomato Salad, 94
Beets and Almonds, 95
Beans Dip, 108
Curd Chicken Salad, 109

Warm Cucumber Salad, 118
Barley and Turmeric Salad, 118
Cod and Cauliflower, 130
Tilapia, Tomatoes and Radish Saad, 136
Shrimp and Radish Curry, 137
Shrimp and Okra, 138
Tuna and Avocado Mix, 139
Tilapia Curry, 142
Cumin Chicken and Artichokes, 154
Chicken, Avocado and Turmeric Rice, 159
Chicken with Cauliflower and Pomegranate Mix, 171
Chicken, Zucchini and Mushrooms Curry, 175
Lemony Beef Mix, 184
Kheema Masala, 185
Cheesy Beef and Rice, 190
Creamy Lamb with Carrots Curry, 193
Minty Lamb Mix, 196
Spicy Pork and Artichokes, 209
Turmeric Zucchini, 220
Spiced Okra, 222
Spiced Eggplant Mix, 227
Zucchini and Cauliflower Mix, 229
Orange Zucchinis, 230
Shrimp Biryani, 53
Beef Stew, 63
Tomato Chutney, 101
Tamarind Dip, 103
Shrimp and Green Beans Bowls, 123
Cod Curry, 126
Chicken with Chili Onions, 178
Sweet Pork Chops, 200

RED PEPPER
Indian Beef and Pumpkin Mix, 189
Pandi Masala, 203

RED PEPPER FLAKES
Chickpeas and Tomatoes Masala, 65
Squash and Lentils Stew, 67

Quinoa and Chickpeas Mix, 76
Spicy Artichokes and Rice, 95
Spicy Shrimp Mix, 105
Chickpea Dip, 114
Tilapia, Tomatoes and Radish Saad, 136
Spicy Tamarind Clams, 145
Chicken with Turmeric Cabbage, 169
Beef with Cinnamon Zucchini Mix, 190
Cocoa Zucchinis and Peppers, 230
Spinach with Broccoli, 234

RED QUINOA
Spiced Quinoa, 74
Quinoa, Almonds and Avocado Salad, 120

RED RICE VERMICELLI
Rice Kheer, 238

RED WINE
Figs and Tomatoes Salad, 42

RHUBARB
Rhubarb Quinoa, 252

RICE
Potato Poha, 17
Chura Matar, 20
Sweet Pongal, 21
Poha Bowls with Sprouts, 37
Veggie Khichdi, 46
Curry Turkey Soup, 62
Garlic Rice Mix, 91
Shrimp and Lime Rice, 128
Spicy Tuna, 134
Cinnamon Chicken and Rice Mix, 155
Payasam, 237
Banana and Rice Pudding, 240
Grapes Rice, 241
Almond Pudding, 243
Coconut and Rice, 243

Raisins Pudding, 244
Raspberries and Rice, 247
Apricots Rice, 249
Pineapple Pudding, 251
Onion Rava Dosa, 16
Pistachio Phirni, 237
Ada Pradhaman, 239

RUTABAGA
Beans and Rutabaga Soup, 60

SABUDANA
Sabudana Knichdi, 33

SAGE
Coconut Pork Mix, 181

SALMON
Salmon, Spinach and Coconut Mix, 136
Salmon Curry, 125
Salmon and Broccoli, 127
Charred Salmon, 127
Salmon and Chili Sauce, 131
Indian Salmon and Asparagus, 131
Turmeric Salmon and Lime Sauce, 132
Rice Salad, 40
Lentils Dip, 114
Beef with Lemony Scallions, 189

SEA BASS
Sea Bass with Fennel, 137
Classic Indian Sea Bass Mix, 143
Sea Bass and Lentils, 143
Tandoori Sea Bass, 144

SEITAN
Balkan Bean Stew, 68

SEMOLINA
Onion Rava Dosa, 16
Paneer Spread, 30
Apricot Rava Pudding, 40

SERRANO PEPPER
Toor Dal, 51
Potato and Pea Curry, 52
Kidney Beans Curry, 55

SHALLOT
Mango Moong Dal, 28
Tomato Rice, 29
Cardamom Shrimp and Zucchinis, 140
Kadala Curry, 22
Beans Masala, 38
Beet Thoran, 78
Endives and Walnuts Mix, 97
Salmon Curry, 125
Seafood Salad, 129
Tuna and Turmeric Green Beans Mix, 139
Curry Chicken and Eggplants, 154
Chicken and Masala Fennel, 160
Paprika Turkey Mix, 164
Chicken Wings and Turmeric Sauce, 174
Lime Turmeric Chicken Wings, 176
Chicken with Chili Onions, 178
Indian Beef and Pumpkin Mix, 189
Tamarind Pork, 208
Coconut Beets, 215
Creamy Potatoes, 219
Spinach Mix, 221
Minty Tomatoes Mix, 233

SHRIMP
Shrimp Curry, 50
Shrimp Biryani, 53
Coconut Shrimp Stew, 63
Marinated Shrimp Bowls, 105
Spicy Shrimp Mix, 105
Hot Shrimp and Peppers Salad, 106
Turmeric Shrimp Salad, 109
Saffron Shrimp, 113
Shrimp and Green Beans Bowls, 123
Shrimp and Lime Rice, 128
Seafood Salad, 129

Shrimp and Radish Curry, 137
Shrimp and Okra, 138
Shrimp and Spiced Potatoes, 138
Lemongrass Shrimp and Corn, 140
Cardamom Shrimp and Zucchinis, 140

SPINACH
Spinach and Lentils Rice, 32
Figs and Tomatoes Salad, 42
Palak Paneer, 45
Palak Soup, 59
Turnips Soup, 68
Hara Bhara Kabab, 81
Spinach and Avocado Dip, 107
Spinach Spread, 107
Curd Chicken Salad, 109
Turkey Bowls, 111
Barley and Turmeric Salad, 118
Salmon, Spinach and Coconut Mix, 136
Saag Gosht, 187
Pork Chops with Allspice Spinach, 198
Hot Spinach and Potato Mix, 223
Spinach and Okra Mix, 225
Quinoa and Chickpeas Mix, 76
Spinach Mix, 221
Spinach with Broccoli, 234

SPRING ONION
Chili Paneer, 99
Chili Fish Mix, 125
Salmon and Chili Sauce, 131
Turmeric Broccoli and Onions, 222
Coconut Tomatoes, 228
Cumin Potato and Carrots Mix, 232

SQUID
Seafood Salad, 129

STRAWBERRIES
Apricot Rava Pudding, 40
Coconut Strawberry Mix, 251

TAHINI PASTE
Garam Masala Hummus, 102
Chickpea Dip, 114

TAMARI SAUCE
Quinoa Curry, 75

TAMARIND PASTE
Pork Vindaloo, 49
Fish Pulusu, 124
Shrimp and Radish Curry, 137
Spicy Tamarind Clams, 145
Crab Curry, 146
Spicy Crab and Eggplant Mix, 146
Pork Indaad, 203
Tamarind Pork, 208

TILAPIA
Tilapia Masala, 141
Tilapia Curry, 142
Tilapia, Tomatoes and Radish Saad, 136
Spicy Tilapia, 142

TOMATO PASTE
Lamb Rogan Josh, 49
Chicken and Turmeric Zucchini Mix, 162
Chicken and Endives Rice Mix, 176
Ribs Curry, 181
Madras Beef Mix, 182
Ginger Beef Curry, 182
Lamb with Spiced Sprouts, 194
Beef and Beets Mix, 191
Coconut Shrimp Stew, 63
Coriander Cod Mix, 149
Turkey Meatballs and Sauce, 151
Curry Chicken and Eggplants, 154
Hot Chicken and Pineapple Mix, 161
Turkey, Cauliflower and Rice Mix, 163
Chicken with Turmeric Beets and Broccoli, 170
Turkey with Chili Black Beans, 173

Pork with Cinnamon Carrots Mix, 199
Hot BBQ Ribs, 209
Spinach Mix, 221
Eggplant Masala, 226

TOMATOES
Poha Bowls with Sprouts, 37
Bell Pepper Omelet, 41
Masala Omelet, 41
Palak Paneer, 45
Veggie Pulao, 46
Goat Curry, 48
Shrimp Curry, 50
Shrimp Biryani, 53
Squash and Lentils Stew, 67
Mushroom Mix, 70
Quinoa Pilaf, 75
Matar Ka Nimona, 82
Eggplant Bhurtha, 83
Curried Brussels Sprouts, 87
Cucumber and Mango Salad, 111
Creamy Chicken Mix, 158
Hot Cayenne Chicken Mix, 172
Chicken Wings and Turmeric Sauce, 174
Kheema Masala, 185
Aloo Egg Curry, 36
Veggie Khichdi, 46
Chicken Masala, 48
Kidney Beans Curry, 55
Fenugreek Tuna and Mushroom Curry, 141
Lamb Curry, 192
Pork and Tomato Chutney, 198
Cumin Chicken with Tomato Chutney, 161
Poori Masala, 18
Tomato Upma, 19
Paneer Butter Masala, 22
Oats Khichdi, 23
Bhindi Masala, 24
Carrot Rasam and Moong Dal, 29
Tomato Rice, 29

Veggie Masala, 31
Green Peas Masala Rice, 31
Spinach and Lentils Rice, 32
Bread Upma, 34
Egg and Broccoli Bhurji, 43
Paneer Butter Masala, 44
Aloo Baingan Masala, 44
Dum Aloo, 45
Chana Masala, 50
Tomato Soup, 61
Spicy Cabbage Soup, 61
Beef Stew, 63
Coconut Veggies, 71
Peas and Mushrooms, 80
Baingan Ka Bharta, 83
Tomato Salad, 94
Spicy Tomatoes, 96
Endives and Tomatoes Mix, 96
Tomato Chutney, 101
Avocado Raita, 102
Tamarind Dip, 103
Peppers Dip, 104
Cumin Eggplant and Tomato Bowls, 106
Curd Chicken Salad, 109
Turkey Bowls, 111
Lentils Dip, 114
Shrimp and Lime Rice, 128
Ginger Trout and Tomatoes, 135
Shrimp and Spiced Potatoes, 138
Classic Indian Sea Bass Mix, 143
Sea Bass and Lentils, 143
Crab Curry, 146
Mustard Seed Mahi Mahi, 147
Coconut Chicken and Tomatoes, 157
Chicken and Masala Fennel, 160
Paprika Turkey Mix, 164
Turkey Bowls, 177
Beef Curry, 180
Beef with Veggies Mix, 183
Beef and Peas, 186
Saag Gosht, 187
Lamb with Spiced Sprouts, 194
Pork Chili Mix, 207

Masala Artichokes, 211

TROUT
Trout and Sauce, 130
Ginger Trout and Tomatoes, 135

TUNA
Chives Tuna Curry, 135
Turmeric Tuna, 134
Tuna and Avocado Mix, 139
Tuna and Turmeric Green Beans Mix, 139
Fenugreek Tuna and Mushroom Curry, 141

TURKEY
Turkey and Curried Lentils, 168
Curry Turkey Soup, 62
Turkey and Coriander Soup, 62
Turkey Bowls, 111
Spiced Yogurt Turkey, 150
Cilantro Turkey and Lemon Mix, 150
Turkey Meatballs and Sauce, 151
Citrus Turkey and Spiced Broccoli, 151
Cinnamon Turkey and Cauliflower, 152
Cardamom Turkey Mix, 155
Turkey with Spiced Potatoes, 156
Curry Turkey, Asparagus and Tomatoes, 158
Cinnamon Turkey and Green Beans, 159
Turkey and Lime Sauce, 160
Turkey, Cauliflower and Rice Mix, 163
Cocoa Turkey and Beans, 163
Paprika Turkey Mix, 164
Cheesy Turkey and Rice, 166
Turkey and Masala Corn, 167
Turkey, Chickpeas and Zucchinis, 168
Garlic Turkey, Tomatoes and Rice, 172

Turkey with Turmeric Yogurt Mix, 173
Turkey with Chili Black Beans, 173
Turkey and Chili Asparagus, 174
Turkey Bowls, 177
Turkey with Brussels Sprouts Rice, 177
Creamy Turkey and Peas Mix, 178
Chicken with Chili Onions, 178
Masala Turkey with Nutmeg Potatoes, 179
Coconut Turkey and Carrots Rice, 180

TURNIPS
Turnips Soup, 68

URAD DAL
Garlic Dip, 101
Rave Upma, 14
Ragi and Kale Idli, 38
Beans Masala, 38
Langar Dal, 54
Beet Poriyal, 77
Beet and Carrot Poriyal, 78

VERMICELL
ISemiya Upma, 20

WALNUTS
Endives and Walnuts Mix, 97
Turkey Bowls, 177
Walnuts Bell Peppers Mix, 216
Walnuts Cream, 250

WHITE FISH
Indian Fish Soup, 59
Fish Pulusu, 124
Chili Fish Mix, 125

WHITE MUSHROOMS
Peas and Mushrooms, 80

WHITE ONION
Salmon, Spinach and Coconut Mix, 136

WHITE QUINOA
Quinoa Curry, 75

YELLOW BELL PEPPER
Veggie Sabjee, 73
Chili Paneer, 99
Beans Dip, 108

YELLOW MOONG DAL
Banana Moong Dal, 27
Carrot Rasam and Moong Dal, 29
Tomato Rice, 29

YELLOW ONION
Rave Upma, 14
Potato Poha, 17
Kanda Poha, 17
Poori Masala, 18
Tomato Upma, 19
Semiya Upma, 20
Oats Khichdi, 23
Bhindi Masala, 24
Banana Moong Dal, 27
Green Dosa, 30
Veggie Masala, 31
Green Peas Masala Rice, 31
Spinach and Lentils Rice, 32
Broken Wheat Upma, 32
Millet Upma, 33
Sabudana Knichdi, 33
Quinoa Poha, 36
Poha Bowls with Sprouts, 37
Beans Masala, 38
Bell Pepper Omelet, 41
Aloo Baingan Masala, 44
Palak Paneer, 45
Dum Aloo, 45
Veggie Khichdi, 46
Veggie Pulao, 46
Chicken Masala, 48

Pork Vindaloo, 49
Shrimp Curry, 50
Chana Masala, 50
Keema Matar, 51
Rice with Lamb, 52
Kidney Beans Curry, 55
Chicken Masala, 56
Cream of Broccoli, 57
Mulligatawny Soup, 58
Curry Cauliflower and Broccoli Soup, 58
Palak Soup, 59
Indian Fish Soup, 59
Tomato Soup, 61
Spicy Cabbage Soup, 61
Curry Turkey Soup, 62
Coconut Shrimp Stew, 63
Veggie Stew, 64
Chickpeas and Tomatoes Masala, 65
Mutton Stew, 65
Broccoli Junka, 66
Zucchini and Peas Curry, 67
Turnips Soup, 68
Balkan Bean Stew, 68
Okra Mix, 70
Turmeric Aloo, 71
Veggie Sabjee, 73
Aromatic Rice Mix, 73
Spicy Rice, 74
Spiced Quinoa, 74
Quinoa and Chickpeas Mix, 76
Beet Sabzi, 76
Beet Rice, 77
Peas and Mushrooms, 80
Matar Ka Nimona, 82
Eggplant Bhurtha, 82
Baingan Ka Bharta, 83
Spiced Gobi, 84
Creamy Cauliflower Mix, 85
Curried Brussels Sprouts, 87
Kale Salad, 87
Orange Pulao, 90
Saffron Red Cabbage, 93
Spicy Tomatoes, 96

Endives with Orange Mix, 97
Peas and Fennel Mix, 98
Avocado Raita, 102
Hot Shrimp and Peppers Salad, 106
Spinach Spread, 107
Mango Salad, 110
Turkey Bowls, 111
Turmeric Onion Dip, 115
Zucchini Salad, 115
Spiced Broccoli Spread, 116
Barley and Chickpea Bowls, 120
Thyme Lentils and Tomatoes Bowls, 121
Mushroom and Broccoli Dip, 122
Creamy Mushroom Spread, 122
Fish Pulusu, 124
Lemon Cod and Rice, 128
Shrimp and Lime Rice, 128
Indian Salmon and Asparagus, 131
Simple Masala, 133
Spicy Tuna, 134
Ginger Trout and Tomatoes, 135
Shrimp and Spiced Potatoes, 138
Fenugreek Tuna and Mushroom Curry, 141
Spicy Tilapia, 142
Sea Bass and Lentils, 143
Curry Clams, 145
Spicy Crab and Eggplant Mix, 146
Cinnamon Turkey and Cauliflower, 152
Curry Chicken Thighs, 152
Cardamom Turkey Mix, 155
Cinnamon Chicken and Rice Mix, 155
Coconut Chicken and Tomatoes, 157
Sage Chicken and Mango, 157
Cinnamon Turkey and Green Beans, 159
Turkey, Cauliflower and Rice Mix, 163
Chicken Meatballs Curry, 164
Chicken and Lime Turmeric Carrots, 165
Chicken, Tomatoes and Mushrooms, 166
Turkey and Masala Corn, 167
Chicken and Chickpeas Mix, 167
Turkey, Chickpeas and Zucchinis, 168
Chicken with Turmeric Cabbage, 169
Chives Chicken and Broccoli, 170
Chicken with Avocado and Cucumber Mix, 171
Hot Cayenne Chicken Mix, 172
Chicken with Coriander Broccoli Sauté, 175
Chicken, Rice and Mango Mix, 179
Coconut Turkey and Carrots Rice, 180
Beef Curry, 180
Ribs Curry, 181
Ginger Beef Curry, 182
Aromatic Beef, 183
Beef and Lentils Curry, 184
Pork with Red Lentils Mix, 185
Saag Gosht, 187
Spicy Beef, 187
Beef and Veggies Curry, 188
Beef with Squash Curry, 188
Cumin Beef, 191
Beef and Beets Mix, 191
Lamb with Coconut Green Beans, 193
Spiced Lamb with Corn, 194
Lamb with Spiced Sprouts, 194
Spiced Lamb and Cucumber, 196
Pork Chops with Allspice Spinach, 198
Pork with Cinnamon Carrots Mix, 199
Pork with Broccoli, 200
Pork Chops and Turmeric Cauliflower, 201
Coriander Pork with Almonds, 201
Paprika Pork with Nutmeg Potatoes, 202
Ginger Pork Mix, 205

Pork Meatballs Mix, 208
Beef and Creamy Turmeric Potatoes, 210
Masala Artichokes, 211
Cinnamon Artichokes and Rice, 212
Turmeric Broccoli and Onions, 222
Cinnamon Potato Mix, 224
Eggplant Masala, 226
Cocoa Zucchinis and Peppers, 230
Tomatoes and Citrus Rice, 231
Allspice Zucchini Mix, 231
Spiced Zucchinis and Carrots, 232
Spinach with Broccoli, 234
Basil Potato and Cream, 235
Spicy Tamarind Clams, 145
Turkey Meatballs and Sauce, 151
Potato Masala, 14
Onion Rava Dosa, 16
Bharwa Karela, 26
Bread Upma, 34
Indian Farro Masala, 34
Aloo Egg Curry, 36
Mushrooms Korma, 37
Egg and Broccoli Bhurji, 43
Paneer Butter Masala, 44
Chicken Biryani, 47
Coconut Veggies, 71
Pyaaz Chutney, 100
Trout and Sauce, 130
Cod and Butter Sauce, 132
Spiced Mussels, 144
Crab Curry, 146
Beef with Veggies Mix, 183
Coconut Beef and Cilantro Mix, 186
Lamb Curry, 192
Beef with Chili Quinoa, 195
Pandi Masala, 203
Pork Indaad, 203
Pork with Bamboo Mix, 206
Kaleez Ankiti, 207
Pork Chili Mix, 207
Beets and Onions Mix, 234

YELLOW POTATO
Matar Ka Nimona, 82

YOGURT
Peach and Mango Lassi, 35
Mushrooms Korma, 37
Chicken Biryani, 47
Chicken Masala, 48
Lamb Rogan Josh, 49
Avial, 56
Aloo Ki Kadhi, 60
Mushroom Mix, 70
Minty Dip, 101
Avocado Raita, 102
Tamarind Dip, 103
Beans Dip, 108
Fish Tikka, 124
Charred Salmon, 127
Seafood Salad, 129
Tandoori Sea Bass, 144
Mahi Mahi Tikka, 147
Spiced Yogurt Turkey, 150
Cilantro Turkey and Lemon Mix, 150
Turkey with Turmeric Yogurt Mix, 173
Aromatic Beef, 183
Saag Gosht, 187
Beef and Veggies Curry, 188
Lamb Curry, 192
Masala Artichokes, 211
Beets with Yogurt, 218
Dill Potatoes, 218
Aam Shrikhand, 236
Coconut Banana Mix, 250

ZUCCHINI
Beans Dip, 108
Chicken, Zucchini and Mushrooms Curry, 175
Turkey Bowls, 177
Zucchini and Cauliflower Mix, 229
Zucchini Curry, 66
Zucchini and Peas Curry, 67
Turnips Soup, 68

Zucchini Salad, 115
Zucchini Dip, 117
Cardamom Shrimp and Zucchinis, 140
Chicken and Turmeric Zucchini Mix, 162
Chicken and Zucchini Rice Mix, 165
Turkey, Chickpeas and Zucchinis, 168
Beef with Cinnamon Zucchini Mix, 190

Turmeric Zucchini, 220
Cayenne Zucchinis Mix, 220
Potato and Zucchini Masala, 221
Lime Zucchinis and Eggplant Mix, 227
Cocoa Zucchinis and Peppers, 230
Orange Zucchinis, 230
Allspice Zucchini Mix, 231
Spiced Zucchinis and Carrots, 232
Saffron Zucchini Pudding, 240
Zucchinis Rice, 249

Copyright 2019 by Mary Goodrich All rights reserved.

All rights Reserved. No part of this publication or the information in it may be quoted from or reproduced in any form by means such as printing, scanning, photocopying or otherwise without prior written permission of the copyright holder.

Disclaimer and Terms of Use: Effort has been made to ensure that the information in this book is accurate and complete, however, the author and the publisher do not warrant the accuracy of the information, text and graphics contained within the book due to the rapidly changing nature of science, research, known and unknown facts and internet. The Author and the publisher do not hold any responsibility for errors, omissions or contrary interpretation of the subject matter herein. This book is presented solely for motivational and informational purposes only.

Made in the
USA
Columbia, SC